SEA SAFARI

A scene once typical of British East Africa in the 1950s— R.M.S.*Kenya*, framed by palm trees and dock cranes, works cargo in Kilindini Harbour, Mombasa, Kenya Colony. *P&O*

SEA SAFARI

British India S.N. Co. African Ships & Services

by

Peter C. Kohler

P.M. Heaton Publishing
Abergavenny, Gwent
Great Britain
1995

To shipmates in R.M.S. *St. Helena*,
last of the British African mailships.

ISBN 1 872006 05 1

© First Edition April, 1995: P.C. Kohler

Printed in Great Britain

Published by P.M. Heaton Publishing, Abergavenny, Gwent, NP7 9UH
Printed by The Amadeus Press Ltd., Huddersfield, West Yorkshire, HD2 1YJ
Typesetting by Highlight Type Bureau Ltd., Shipley, West Yorkshire, BD17 7EG

THE AUTHOR

Peter C. Kohler was born in 1957 in Grand Rapids, Michigan, but has lived since 1958 in Washington, D.C. He graduated from the George Washington University in 1979 with a BA degree in European History.

His first article on liners was published in *Steamboat Bill,* the journal of the Steamship Historical Society, in 1981 and since then he has written 14 major articles for this publication including his ongoing full issue series on American Passenger Liners begun in 1989.

He has also contributed articles for *Sea Breezes, Seascape, Fairplay, Titanic Commutator, Design/Guide* publications and *Ships Monthly*, including originating the "Cruise Ship Review" column. He was co-editor of *Fairplay Cruise Review*, 1987, and his first book *Holland America Line - A 120th Anniversary Celebration in Vintage Postcards* was published in 1993.

A 15 year veteran of the travel industry, he has made some 30 voyages and cruises in over 20 different ships including two in *Uganda* (the inspiration for Sea Safari). In 1990 he served for one voyage as an Assistant Purser in R.M.S. *St. Helena*. Additionally he has done consulting work for St. Helena Shipping Ltd. and Holland America Line and presented lectures aboard many ships.

He also has a great interest in electric tramcars and is Vice-President of the National Capital Trolley Museum, Wheaton, Maryland.

In August, 1993 he married Christine, who is from West Sussex – they met in 1987 on a cruise aboard *Canberra*.

CONTENTS

LIST OF ILLUSTRATIONS

Takliwa.

Sofala.

Malda.

Karanja during Second World War.

Tilawa (painting).

SECTION II

Mantola.

Landaura.

Shirala.

Amra at Durban.

Kilwa at Durban.

Palikonda at Cape Town.

Matiana, aerial view in English Channel.

Tairea.

Kampala on trials.

Karanja on trials.

Madura.

Mombasa on trials.

Leicestershire in BI livery.

Kenya in English Channel.

Kenya, evening view at London.

Uganda on trials.

Uganda on delivery voyage.

Uganda at Mombasa.

Uganda at Rotterdam.

Superstructure of *Mulbera.*

Mantola transiting Suez Canal.

Kampala at sea.

Kampala's First Class lounge.

Uganda's First Class dining saloon.

Kampala First Class cabin.

Modasa and *Uganda* at Mombasa.

Karanja at Mombasa.

Amra at Mombasa.

Mombasa at Zanzibar.

Madura at Dar-es-Salaam.

Amra leaving Durban.

Karanja at Bombay.

SECTION III

Madura, final sailing from Mombasa.
Mulbera, final sailing from Mombasa.
Itinda.
Urlana.
Chupra.
Chantala, BI cadet ship.
Durenda
Nuddea (painting).
Kenya in white livery.
Uganda in white livery.
Amra in white livery.
Uganda and *Nowshera* (painting).
Britannia and *Kenya* at Dar-es-Salaam.
Warla at Durban.
Nyanza.
Mombasa in revised livery.
Santhia at Hong Kong.
Aronda, final sailing from Durban.
Uganda, *Europa* and *Kenya* at Mombasa.
Karanja, *Uganda* and *Kenya* at Mombasa.
Karanja at Mombasa.
Kampala sailing from Mombasa.
Uganda sailing from Mombasa.
Kenya at Cape Town.
Kenya at Mombasa.
Kampala, final sailing from Bombay.
Karanja after refit.
Tairea sailing from Cape Town.
Sirdhana at Bombay.
Chilka sailing from Durban.
Announcement of *Karanja's* last Mombasa sailing.
Nancowry, ex-*Karanja*.

BI Sunday. Mombasa, Kenya, 16 September 1951: *Kampala* (closest camera) with *Mantola* behind and *Tabora* outboard, and *Karanja, Kenya, Mombasa* and *Modasa* astern. *P&O*

10

INTRODUCTION

All in the feathered palm tree tops
the bright green parrots screech
The white line of the running surf
goes booming down the beach.

Harbour Bar – John Masefield

It was called "BI Sunday"— Mombasa, Kenya Colony, 16 September 1951; *Kenya* on her maiden voyage joining *Mantola, Mombasa, Modasa, Karanja, Tabora* and *Kampala* docked in Kilindini Harbour and *Sofala* sitting on the slipway. Altogether, 56,807 gross tons of vessels bearing the black funnel with two narrow white bands of the British India Steam Navigation Co. occupying every berth in the port of a colony whose initial development was the inspiration of BI's founder William Mackinnon.

Twenty-five years after this post-war pinnacle, BI's African passenger services finished in 1976 upon the withdrawal of *Karanja* which was finally scrapped in 1988 as the Shipping Corp. of India's *Nancowry.* Thus ended a not too distant era when "British East" began at Tilbury Landing Stage or Bombay's Ballard Pier and the gangway of a BI mailship Beira-bound.

With Cunard, P&O and Royal Mail, the British India Steam Navigation Co. was among the pillars and prides of the once- supreme British Merchant Navy. The "BI", as it was universally known, was founded in 1856 as the Calcutta & Burmah Steam Navigation Co. to operate a Calcutta-Rangoon Royal Mail service. From two steamers in 1858 to 161 in 1920, BI's growth and prosperity paralleled and, in large measure, facilitated, the growth of the British Empire east of Suez.

British India helped to pioneer steam navigation in the Bay of Bengal, Indian Ocean, Persian Gulf and the Straits. Its vast network of routes encompassed India, Burma, Arabia, Malaya, Australia, Japan, China and Africa. Its fleet included passenger liners, troop transports, cargo vessels, river steamers, tugs, coasters and barges. Its passengers included the administrators, soldiers, tradesmen, missionaries and native labourers who developed, governed and protected the Empire. Its holds carried the Royal Mail and cargoes of Imperial communication and commerce.

The line's roots were Scottish, but its heart and soul lay in the Bay of Bengal. Rangoon, the BI hub, had more than 500 calls by company ships a year. With its own repair yards, coal mines, officers' clubs and residences in India, BI maintained its Eastern Fleet, a unique foreign service. Its Indian agency, Mackinnon Mackenzie & Co., was one of the mainstays of the Raj.

The line's commanding Indian presence spread westwards across the

11

Indian Ocean to East Africa. This vast region was opened to steam navigation and secured for the Crown largely due to the pioneering efforts of William Mackinnon and its development was closely tied to the Raj. Indian labourers built the great African railways, Indian tradesmen dominated African commerce—whose pre-First World War currency was the Indian rupee—and ports like Durban, Mombasa and Zanzibar boasted large Indian communities for which BI ships, with their largely Indian names, crews, deck passengers and cargoes, were the principal link across the Indian Ocean.

The story of BI ships and services in Africa is intertwined with the modern history of that continent—the slave trade of the Sultans of Zanzibar, the exploits of H.M. Stanley and the intrigues of King Leopold, the African Scramble and Mackinnon's own Imperial British East Africa Co., the heyday of British East Africa and the Kenya of Lord Delamere, the wars of the African bush and veldt from Rorke's Drift to Keren, the construction of the Uganda Railway and Kilindini Harbour to convey newly developed cargoes of sisal, coffee and cotton, and finally the transition from protectorates and colonies to fledgling independent nations.

Despite the burgeoning bibliography on merchant shipping, BI has been unfortunately if understandably overlooked. Its fleet was the largest in the greatest Merchant Navy and its services widespread, yet they were largely "East of Suez"; its ships, only a few exceeding 10,000 grt, were generally small, slow and conventional; many of the services were of the localised

"feeder" type, and its corporate image remained quiet and unassuming. Yet these largely workaday vessels bound together much of the Empire, carrying the merchandise and mails, the coolies and colonists, giving purpose and profit to the ever-expanding company.

The heart of BI was its remarkable system of interconnecting feeder lines. The African services began in this manner, yet within a few decades rivalled the traditional Bay of Bengal-based routes and evolved into two main lines, one from Britain via Suez and the other from Bombay, augmented by various East African coastal runs. With the post-war independence of India and Burma, BI's African routes assumed a new importance and indeed its African business was better towards the end than at the beginning and eventually was served by some of the company's best and most notable vessels.

Whilst the lavender-hulled "Round-Africa" ships of Union-Castle, larger and faster, were often in the vanguard of the East Africa run, those of BI played as prominent a part in the development of "British East". They were splendid ships all—the clipper-stemmed *Abyssinia,* with coal smoke and billowing sail, cleaving the monsoon swell; one of the doughty "M"s working cargo in the chilly gloom of Middlesbrough or in sultry Beira; the graceful *Tairea,* her three funnels silhouetted against Durban's Bluff, Bombay-bound; the varnished teak and polished brass of *Amra's* bridge; the bustle and babble of *Kampala's* 'tween decks and the elephant tusks and over-stuffed leather armchairs of *Uganda's* smoking room.

13

The company's final and finest liners, the "BI Sisters" *Kenya,* and *Uganda,* figured prominently and poignantly in the gathering dusk of both British India Line and British East Africa; *Kenya* was the last Red Ensign liner on the East Africa run whilst her sister, one of the most beloved ships of the post-war era, was the last to fly the BI houseflag and served valiantly during the Falklands War.

To Tilbury Landing Stage then, steamer trunks packed with safari kit and dinner jacket, where R.M.S. *Uganda,* Beira-bound, loaded to the marks with Commonwealth commerce, Blue Peter and Royal Mail pennant whipping at the fore truck, awaits with wisps of steam hissing impatiently from polished brass whistles on that memorable funnel. A 6,000-mile voyage, from the cliffs of Dover to the cliffs of Kilindini, beckons with the once-familiar shipboard pleasures of awakening to *chota hazri* ("small breakfast"), watching the flying fish skim the bow wave, tucking into a BI curry luncheon, a siesta in the shade of the promenade deck and dancing in the verandah with its French doors opened to the breezes of a tropic evening. A voyage in time and space, of pleasure and purpose, that once, not so long ago, defined ocean travel to British East Africa.

Peter C. Kohler
April, 1995.

14

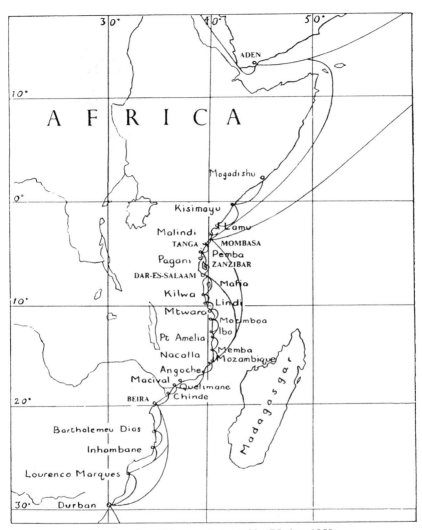

Map showing African ports served by BI circa 1950.

15

1.   BI BEGINNINGS

Any soundly established British shipping line is one of the finest expressions of the genius of an island people. It has been the lot and fortune of the British India Company to play a unique part in British imperial history as well.

BI Centenary, 1856-1956

In the vanguard of the progress that marked the Victorian Age frequently stood an enterprising Scot. Scottish entrepreneurs and engineers built much of the commercial and civic infrastructure of the British Empire and expanded its bounds. Calcutta, the business centre of the British Raj, with its ornate houses of commerce along the Hooghly evoking Argyle Street in architecture, became a palm-treed extension of Glasgow, exerting a call to the ambitious and adventurous of a remarkable generation of Scots. The BI story begins with two such men, William Mackinnon and Robert Mackenzie, both of Campbeltown, Argyll.

Robert Mackenzie arrived in Calcutta in 1836 and set up an oil goods import/export business there as well as being the agent for the India General Steam Navigation Co. Indian commerce and eastern overseas trade were then entering a period of enormous expansion occasioned by the ending of the Honourable East India Company's long held monopoly and rapid developments in steam navigation. Because of reasonable distances and availability of Bengal coal, steamship services were established in Indian waters well in advance of other regions. Indeed, the first regular scheduled overseas steamer route, Bombay to Suez, was begun in 1829 by the East India Company, four years before *Royal William* crossed the North Atlantic.

The man who would establish steam navigation along India's coasts, the Bay of Bengal and Persian Gulf, was born William Mackinnon on 31 March 1823 in Campbeltown, Argyll. Beginning his career in commerce with a Portuguese East India merchant in Glasgow, he too, was drawn to greater prospects in India where he arrived in 1847. His business relationship with Robert Mackenzie began almost at once and the partnership of Mackinnon, Mackenzie & Co. was founded in December 1847. So too was its involvement in shipping, mainly chartered sailing vessels running between India and Australia. It was on passage from Australia to Calcutta that Robert Mackenzie was lost in a shipwreck in 1853.

The firm continued to prosper, additional capital was raised in Scotland and Mackinnon took an increasing interest in shipping. "A shrewd little man who loved to pore over maps and perceive where a ship might carry, or take up, a profitable cargo," as he was described in *BI Centenary,* Mackinnon hit upon the idea of opening up India's vast coastline to steam navigation to reach

16

the many places where railways did not touch.

> *The stately homes of England*
> *Shake hands across the sea,*
> *And colonists, when writing home,*
> *Pay but a penny fee.*

Nowadays in an age of instant communication, it is worth recalling when the mails, transported by stage, railway or ship, were the only means of keeping in touch, especially in the far-flung colonies where those early settlers endured almost unbearable conditions. Letters from home assumed an immense importance and quantity; by the 1890s some 22 million pieces of mail were posted annually from Britain to the Empire. In an age whose credo was "transportation is civilisation", getting the mails through safely and speedily became a Victorian obsession.

The steamship, by virtue of its regularity even more than speed, revolutionised worldwide mail communications and there was no prouder vessel than one bearing the imposing prefix "R.M.S.", Royal Mail Steamship, "conveying the Mails and Dispatches, under contract with Her Majesty's Government." Today only one such vessel, R.M.S. *St. Helena,* remains in ocean service between Britain, the South Atlantic islands and Cape Town, but at the turn of the century a large yet elite company of crack mailships were the "shuttles of an Empire's loom."

For the traveller, taking passage in an R.M.S. meant safety and speed, and promised the Victorian virtues of seasoned British officers, stout seamen whether from Bristol or Bengal, a plentiful bill of fare and an irreproachable dignity derived from sailing with the English Mails. There were practical advantages, too; in any civilised harbour, the Royal Mail pennant at the foretruck guaranteed priority berthing, coaling and provisioning. For the Colonial Office, mailships running to a regular timetable were a vital part of the "trade follows flag" imperial credo. Machinery had mastered the monsoon, and the whole of the coastline round India and Burma fell within reach of British trade and influence.

For an aspiring steamship line, securing a coveted Royal Mail contract guaranteed a minimum revenue beyond the carriage of cargo (the quantity of which was limited aboard early steamers due to amount of coal required) and passengers and conferred an enormous cachet. There also came a heavy burden of running to a fixed contract over a set number of years, maintaining an often rigorous schedule in all conditions and submitting to the whims of the Admiralty, Post Office or whatever authority conferred the contract. Competition for such contracts was keen, often cut-throat, but once won, could make or break a company.

The Honourable East India Company, which had only just annexed the southern half of Burma, opened the door to Mackinnon Mackenzie when in 1855 they invited tenders for a regular mail steamship route between Calcutta and Rangoon. The Scottish partners were successful with their bid and set out to establish the first reliable scheduled steamship service in the Bay of Bengal.

Eighteen fifty-six. Queen Victoria establishes the Victoria Cross to award extraordinary valour by British redcoats then fighting in the Anglo-Chinese and Anglo-Persian Wars. Natal becomes a Crown Colony, Tasmania is granted self-government and Marthinius Pretorius establishes the South African Republic (Transvaal). Woodrow Wilson, Sigmund Freud, George Bernard Shaw and Oscar Wilde are born. The Khedive of Egypt grants Ferdinand de Lesseps the concession to construct the Suez Canal. And on 24 September the Calcutta & Burmah Steam Navigation Co. is registered with £35,000 in capital.

Choosing the peacock of Burma for the company crest and houseflag, Mackinnon acquired a small fleet of second-hand steamers for his new Royal Mail service. In a sense, the future BI's African connection began at once for the second vessel purchased was *Cape of Good Hope,* a new 500-grt steamer built for the London-South Africa service of the defunct General Screw Co. She and *Baltic* (1854/535 grt) maintained the initial fortnightly run between Calcutta, Akyab, Rangoon and Moulmein.

The company's association with the Peninsular & Oriental Steam Navigation Co. (P&O) began at an early date, if under rather regrettable circumstances, when on 23 March 1859 *Cape of Good Hope* was rammed and sunk by P&O's aptly named *Nemesis* in the Hooghly River. Apart from this and other setbacks, including the loss of the line's first newbuilding, *Calcutta* (1860/527 grt) in Irish waters even before entering service, the company persevered.

India was transformed after the Indian Mutiny in 1857 during which the infant Calcutta & Burmah carried troops, thus starting a long tradition between the company and Her Majesty's Forces. The mandate of the long moribund Honourable East India Co. was ended and direct rule from Whitehall brought far-reaching developments in trade and a large influx of civil servants. It was the beginning of the modern British Empire, one in which Mackinnon's fledgling little line of steamers would go on to play a considerable role.

In 1862 an important and long-lasting friendship was begun between Mackinnon and Sir Bartle Frere, a member of the Viceroy's Council and chief administrator of the Bengal Government, that was to have a big impact on the company's fortunes and indeed those of the British Raj itself. As a result Mackinnon was able to propose to the Viceroy, Lord Canning, that a scheduled mail service linking Calcutta and Bombay with calls at numerous intermediate ports should be instituted. Frere was enthusiastic about the scheme, which also interested the Viceroy, but the Bombay Government's approval had to be sought too. With the appointment next year of Frere as Governor of Bombay this idea, that depended on a financial grant, became a reality. Of greater importance still was the granting by the friendly Governor of two mail contracts, one for a fortnightly service between Bombay and Karachi and the other for an eight times a year service between Karachi and Persian Gulf ports. Prior to this act the new routes had already been tested so the carriage of the mails was quickly and easily implemented, the arrival and departure dates having to dovetail in with those of the P&O schedule for the English Mails. *

Apart from enabling the company, since 28 October 1862 reorganised and restyled as the British India Steam Navigation Company Limited (BI), to switch vessels between its eastern and western wings, the monthly coasting services acted as a more efficient feeder for P&O for goods such as coir yarn and Mangalore tiles, as well as valuable foodstuffs like spices, coffee, pepper and coconut oil. Within two years the frequency of this schedule had to be doubled and the Persian Gulf Line's departures increased to one a month. One other feature of the coasting line was an important new agreement with P&O's arch-rival, the French mail company, Messageries Imperiales (later to become the Messageries Maritimes) enabling some interchange of passengers and cargo at both Galle in Ceylon and Pondicherry in India. British India was to benefit in future years from this good relationship even, as will be seen, in East African waters. *

Thus within a year BI was operating the following services:
Calcutta-Akyab-Rangoon-Moulmein (fortnightly)
Calcutta-Rangoon-Moulmein-Penang-Malacca-Singapore (monthly)
Rangoon-Port Blair, Andamans (monthly)
Bombay-Karachi (fortnightly)
Karachi-Persian Gulf ports (eight times yearly)
Calcutta-Bombay via coast ports (monthly)
As indicated, some of these were to be improved in frequency and over the next few years many new routes were to be opened up. The network of services was not unlike that of a large water-bus company, whose reputation for reliability became steadily more firmly established, as did that for the service and discipline provided by the British officers and Indian crews to whom wearing the company uniform was an object of immense pride.

The ships, despite their small size, quietly assumed a smartness of their own as regards appearance and performance. This was an age when a warship of the Royal Navy, elegant in black hull and yellow upperworks, was more gaily turned out than most merchantmen. British India's sombre livery of black hull, funnel and boats, dark brown masts and dark varnished deck houses was enlivened only by a white sheer line and the two narrow white bands separated by a thin black line that ringed the funnel. The houseflag was a white swallow tail burgee emblazoned with the cross of St. Patrick in red and the crest was among the most symbolic imaginable, the figure of Britannia backed by the British lion with one paw resting imperially on top of a globe. There was something else about these ships: the polished copper steam pipes, the glistening black varnish of the lifeboats, the bleached-white teak decks and vessel names like *Cashmere, Kurrachee, Satara* and *Coconada* that bespoke a pride of purpose and place as belonging to the British India Line of Royal Mail Steamers.

In 1863 alone BI added nine ships to its fleet and quickly acquired a distinctive look about its vessels. Nothing revolutionary was to be found in the design and construction of a BI ship; pace-setting usually proved, if at all, fleetingly profitable. The company did not design its own vessels, preferring to order "off the peg" to its own exacting specifications. These included the ability to operate on any of BI's services and to have spacious 'tween decks for the carriage of cargo, livestock, troops or deck passengers. Additionally the vagaries of Calcutta's meandering Hooghly River with its maximum depth of 27 feet, restricted the size and draught of the ships. Like most lines, BI enjoyed a special relationship with one builder, Wm. Denny & Bros. of Dumbarton, that began with *India* of 1862 and carried on through to *Ordia* of 1950. Another important early builder was A. & J. Inglis, Glasgow.

The 1,059-grt, 239 ft. by 30 ft. *India* was really a one-off ship spotted by Mackinnon in his desperate and urgent Clydeside search for new tonnage to enable him to fulfil his new commitments. She had been intended for trans-Atlantic use, but was still unfinished. Completed therefore to Mackinnon's specification she joined his fleet as the first ship with a gross tonnage exceeding 1,000 grt. Two-masted and rigged as a brig, the new single-screw steamer was powered by a simple direct-acting two-cylinder engine and capable of carrying 28 Saloon passengers and 600 on deck. So satisfied was BI with her suitability for the trade and performance that it quickly ordered from Denny's four very similar vessels, which were two pairs of sisters with identical hull dimensions, but three-masted and barque rigged without forecastles. Later, however, these were added and Saloon accommodation, at that time always in the poop, was enlarged. Named *Burmah* (II) (1863/1,081 grt) and *Arabia* (1863/1,081 grt) the first pair were followed by *Punjaub* (1864/1,080 grt) and *Cashmere* (1864/1,083 grt). Larger versions would be built later, but the company continued to need many small vessels also, these being for particular coastal routes which were often affected by draught and other limitations. *

In this, the era of sail and steam, all of these early BI steamers were brig or barque rigged. It is recorded in *BI Centenary* that *Baghdad* once "sailed from Mombasa to within a day's run of Aden without the propeller having turned once." In addition to being essential in case of mishaps with machinery or screw (which were then common), sail was routinely employed to get extra speed during the monsoon and to steady a vessel heavily laden with deck passengers. Indeed, BI ships used auxiliary sail right through to the First World War and stay sails were used into the 'twenties.

Such was the pace of steamship development that all of the initial simple engined vessels were made obsolete within a few years with the rapid improvement of the compound engine. In effect, using the steam twice through compounding halved coal consumption and enabled steamships to compete economically with sail. British India, already known for having its entire fleet composed of modern screw steamers, made the considerable investment of refitting its still new vessels with the improved engines.

Saloon accommodation of the early BI ships was invariably small and usually divided into two grades, the better being traditionally sited in the poop and the lesser amidships. This was based on the prevailing thought that the throbbing of the screw was preferable to being in close proximity with the vibration, heat and clanking of the machinery and boilers. From the beginning BI shunned ostentation in on-board services or accommodation, but its service by Goan stewards and bill of fare were certainly on a par with those provided by P&O steamers, including the huge Victorian menus and the inevitable luncheon curries which quickly became a hallmark. Far from today's frivolous shipboard lifestyle, BI ships (and most passengers) took themselves seriously, perhaps too much so:

> The Austrian traveller Baron von Hubner, who made a long voyage in the British India liner *Dorunda* in 1885, recorded in near-despair the awfulness of a shipboard Sunday— no whist, no bezique, even smoking was unpopular. 'Young M. caught with a novel in his hand: a lady looks at him fixedly, utters the word "Sunday", takes away the novel and slips into his hand a hymnbook instead.'
>
> James Morris, *Pax Britannica*

Far more numerous than the travellers in Saloon were the deck or unberthed passengers who found shelter in the 'tween decks or under awnings topside, providing their own bedding. Their numbers aboard depended on the weather conditions, fine or foul, as during the monsoon, and the length of the voyage, long or short. On average, the larger ships could carry approximately 875 deck passengers during fair-weather voyages. In charge of deck passengers' needs was the Chief Officer who bore a considerable responsibility indeed, given the numbers carried aboard in very limited space, yet BI from the start insisted that deck passengers be afforded the best possible treatment. Their meals were prepared by *vishiwallahs,* normally separate ones for Hindus and ones for Moslems, who received free passage but were not part of the ship's company. These huddled masses were to form the bulk of BI's passenger trade for the life of the company. Most were Indians, the migrant labourers for much of the Empire, who built the railways, harvested the crops and toiled in the mines when local labour was found unwilling or unable. Upon their backs were largely carried the trade and development of the Empire and BI conveyed no more important passengers in terms of company profit and Imperial progress.

From the start, the heart of the BI was its localised services as exemplified by the legendary "umbrella ships", the coasters that were originally summoned, legend has it, to collect cargo or passengers by a merchant hoisting an umbrella, or later a flag, to attract the captain's attention. It is all the more remarkable to consider that BI achieved a reputation for the regularity and safety of its services at a time when the Indian coast, Bay of Bengal and Persian Gulf were among the poorest charted waters in the world and each beset with its own peculiar climatic and geographic conditions. Thus Mackinnon's entrepreneurial ambitions were realised by good seamanship and well found ships that truly went where no others had plied before. Many an eastern port was surveyed, buoyed and lighted by BI enterprise and at BI's expense.

There were pirates to fend off in the Gulf, inter-racial or religious fights among deck passengers as well as the whims of *burra sahibs* in Saloon to cater for. The little steamers of BI came to play an important role in the lives of scores of small coastal communities and to both native and European, they were the sinew and symbol of the British Empire. Now BI was to do for East Africa what it had done for Burma, India and the Gulf and begin one of the most exciting and far-reaching chapters in its history.

2. RED ENSIGN TO DARK CONTINENT

There seems good reason to believe that the eastern coast of Africa will within the next twenty years receive much more attention both from the commercial and philanthropic worlds than it does now....No line of coast with equal resources in the background is more out of reach of anything like systematised communication.   The Argus (Cape Town), 3 September 1870

Kipling's "Far-Flung" British Empire was indeed just that and its bounds, "wider and wider still", were expanded largely because of the revolutionary developments in communications during the Victorian Age. The railway, steamship and telegraph all played their role, but it was a fixed artery, the Suez Canal, that proved pivotal.

The opening of the Suez Canal on 9 November 1869 would revolutionise maritime trading patterns, consign the sailing ship to commercial oblivion and alter what we now call geopolitics in the Mid and Far East. Yet what was soon heralded as the "Lifeline of Empire" was greeted with varying emotions by the established British lines. It was telling that whilst BI's *India* was among the first to make a northbound transit of the Canal, en route to her Dumbarton builders for compounding of her engines, the P&O paddle steamer *Delta,* participating in the opening ceremonies, went half-way through and then turned back! With its huge investment in two separate fleets (composed of now obsolete Mediterranean-based paddlers like *Delta* and Indian-based ships with too much draught for the Canal) and an overland route through Egypt, it was little wonder that P&O may have shared the British Government's initial view that the waterway was little more than a French plot to achieve hegemony in the region and further the ambitions of the Messageries Maritimes.

> The opening of the Suez Canal, by which a new expeditious route is provided for general traffic between Europe and India, is likely to have an important bearing on the Company's interests.
> BI Annual Report, 1870

> The Directors believe that the opening of the Suez Canal may, on the whole, prove not to be prejudicial to the prospects of the Company.
> BI Annual Report, 1871

With no established long-distance routes or binding mail contracts suddenly made incompatible with the opening of the Suez Canal, BI could view the situation rather more sanguinely. If nothing else, the waterway meant that BI's major engine-compounding programme could now be undertaken at substantial savings in cost and time by sending the ships, like *India*, home via the Canal instead of round the Cape. More importantly, BI was quick to exploit the changes in marine commerce wrought by the new artery.

By shifting the axis of trade routes from Europe to India and Asia, the Suez Canal created a maritime trading triangle, Aden-Zanzibar-Bombay, in the Western Indian Ocean. Aden, British since 1839, took on enormous potential by its unique situation linking African, Persian Gulf and Indian-based commerce as well as being an important coaling station. Zanzibar began to supply water to trans-Suez ships and profit from expanded trade; to the east Bombay became the closest Indian port from Suez. Bombay's ideal location as a base for new services in the Persian Gulf and Indian Ocean, its new rail link to Calcutta and its superb natural harbour, prompted BI to develop it as a centre of operations that would soon rival Calcutta. Towards this end BI leased from P&O the South Yard of the Mazagon Dockyard, Bombay, in 1870.

British India's expansionist aims now looked to horizons beyond the Bay of Bengal and Persian Gulf. Firstly there was the establishment of what the company always quaintly referred to as "Home Lines" to and from England via Suez. The first of these, from London to Basra via Lisbon, Algiers and Red Sea ports, began in 1871, followed five years later by what would become the principal Home Line from London to Calcutta via Colombo and Madras. And to the annoyance of P&O, BI won a share of the lucrative Indian trooping contract which was soon to become a major part of its business.

The Persian Gulf Line had brought to light the seasonal dhow-carried traffic between northern Arabia and Zanzibar including the slave trade, whilst East African merchants had been crossing to southern Malabar for years. Extending from the Persian Gulf and down the coasts of both India and Africa, this is one of the world's oldest trade routes and was first plied by the Sumerians some 4,400 years ago. Arab seafarers learned to exploit the unique monsoon wind pattern of the region: southwesterly from May to September and northeasterly from October to April. This was sufficient to fill the lateen sails of their dhows for one voyage a year carrying ironware, glassware, textiles, wine and wheat to Africa and returning to Arabia with slaves, ivory and tortoise shell. Upon this was established an Arab maritime empire extending from the Red Sea and Persian Gulf down the East African coast from Somalia to Mozambique. This Islamic influence survived the arrival of Portugal's Vasco da Gama who first rounded the Cape of Good Gope and sailed up the East coast in 1498. Portuguese forces conquered the coastal towns and fortified Mombasa, whose old port is still dominated by Fort Jesus, but after two centuries the Arabs wrested back control, except in Mozambique.

East African commerce had long attracted the aspirations of Indian merchants, *banyans,* who made annual voyages from India to Zanzibar for trading and to finance the slave trade. There was a growing Indian merchant population on the island as well. Thus, BI's interest in the area was both understandable and longstanding. As early as 1864 James Liddell declined an offer to establish a BI agency at Zanzibar saying he had met "another man who was able to give me some information about Zanzibar, and as his knowledge of the place somewhat tallied with that which I had already heard before, it rather unsettled my mind as to desirability of going."

Mr. Liddell knew considerably more about the Dark Continent than most Europeans of his day. Fringing the great unexplored interior, populated by fearsome tribes like the Masai, was a coastal strip, centred on the spice-scented island of Zanzibar. This traditional meeting ground between the African and Asian, 20 miles off the coast, was seized by Seyyid Said, Sultan of Muscat and Oman, around 1820 and became the centre of the still-flourishing slave trade and an important entrepôt for commerce in the region. As such it attracted the interest of the growing abolitionist movement in Britain. In 1822 Captain Moresby, on behalf of the Bombay Government, signed a treaty with Seyyid Said which prohibited the slave trade between the Omani sultanate and any Christian, but by permitting slaving between Moslems along most of the East African coast, it actually encouraged the Sultan to extend it further into the interior.

In 1824 Captain William Owen, Royal Navy, established a small detachment at Mombasa and offered protection to the local Mazrui family rulers from the Sultan's slavers. This was done without consultation with the British Government which had no ambitions in the region. In 1826 British forces left Mombasa to its eventual occupation by Said in 1837, who moved his government from Oman to Zanzibar three years later and claimed sovereignty over the coastal mainland. Clove and palm oil trees were planted on Zanzibar and Pemba islands which established a lucrative plantation economy built on slave labour which in turn prompted extensive Arab caravans to penetrate deep into the interior hunting for slaves and ivory, the so-called black and white gold of Africa.

Seyyid Said eagerly opened up Zanzibar to world trade, but American, German and French mariners and merchants were first to answer the call of commerce, not British. Only the continued presence of Indian traders in East Africa and the growing anti-slavery movement prompted any British political presence there. That slavery still prospered in the unknown East African hinterland, despite attempts by Royal Navy gunboats to intercept dhows in the Gulf, inspired its exploration by abolitionists, not the least of whom was David Livingstone, who believed that the three Cs, Christianity, Civilisation and Commerce, would ultimately consign slavery to history. He and others, like Richard Burton and John Speke, were also intent on discovering the relationship between the great African rivers, the Nile, Congo and Zambezi. It was the beginning of the great era of African exploration, culminating in the legendary meeting between the "lost" Livingstone and American journalist-explorer H.M. Stanley in 1871 which made East Africa the topic of discussion in every Victorian parlour.

The opening of Suez also thrust a reluctant Great Britain into empire building in the region, if only to secure the shorelines of new routes to India. The canal put the East African coast 2,000 sea miles closer to Britain and Europe. Gladstone's Liberal government was loathe to assume binding colonial responsibilities, preferring "trade not territory" and an informal empire built on private enterprise. Four years after the establishment of British West Africa, a House of Commons committee suggested that no further expansion take place, but it could not halt the "civilising mission" of individuals. Abolition of slavery remained the principal concern. The tactic decided upon was more mercantile than moralist: to lessen the Sultan of Zanzibar's dependence on the slave trade by opening up Zanzibar to commerce with Europe via the new Suez link and in effect supplant the ancient Arab dhows with British steamships.

The 1870s also gave rise to the concept of national self-sufficiency built on mercantile overseas empires that would provide the industrialised mother country with raw materials and overseas markets. This had particular appeal to those nations to whom the industrial revolution came later than Britain's: France, Germany, Portugal and especially Belgium, whose King Leopold II became a fervent African empire builder, seeing in H.M. Stanley's newly discovered Congo the makings of a Belgian commercial base.

In 1866 Dr. John Kirk, who had accompanied Livingstone on one of his explorations, was appointed British Consul at Zanzibar and became an influential confidant of the Sultan from whom he was determined to obtain a meaningful anti-slavery treaty. The diplomat whom the British Government dispatched in 1871 as a special envoy to "have a look at things" in East Africa and negotiate the anti-slavery treaty with the Sultan, Sir Henry Bartle Frere, was from BI's perspective an ideal choice, given his friendship with Mackinnon and past support in the granting of mail contracts to the company. It was Kirk, however, who prevailed upon the Sultan to sign an agreement in 1873 which effectively ended the slave trade along the coast, but had little effect in the interior.

> I believe that as Mackinnon, since he had made his fortune and was childless, devoted his ripest and wisest years and the greater part of his fortune to this idea, which like the King of the Belgians, he had making an African State valuable to his Government and people...

So H.M. Stanley described his old friend and colleague in African adventure and empire building. Like many of his contemporaries, Mackinnon became obsessed with Africa; the exploits of Stanley and others recalled his adventurous youth and Livingstone's ideals of supplanting the slave trade with legitimate commerce appealed to his deep religious and moral convictions and renewed his mercantile zeal. In the absence of any formal interest or encouragement by the British Government, those with ambitions in Africa, whether abolitionist, avaricious or simply adventurous, looked to other sources of moral and financial support—Belgium's King Leopold and William Mackinnon who was once described as "occupying that interesting borderland, between philanthropy and high finance."

Bartle Frere and John Kirk, knowing what Mackinnon had done with BI in India and playing to his newfound African interests, hit upon him as the man with the experience, resources and expansionist vigour to establish a similar network of steamship services in East Africa which would connect with existing ones to the north at Suez and from Cape Town in the south. In this way East Africa would be opened up to international commerce, but unlike in India, Burma and the Gulf where BI ships served lucrative established markets and trade routes, similar services in Africa would be speculative empire building projects whose initial purpose was more about politics than profits.

Before the First World War, local connecting steamship routes were an integral part of the Empire's chain of communications. To generations of Victorian timetable readers, these intricate inter-connecting mail services had a certain fascination as well as practical utility. As one progressed out East along the Imperial waystops—Gibraltar, Malta, Suez, Aden, Bombay, Calcutta, Singapore and Hong Kong—passenger lists and cargo manifests thinned out, making direct through services unprofitable. East Africa was in an odd corner for the existing trunk routes, being too far north to be served by an extension of the Cape Mail and too far west to permit the Bombay Mail to detour there. P&O had helped to pioneer transhipment services on trunk routes whilst BI had established an effective feeder network in Indian and Asian seas; now the pattern of operations would extend to East Africa.

Prior to 1863 Zanzibar had no regular steamship service with any other port and was effectively cut off from mail communication. Captain C.P. Rigby, British consul at Zanzibar prior to Kirk, argued that without regular mail service, British trade could not be developed and suggested that a Lascar-crewed schooner be put on a scheduled connecting service from Zanzibar to the Seychelle islands. Lying approximately midway between Africa and India, the Seychelles offered a convenient connection point with the Aden-Mauritius trunk line. The proposal was rejected by the Treasury Department, but in 1863 it was arranged to have a naval vessel make a monthly mail run between Zanzibar and the Seychelles. This lapsed after a short period and it was not until 1871 that Sultan Barghash had his own steam yacht perform the service.

The revolution in world communications wrought by the Suez Canal and the completion of the telegraphic cable from Falmouth to Bombay in 1870 put Aden at the crossroads of imperial commerce and communications by virtue of its pivotal role as a coaling and cable relay station. Aden and not the Seychelles became the link between Zanzibar and the outside world desired by John Kirk and two Cape Town residents: D.C. Stevens, a local shipping enthusiast, and Edgar Layard, the British Slave Trade Commissioner there.

In a series of letters to Cape Town *Argus,* D.C. Stevens urged that the Suez Canal be exploited to its fullest potential by re-routing Union Steam Ship Company's Cape Mail into a full round-Africa service, out via the Cape and return via Suez. For South Africans, the canal was both a threat (siphoning off the India-bound trade via the Cape) and a promise (permitting a potentially faster link with England and India via Aden and accessing the Aden cable), whilst Layard, in a letter of 2 October 1871 to authorities in Britain, argued that an East African service be used "as the means of opening up the east coast of Africa, Madagascar and the Comoro Islands not only to trade but to the spread of civilisation and the abolition of slavery." He added that "much better results would accrue from subsidising a company to run steamers as suggested than spending double the sum in increasing our squadron [of Royal Navy gunboats on anti-slavery patrols] on that coast."

Layard's letter was forwarded from the Foreign Office to the Treasury and Robert Lowe, Chancellor of the Exchequer, asked the Post Office to make tentative enquiries with steamship companies regarding the possibilities of establishing two feeder services to Zanzibar, one from Cape Town or Natal connecting with the Cape Mail, and another from Aden connecting with the Bombay Mail. Thus Steven's call for a round-Africa route was not heeded. The East African coast, poorly surveyed, fraught with natural hazards, and, except for Zanzibar, lacking commercial prospects, would have been a dangerous, lengthy and unprofitable diversion for Union's deep-draught mailships coming up from the Cape. The dual feeder service proposal was, however, a promising one, connecting as it would East Africa with the two most efficient of Britain long-distance mail routes.

Negotiations for the East African feeder contract began in 1871 and were hotly contested. On 21 November 1871 Union Line asked for £29,000 annually to undertake a monthly Cape Town-Zanzibar service for a period of seven years. The next month the Director of Posts in India replied with BI's bid of £27,365 annually for a monthly service from Aden to Cape Town via Zanzibar. This competitive bid, lower than Union's and fulfilling both functions of the proposed service, was muddled by BI's insistence on granting of certain other contracts relating to its existing Indian routes. Union's bid was complicated by its renegotiation of the Cape Mail contract which expired in 1876 amid the expectation of new competition from Donald Currie's Castle Line. Negotiations were also undertaken between Union and BI regarding their respective bids for the East Africa run and it was eventually decided that the two should split the service, as originally intended.

A joint tender was offered in June 1872 proposing that Union Line serve Zanzibar from the Cape and BI from Aden. On 29 October BI was awarded a Royal Mail contract worth £6,000 between Aden and Zanzibar whilst the Union Line won a contract from Cape Town to Zanzibar.

MAILS FOR ZANZIBAR—Mail for Zanzibar will be made up at the General Post-Office and forwarded to Aden, *via* Southampton, on the morning of the 14th inst.; *via* Brindisi; on the evening of the 22nd inst., and thence forward every four weeks. These mails will be conveyed from Aden to their destination by a steam vessel provided under an agreement recently concluded with the British India Steam Navigation Company. The costs of postage, which in all cases be prepaid, will be as follows:— *via* Southampton—letters, 9d per 1/2 oz.; newspapers each, not exceeding 4 oz., 2d; books and patterns, not exceeding 1 oz., 1d; above 1 oz. and not exceeding 2 oz., 2d; above 2 oz. and not exceeding 4 oz., 4d; every additional 4 oz., 4d. Via Brindisi—letters 1s per 1/2 oz.; newspapers, each, not exceeding 4 oz., 3d; books and patterns, not exceeding oz., 2d; above 1 oz. and not exceeding 2 oz., 4d; above 2 oz. and not exceeding 4 oz., 7d; every additional 4 oz., 7d.—by Command of the Postmaster-General.

The Times, 7 November 1872

THE EAST COAST OF AFRICA—The Union Steamship Company have made arrangements for the establishment of a mail packet service between the Cape, Natal, and Zanzibar, and the British India Company, in conjunction therewith, have undertaken the service from Zanzibar to Aden. The East Coast of Africa will thus be in communication with England and India, and the establishment of this service will supplement the operations of the Government for the forcible suppression of the slave trade by encouragement of legitimate commerce in its stead, the beneficial effects of which have been so successfully exemplified on the West Coast.

The Times, 8 November 1872

STEAM TO ZANZIBAR—Steamers of the British India Steam Navigation Company will leave Aden for Zanzibar every four weeks, carrying Her Majesty's Mails, commencing with the

India Mail leaving London on 22nd November. Arrangements have been made with the Peninsular and Oriental Company for the conveyance of passengers and cargo from the United Kingdom to Zanzibar, to be transhipped at Aden.

BI advertisement, *The Times,* 11 November 1872

The service, a 2,000-mile run to be covered in nine days southbound and 11 northbound, was to carry the mails once every four weeks to connect (at Aden) with outward and homeward P&O steamers carrying the British Overland Mails which unfortunately did not call on the same day, the outward ship arriving on a Thursday about noon and the latter during the night between Monday and Tuesday. So the BI branch line vessel would have to remain in Aden for about four days to make the connection with both, but this would also allow time for other transfers to be carried out. *

Beginning a tradition of BI ships serving Africa that would endure for 104 years, R.M.S. *Punjaub,* under Commander Hansard, first arrived at Zanzibar with Her Majesty's Mails on 15 December 1872 and according to *BI Centenary,* "astonished at least the European residents by carrying news of recent date."

In addition to the P&O transhipment at Aden, BI sailing lists also showed an all-BI service from London to Zanzibar with the 30 November 1872 London sailing of the brand-new *Agra* to Madras and Calcutta via Aden where a transfer could be made to the BI Zanzibar vessel. A similar arrangement was made with the new *Java's* 30 December delivery voyage from London to Calcutta.

In the BI *Handbook* the Aden-Zanzibar service was given the line number 12 initially, following the Bombay, Karachi and Gulf lines which by then were numbered 10 and 11, but after a year the Aden branch line became No. 13. The 1873 *Handbook* listed the initial timetable:

LINE NO. 12 ADEN-ZANZIBAR

3 January	sail ADEN
12 January	arr. ZANZIBAR
16 January	sail ZANZIBAR
27 January	arr. ADEN

The northern connection started operating in December 1872, but it was not until February 1873 that the Union Line's 613-ton *Natal* arrived at Zanzibar, having left the Cape earlier that month. Union's *Kaffir* and *Zulu* soon became the principal ships on the run for a number of years.

For the new Zanzibar run, BI assigned a variety of tonnage, old and new. The 1,080-grt *Punjaub* was a handsome vessel with her clipper bow and barque rig, but she was already nine years old. Less rakish looking, but brand new were the sister ships *Calcutta* and *Coconada* of 863 grt, designed for the

Calcutta-Chittagong run and delivered by A.&J. Inglis, Glasgow, in August and September 1872, respectively. They were among the first BI ships with straight stems and were built with compound engines of 129 hp giving 10 knots in addition to being schooner rigged. They could carry 35 First, 14 Second and 969 deck passengers.

Calcutta (Captain Atkinson) began her stint on the Zanzibar run on 14 February 1873, transhipping mail from P&O's *Deccan* and arriving at Zanzibar on the 23rd. On 21 April *Punjaub* anchored at Aden from Zanzibar for the last time and proceeded directly to Bombay for new duties. In her place *Cashmere* made her first Aden arrival from Zanzibar on 14 June and ran with *Calcutta* until October. For 1874 *Euphrates* (1863/488 grt) entered service upon her 19 May arrival at Aden from Bombay and plied the route until 21 November when she left Zanzibar for Bombay and was replaced by *Coconada* which undertook her maiden sailing from Aden on 27 December.

Considering the Bombay Governor's contributions to the line, BI might have retained the ship's original name when it acquired the 811-grt *Sir Bartle Frere* (1865) from the Bombay River & Coast S.N. Co. As *Medina* and re-engined (becoming BI's first twin-screw ship), she carried 12 Saloon and 500 deck passengers and joined the Zanzibar run in 1875. Another newcomer that year was the new *Akola* (1875/578 grt) with accommodation for 28 Saloon and an unspecified number of deck passengers. In June a somewhat similar ship to the *Calcutta* sisters, *Umballa* (1875/840 grt), a product of Caird's, joined the service for a short time and later was transferred together with her sister *Puttiala* (1875/839 grt) to BI's associate firm, the Netherlands Indies Steam Navigation Co.

The pattern of BI success in the Bay of Bengal—a network of connecting feeder routes—was being duplicated in the Indian Ocean and so too was an expansion-minded local agency system. British India was the first steamship line to have its own representative in East Africa. Captain H.A. Fraser, ex-Indian Marine and owner of a sugar plantation in Zanzibar, was appointed BI agent there, but proved a bit of a scoundrel who ran his plantation with slaves in defiance of Sir Bartle Frere's anti-slavery laws by hiring them from their Arab masters at £5 per annum and who later fled to South Africa when he went bankrupt.

Mackinnon Mackenzie & Co. acted quickly to put things right and dispatched Archibald Smith from the Glasgow office to Africa and shortly thereafter sent E.N. Mackenzie and Archibald Brown from BI's Calcutta office to establish Smith, Mackenzie & Co. Ltd. in 1877. Lighterage and victualling facilities at Zanzibar included a small steam launch, five wooden boats each with a 50-ton capacity and another boat capable of holding 400 gallons of fresh water. In addition to its BI-related duties, Smith Mackenzie, with characteristic Victorian enterprise, also acted as Reuter's East African news bureau, served as Lloyd's agents, imported British goods (for which the Sultan proved a steady customer, doing £1,800 in trade in the first half of 1877) and traded in rubber and ivory.

The last of Africa's great slave markets was closed in Zanzibar on 5 June 1873, but slavery remained in the interior until European missionaries finally put it down, and was not formally abolished until 1897.

Mackinnon set about to build a network of BI services in the Indian Ocean just as he had done in the Bay of Bengal. Sandwiched as it was between the well-established P&O to the north and Union Line to the south, BI began a cordial and co-operative relationship between the lines which was to last for the respective lives of the three companies. Although BI was disappointed at not being able to extend its service farther south, it had every reason to be satisfied, for its foot was in the East African door, which would soon be pushed open wider.

In 1873 BI was awarded a French Government contract for a mail service connecting Zanzibar with the Comoro Islands, Mayotte, Nossi-Be and Majunga in Madagascar. The new service commenced on 12 March 1874 with the departure from Aden for Nossi-be of *Calcutta* (Captain Hansard) which was soon replaced by *Malacca* (1864/592 grt), ex-*Lord Clyde*. The service connected at Zanzibar with the Aden branch-line steamer.

After a year's operation the new line (No. 14) was extended south to Mozambique, the Portuguese colonial port. This happened when a mail contract had been secured from the Portuguese Government for the carriage of that country's mails between Lisbon and Goa and between Lisbon and Mozambique. The London-Persian Gulf line (No. 15) which commenced four-weekly sailings in the autumn of 1874 started to make calls at Lisbon in the following year. From the beginning there was an Algiers call where mail was exchanged with the Messageries Maritimes steamer from Marseilles under contract with the French Government. *

As the first of BI's home-based services, the new line was therefore a challenge to P&O. The BI line, of course, was mainly for cargo and was never intended to be an express service. Nevertheless, it had the role of connecting at Aden with the Zanzibar branch line steamer, which in turn had yet another mail connection to make in both directions with the French and Portuguese colonial possessions. The itinerary did not include Goa or Bombay so mails for the former place were presumably transhipped initially at Karachi or Aden. In the latter case that would have involved onward transmission by P&O. Calling at Jeddah and sometimes Yanbo and Hodeida in the Red Sea and Karachi, Bunder Abbas and Bushire en route to and from Basra, the line provided most important connections between various parts of the Islamic world. Pilgrims could thus travel to Jeddah en route to Mecca and Medina or to Basra for Kerbela and Kadhimain from as far away as North Africa or

Zanzibar and farther south as has already been related. As an important junction Aden was following in the steps of Galle and Singapore. *

The westbound BI Home steamer having left Karachi on a Saturday, eight days earlier, would reach Aden on a Monday. The eastbound vessel would be there already, having left Suez ten days before and was scheduled to leave for Karachi on the Wednesday and arrive there nine days later. Also in port from Monday to Friday would be the Zanzibar branch steamer which had also to connect with the P&O mail steamers. When one realises that all these transfers had to be effected in the Aden anchorage with the use of barges and tugs in all types of weather, one can but marvel that they ever worked. *

More difficult, however, were the customs and other formalities at some of the Gulf and Arabian ports of call where annoying delays threatened the necessarily accurate timing of the Aden call. Few Muslims were impressed, moreover, with the improved standards and speed of travel, and many thought the BI services an impertinent intrusion into the austere, conservative and rigidly orthodox domains of the Mohammedan faith. Furthermore, as had been the original intention, they interfered with the age-old slave trade in those parts. Delays to the local Bombay ships did not matter so much, but when the Home Line vessel due to connect at Aden with the Zanzibar ship was held up by dissatisfied officials that was another matter. *

By the 1870s, Aden had become a Clapham Junction for sea travellers, particularly those of the Moslem faith whether they were bent on trading, performing a pilgrimage or just emigrating. Aden Roads became a great maritime meeting point and in bad weather, especially during the southwest monsoon period, adherence to the myriad connecting timetables must have been quite a feat. The Zanzibar vessel was normally in port for four days, her arrival on a Monday being timed to occur shortly before that of the mailship from Bombay and her departure on Friday coming within 24 hours of the arrival of the P&O liner carrying the Overland Mails from Europe. The other transfers of mail, passengers and cargo between BI ships on the London, Lisbon and Algiers run via Hedjaz and Egyptian ports, the Karachi, Persian Gulf and Eastern Arabian runs and the Zanzibar Branch line with its extensions to Madagascar, Mozambique and South Africa (by the Union Line's mail steamer) were all sandwiched in between. *

British India quickly figured in Victorian Africana when in 1874 *Calcutta* carried David Livingstone's remains (he had died on 1 May 1873) to Aden where they were transferred to the P&O *Malwa* bound for England. The sun-dried body was brought by his faithful African followers, Chuma and Susi, to the Smith, Mackenzie office in Zanzibar where it was prepared for transport back to England. It was a courtesy that did not go unnoticed by Sir Bartle Frere who expressed the appreciation of the Royal Geographical Society (of which he was President) in a letter to BI's Secretary P. Macnaughtan on 27

April 1874:

> I am charged by my Colleagues of the Council of this Society with the welcome duty of expressing through you to the Directors, British India Steam Navigation Co., their cordial thanks for the liberality of the Board in conveying free of charge the body of the late Dr. Livingstone from Zanzibar to Aden.
>
> They wish me also to state that they consider the merit of this Act enhanced by the feeling terms in which the wishes of the Directors are in expressed in your letter.
>
> I am empowered to add to the thanks of the Council and myself those of the family of our Great Traveller, and it is the wish of all of us that the Directors should convey to Captain Henderson of the Company's Mail Steamer *Calcutta* and the Officers, Engineers, & Crew our warm acknowledgements of the respect and good feeling they displayed at the embarkation and disembarkation of the honoured remains.

H.M. Stanley and Sir John Kirk were both present at the state funeral in Westminster Abbey.

The Sultan of Zanzibar was also an early BI passenger, leaving Zanzibar on 9 May 1875 and transhipping at Aden to *Canara* (1874/1,903 grt) for passage to England, his entourage, including John Kirk, occupying most of the 27-berth First Class.

Mackinnon's commercial interests in Africa and commitment to carry on the work of Livingstone went well beyond his line's opening up the East African coast to steam navigation. The key to African commerce lay in the vast expanses of the interior and it was Mackinnon who first formulated schemes to open up the hinterland to legitimate trade and development. Together with Sir Thomas Fowell Buxton, a leading exponent of the theory of commerce as a weapon against slavery, Mackinnon would dedicate the last years of his life and his fortune towards furthering the work and ideals of Livingstone as well as the exploits of Stanley and intrigues of King Leopold.

Sir William was a member of the British delegation at an international geographical conference convened by King Leopold II in Brussels in September 1876 which created the International African Association, an ostensibly scientific and altruistic enterprise that was really a front for Leopold's ambitions in the Congo. Meanwhile, John Kirk actively encouraged Mackinnon's own East African ambitions. At his urging a road was constructed, solely at Mackinnon and Buxton's expense, to link Dar-es-Salaam, then the only good natural harbour on the coast, and Lake Nyasa, to "open the Nyasa country to legitimate trade and so assist in replacing that in slaves." Work began in 1876 and the 73-mile road did much to establish Dar-es-Salaam as a commercial centre and port.

As had been John Kirk's intention, BI's original Aden-Zanzibar run had opened up Zanzibar to world trade and considerably enhanced the position and fortune of the Sultan whose revenue from taxes and customs alone totalled £300,000 per annum. With its trade valued at £2 million and largely controlled by 4,000 Indians, Zanzibar had become a valuable extension of British Indian commerce. And it was overwhelmingly carried in British ships; in 1877 48 merchantmen flying the Red Ensign called at Zanzibar compared to 15 under German colours. Within two years the number of British ships using the port had climbed to 69. Kirk's and Mackinnon's influence and power with the Sultan grew as a result.

Opposition to the slave trade came from other quarters, in particular from Colonel Charles Gordon, Governor General of Egypt's Equatorial Provinces, who, in the service of the Khedive Ismail, sought to expand Egypt's control into what is now Uganda to put down the slave trade there. His encroachment on the Sultan's territories brought immediate protests and fearing for his newly developed commerce, Sultan Barghash sought the protection of a European Power. In summer 1876 he advised Lord Derby, Britain's Foreign Minister, that he wanted British capitalists to develop the interior. Mackinnon was the obvious choice and he and Buxton had already approached Gordon with a development scheme. Instead of Gordon, Mackinnon sent Gerald Waller to Zanzibar in April 1877 with a concession agreement for the Sultan.

The Mackinnon Concession, "for 70 years of the customs and administration of the dominions of Zanzibar, including all rights of sovereignty", would have ceded political and commercial control of a vast area, comprising the present day Tanzania (except the islands of Zanzibar and Pemba), Kenya and Uganda, to Mackinnon in return for 20 per cent of the company's profit, customs duty and royalties on exported minerals. The scheme won the approval of both Kirk and the Sultan and had tacit Foreign Office encouragement. Mackinnon, initially confident of gaining the concession, laid plans for the penetration and development of the interior, building on his Nyasa road project. However, opposition from Arab traders, tepid British Government support, and hesitancy by Mackinnon and his backers who did not have the financial resources to act as a colonial government, saw the Mackinnon Concession never realised. It was a tremendous opportunity that unfortunately came too early.

Meanwhile Mackinnon, like Stanley, was drawn further into the schemes of Leopold. With an eye to securing potentially lucrative railway concessions in the Congo, Mackinnon invested heavily in the Comite d'Etudes du Haut Congo, another of Leopold's schemes, which sent Stanley off to explore the region in 1879. And Mackinnon further expanded BI's Indian Ocean network.

In 1879, following the speeding up of the P&O services to India and elsewhere under the terms of a postal contract awarded by the home government, it was necessary to change the timings of the BI connecting service to Zanzibar, and the opportunity was taken not long afterwards to substitute a new service starting and ending at Bombay, instead of Aden, the extra part of the voyage between these ports being free of any binding contract as cautioned by the 1881 BI *Handbook,* "the line between Bombay and Aden is non-contract and may be suspended at any time."

The new Bombay-Africa line (No. 12 in 1881) was, like its predecessor, a four-weekly one and was operated for the next ten years. And as with many of BI's early lines, the new service underwent a variety of changes both in vessels and ports of call and was connected with other routes. The sailing schedules listed it initially as Bombay-Aden-Hodeida-Jeddah-Zanzibar-Mozambique-Port Natal (Durban), but in fact the latter two ports were served by the Union Line connecting steamer which was timed to depart Zanzibar 24 hours after the arrival of the BI vessel.

Additionally the Persian Gulf Home Line ship's schedule included a Lisbon call in both directions, thereby providing the postal contract link between Portugal and its Indian and East African possessions. What was different was the length of stay at Aden; instead of just a few hours there the call was lengthened to one of three days in both the outward and homeward programme thereby allowing not only greater latitude in the connecting and transferring arrangements for passengers and cargo between the two BI ships, but also much more time for handling the increasing amount of freight involved. *

This direct India-Africa link, which was destined to become one of BI's most important trunk routes and play a prominent role in the development of East Africa, was inaugurated on 7 May 1879 with the departure from Bombay of *Chinsura* (1877/2,033 grt) commanded by Captain J.R. Gavin. The meagre passenger list comprised two passengers destined for London and three for Suez, via the Aden connection, and just two for Zanzibar plus 22 deck passengers. The first Aden transhipment was made with the London-bound *Java* (1872/1,477 grt). The pioneering *Chinsura,* which would not again sail to Africa, was followed by *Burmah* from Bombay on 31 May 1879, *Abyssinia* (1868/1,129 grt) on 28 June and *Punjaub. Java* joined the service on 16 January 1880.

Union Line's eight-year Zanzibar mail contract expired in 1880 and the company began an intermediate line from Southampton as far as Zanzibar. The BI India-Africa service now directly called at the Portuguese East African ports of Mozambique, Inhambane, Quelimane and Lourenço Marques where the connection was made with the Union intermediate ship from Natal and the Cape. A sample itinerary from the 1881 *Handbook*:

LINE NO. 12 BOMBAY-ADEN-ZANZIBAR-MOZAMBIQUE-
LOURENÇO MARQUES
13 January   sail BOMBAY

22-26 January	call Aden
4-6 February	call Zanzibar
10 February	call Mozambique
13 February	call Quelimane
16 February	call Inhambane
17 February	arr. LOURENÇO MARQUES

The BI ship was scheduled to be at Aden from Sunday afternoon to Wednesday afternoon, but in any case waited to receive the mails from Europe which were due late on Tuesday or early on Wednesday. In the reverse direction the ship from East Africa would be in Aden from Thursday to Saturday, i.e., allowing only two days during which mails for Europe would be transferred to the P&O mailship which called there on Friday. *

Punjaub (Captain K. Macaulay), which had pioneered BI's African services, was also first on the new Bombay-Aden-Zanzibar-Mozambique-Inhambane-Quelimane-Lourenço Marques routing with her sailing from Bombay on 21 October 1880 with three Saloon and 40 deck passengers. She was followed by *Java* on 18 November, *Assyria* (1872/1,495 grt) on 14 December and *Abyssinia* on 13 January 1881, these three steamers maintaining the monthly service thereafter. Starting with *Assyria*'s 9 March 1881 departure from Bombay, BI sailing lists included calls south of Lourenço Marques at Durban and Cape Town, although these ports again were served by Union Line.

Making their first East African voyages in 1881 were *Baghdad* (1871/1,271 grt), a handsome brig-rigged vessel with accommodation for 46 First and 13 Second Class passengers, from Bombay on 23 July; the straight-stemmed *Mecca* (1873/1,450 grt) on 17 November and *Oriental* (1866/1,481 grt) which supplanted *Assyria* and *Abyssinia* by the next year. Also joining the service in 1882 was *Simla* (1878/1,615 grt) which left Bombay on 14 October. She took the last sailing (10 August 1883) to call at Lourenço Marques and after a month without a departure from Bombay service to Aden, Zanzibar and Mozambique only was resumed by *Java* on 11 October. Mozambique was designated as a new interchange point, this time with the Castle Line that now provided the link with Durban and Cape Town instead of Union Line.

In 1884 calls were added at Lamu, Kilwa and Lindi and a typical voyage was as follows:

11 September	sail BOMBAY
20-24 September	call Aden
3 October	call Lamu
4 October	call Mombasa
6-9 October	call Zanzibar
10 October	call Kilwa

37

12 October	call Lindi
14 October	call Ibo
15 October	arr. MOZAMBIQUE

In BI's 1883 Annual Report, it was noted that the "punctuality of the steamers on the Home and Zanzibar lines has been greatly interfered with by the delays in the Suez Canal, occasioned by the congestion of traffic." In June 1884 a new five-year mail contract for the Aden to Zanzibar route, with the extension to Lindi, was signed.

African waters claimed their first BI victim when on 31 March 1886 *Abyssinia* (Captain M. Macfarlane), whilst northbound, was wrecked on the Pinda Shoal, 50 miles north of Mozambique, but fortunately with no casualties among her crew or passengers. Judged too costly to salvage and repair, she and her cargo were auctioned off.

Apart from vessels on the regular India-Africa line, which sometimes carried Portuguese inter-colonial mails, *Canara* was chartered by the Portuguese Government about the beginning of 1886 to transport troops from Goa to Quelimane and Mozambique.

Opposition to the new service came from no less an exalted personage than the Sultan of Zanzibar who ran his ex-P&O and Union Line paddler *Nyanza* direct between Bombay and Zanzibar with accommodation for 80 First and 40 Second Class passengers, besides an unspecified number on deck. His advertisement in the *Times of India* included a claim that his ship took less than half the time taken by those of the BI, e.g. "Average time 10 days. Steamers for Zanzibar via Aden take nearly 24 days." He certainly had a point here and presumably his line was reasonably patronised, for before long another old P&O ship, the 1,482-grt *Avoca*, was running in it also and these two were joined by others a few years later (e.g., the former P&O *Malacca* of 1866 was shown on the run in 1889). Of course, BI was obliged by its mail contract to maintain the Aden call. *

Moreover, Bullard King, whose Natal Direct Line had maintained sailings from London to Durban via the Cape since 1869, secured a lucrative contract with Natal Colony in 1889 for the transport of Indian coolies to work the sugar plantations. This Calcutta-Madras-Colombo-Durban-Cape Town service proved a potent rival to that of BI.

In 1889 the BI fleet steamed a total of 2,301,204 miles and carried more than 400,000 deck passengers. The company's enviable and efficient network of steamship services in the Indian Ocean had forged the East African coast into an integral link in the imperial sea chain of communications. From its virtual isolation just 15 years previously, Zanzibar now enjoyed the following services as listed in the 1887 BI *Handbook*:

Four-weekly to London, via Aden.

Four-weekly to Kilwa Kinvinge, Lindi, Ibo and Mozambique and
to Mombasa and Lamu, and Aden.

Four-weekly to Karachi, Persian Gulf and Baghdad, via Aden.

Four-weekly to Bombay direct, transhipping there for
Colombo, Madras and Calcutta, touching at all the important
Malabar and Coromandel Coast ports en route.

Four-weekly to Burmese ports and Straits Settlements, via
Bombay and Calcutta.

Four-weekly to Red Sea ports, via Aden.

Four-weekly to Java and Queensland Ports, via Aden.

It was now possible to circumnavigate the whole of Africa in British
mailships, and for 100 guineas a Victorian traveller could, with reasonable
speed, comfort and safety, undertake the following journey in 1887:

BY CASTLE MAIL PACKET   OUTWARD VIA THE CAPE
Portuguese Royal Mail Service U.K.-Lisbon-Mozambique Coast

20 January	sail DARTMOUTH
24 January	call Lisbon
10 February	call Cape Town
16 February	call Durban
20 February	call Lourenço Marques
23 February	call Inhambane
26 February	call Quilimane
2 March	arr. MOZAMBIQUE

BY BRITISH INDIA PACKET

Line No. 12 Bombay and East Africa Line

5 March	sail MOZAMBIQUE
6 March	call Ibo
8 March	call Lindi
10 March	call Kilwa
11 March	call Zanzibar
28 March	arr. ADEN

N.B. steamer proceeds to Bombay, arriving on 9 April

BY BRITISH INDIA PACKET   HOME VIA SUEZ

Line No. 11 London-Karachi-Bombay Line

2 April	sail ADEN
8 April	call Suez
	transit Suez Canal
10 April	call Port Said

| 15 April | call Malta |
| 25 April | arr. LONDON |

British India's African services, having already fulfilled the original intention of banishing the slave trade and opening up the East African coast to Western commerce and civilisation, would now assume wider-ranging political and strategic responsibilities. In addition to Her Majesty's Mails, merchants, missionaries and Manchester piece goods, the pioneering BI packets would bring European empires to East African shores and beyond.

3. EMPIRE BUILDING

East Africa had become Mackinnon's love, his pride, and the one important object of his life. H.M. Stanley

"Shuttles of an Empire's loom" BI's ships and services did indeed become, but more than that in East Africa where they were pivotal in expanding the bounds of the Empire itself. The shipping entrepreneur as empire builder was a common theme in Victorian Africa: Elder Dempster's Alfred Jones in West Africa, Castle Line's Donald Currie in South Africa and, most remarkably, BI's William Mackinnon in East Africa where Red Ensign preceded Union Jack. By the mid 1880s, British and European imperialism had caught up with the pioneering steamship services to East Africa where the old imperial bromide of "trade follows flag" had been reversed.

Hitherto African exploration, preoccupied with finding the source of the Nile, had left Kenya largely uncharted. Few dared enter the domain of the fierce Masai. In 1883 Joseph Thomson, a young Scot appointed by the Royal Geographical Society, began his epic 14-month long exploration of Kenya. His adventures, popularised by his account *Through Masai Land,* refocused European attention on East Africa and revitalised the interests there of fellow Scotsman William Mackinnon and a 28-year-old German metaphysician, Carl Peters.

The scramble for Africa was on. Mackinnon, businessmen and missionaries founded the East African Association in 1884 to co-ordinate their interests there. That same year Carl Peters and other German imperialists began the Society for German Colonisation. Like their British counterparts Peters' group initially received no government support as Chancellor Bismarck shared many of Gladstone's reservations about African adventures. Disguised as mechanics and under assumed names, Peters and three compatriots sailed from Trieste for Aden in September 1884. Ironically Mackinnon's greatest rivals for East Africa reached their destination, Zanzibar, aboard a BI mailship on 4 November, travelling as deck passengers. The Germans set out into what was ostensibly the Sultan of Zanzibar's territory and signed some 120 treaties with the local chiefs. Peters then secured a charter and government backing for his German East Africa Company which eventually developed what became Tanganyika.

This German intrusion prompted an immediate protest by the Sultan to the British Government and renewed Kirk's calls for intervention. He also continued to encourage Mackinnon to form his own chartered company to secure the territory around Mount Kilimanjaro. In the meantime, the Germans extended their control in this area and to show they meant business sent a gunboat to Zanzibar in August 1885. Yet, instead of alarm, the successive governments of Gladstone and Salisbury were content to have the German taxpayer subsidise the introduction of order and civilisation in East Africa.

One of the more remarkable endeavours that Mackinnon involved himself (and BI) in was the relief expedition of Emin Pasha in 1887. The German-born Edward Schnitzer, who had become known as Emin Pasha, Governor of Equatoria Province, was holding out against the onslaught of the Mahdists and became in the public eye another Gordon of Khartoum who had to be rescued lest he suffer the same fate. Mackinnon's motives behind the enterprise were, as with most of his African endeavours, both commercial—laying claim to the rich ivory trade of Equatoria by the relief expedition taking the East Coast route and signing treaties as they advanced into the interior—and charitable—saving Emin Pasha from Moslem fanatics. Yet at King Leopold's urging the relief expedition would approach instead from the Congo although with the prospect of returning via the East Coast to accomplish Mackinnon's aims. Beyond committing more than £5,000 towards the £21,000 total cost of the enterprise, Mackinnon offered BI's *Madura* (1874/1,942 grt) to carry the expedition from Zanzibar, round the Cape, to the mouth of the Congo.

Under Red Ensign and BI houseflag, the relief of Emin Pasha got underway as *Madura* steamed out of Zanzibar, Cape-bound, on 25 February 1887 and arrived at Matadi on 18 March. Of the ship, Mr. Stanley wrote *In Darkest Africa*:

> The *Madura* is a comfortable steamer. 'Tween decks abreast of the boilers is rather a hot place for the people, but we have had agreeable weather and the men have preferred to stow themselves in the boats and among the donkeys and on deck to the baking heat below... [the] expedition were in such an overfed condition after the glorious plenty on board the *Madura* that they straggled in the most disheartening manner.

After almost three years of slogging from the Congo to the upper Nile, Stanley reached Emin Pasha and urged him to withdraw his garrison to Lake Victoria where it could be resupplied from Zanzibar, as proposed by Mackinnon. Instead the Emin's troops mutinied and Stanley and the Emin left the territory to the Mahdists. And the area between Mombasa and Equatoria that Mackinnon wished to annex was just as ripe for the picking by the Germans as before.

Years after its coasts were traced by a web of BI routes, the map of East Africa finally assumed the pink hue of the British Empire. In 1887 BI's agent E.N. Mackenzie joined General Sir Lloyd William Matthews in an exploration, sponsored by the British East Africa Association, of the country around Mombasa, an island affording a protected anchorage which was

42

separated from the mainland by a narrow tidal strait. Whilst the British General, acting on behalf of the Home Government and the Sultan of Zanzibar, made treaties with the local tribes, Mackenzie appraised the commercial prospects. In September 1888 an office of Smith, Mackenzie & Co. was established on Mombasa island by J.W. Buchanan.

Political events, caught up in the African scramble, now assumed a fast and far-reaching pace. On 24 May 1887 the Sultan of Zanzibar granted the British East Africa Association political control of the territories in the northern mainland. In effect, the Sultan retained control of the ten-mile-wide coastal strip and Zanzibar island whilst giving Britain a free hand in the vast interior of what is now Kenya and Uganda. More important than the Sultan's blessing was that of Lord Salisbury who, now convinced that East Africa had to be secured to protect the flank of the Sudan and Egypt, cleared the way for Mackinnon to develop the territory with a chartered company, the Imperial British East Africa Company (IBEA), which was granted a royal charter by Queen Victoria on 3 September 1888.

The initial £240,000 share capital of this enterprise was held by the Mackinnon family, Sir William alone holding £25,000 in shares, Sir George S. Mackenzie, James Hutton (the Manchester cotton tycoon) and leading anti-slavery and missionary personalities, notably Sir John Kirk who had retired from the Foreign Service in 1887. Thus a decade after the original Mackinnon Concession was conceived, the Scottish shipowner and imperial grocer became an empire builder.

Adopting a rising sun over the Union Jack as its flag and "Light and Liberty" as its motto, the Imperial British East Africa Company was an audacious and, in many aspects, noble enterprise, its aim being to end the vestiges of the slave trade in the great hinterlands of East Africa and open them up to exploitation and development. Noble and audacious, but severely undercapitalised, pursuing often elusive commercial prospects and saddled with purely political functions in the continued absence of any government support, IBEA was destined never to make a penny for its investors. Sobered perhaps by financial losses, Sir George S. Mackenzie later confided that, "The Imperial East Africa Company never expected to receive any dividends during the lifetime of its founders. The result of their labours they only hoped to leave as a legacy to posterity."

When one today thinks of British East Africa, the territory which became Kenya usually comes to mind and it was eventually the most prosperous and developed colony. Not so in the 1870s when Zanzibar was the focus of British interests or in the 1880s when attention turned to the Kingdom of Buganda (Uganda). In imperial strategic theory, Uganda was the object of British interest now that the slave trade was more or less put down.

The Suez Canal, that now indispensable "lifeline to India", ended any lingering hopes of an informal empire. The Canal was a fixed artery which required a permanent British presence in Egypt to protect it. Now the scientific pursuits of Burton, Speke, Livingstone and Stanley to locate the Nile headwaters were perverted into a strategic domino theory by the pro-imperialists who argued that whoever controlled the source of the Nile, Uganda, effectively controlled Egypt and thus threatened the Canal. Within IBEA itself, John Kirk actively pushed for an immediate thrust deep into the interior, fearing that Lord Salisbury would let Uganda and Equatoria fall into the hands of the Germans.

Thus IBEA, dedicated to commercial and moral pursuits, found itself thrust into this great inland region for largely political and strategic reasons. Uganda, the name borne by BI's last and best remembered African liner, proved to be the final frontier for Mackinnon's African enterprise, but also its greatest success.

Uganda in the 1880s belonged to the Baganda, one of Africa's most developed and sophisticated peoples, ruled by Kabaka (King) Mutesa. This peaceful and prosperous kingdom was torn asunder by rival British Protestant and French Catholic missionaries as well as by Arab slavers. Mutesa's successor, Mwanga decided to rid his kingdom of European influence before himself being driven from power by a coalition of Christians and Arabs in 1888. In 1889 Mwanga, now supported by the Christian missionaries after promising religious freedom to all, invaded Uganda and appealed to IBEA for support in regaining his throne.

Mackinnon, already drawn to potential trade with the Baganda and hoping that here he could enlist real government assistance, plunged IBEA's already hard-pressed resources into Uganda. Hitherto the farthest the company had extended itself was Machakos, 250 miles inland, and prudence would have dictated solidifying coastal and immediate hinterland trade and influence rather than reaching deeper into the interior. Mackinnon and other directors believed that the richest commercial prospects lay in Equatoria where an initial company presence would draw the attention of investors. Any inclinations that Mackinnon and Kirk had towards an expedition into Uganda were reinforced by lobbying of IBEA's George Mackenzie by Colonel Charles Euan-Smith, who had replaced Kirk as British Consul in Zanzibar.

In August 1890 the company sent Captain Frederick Lugard, 50 Sudanese troops and 270 porters into Buganda. Lugard soon obtained a claim on behalf of IBEA over Buganda and later Toro and Ankole. This was real empire building, but ruinously expensive and as H.M. Stanley recalled, "The capital that rightly was called for the development of the commerce of the maritime region [East African coast], and would surely have been remunerative, was thus wasted on purely political work; which the national exchequer should have paid for....The Company bravely and patriotically held on, however, and

44

sustained the enormous expense of maintaining the communications open between Uganda and the sea; but it soon became evident to Mackinnon, who was always so hopeful and cheerful, that the responsibilities were becoming too great for his Company."

In December 1891 Lugard was instructed by IBEA to withdraw from Uganda, but to protect its missionaries and carry on Lugard's good work, the Church Missionary Society agreed to fund his staying for an additional year.

In the meantime, rival British and German claims in East Africa were threatening relations between the two powers. Despite Kirk's anxiety, Lord Salisbury had proved to be a closet imperialist and he skilfully exploited the departure of Bismarck and the interests of the new Kaiser, Wilhelm II, whose ambitions lay in North Sea naval strategy, not African colonies. A conference was held leading to the 1890 Heligoland Treaty by which Germany recognised IBEA's claim to Uganda and Britain conceded what became Tanganyika, including Mount Kilimanjaro which was presented by Queen Victoria to her grandson, Kaiser Wilhelm. In return, Germany was given the North Sea island of Heligoland, a bargain that Carl Peters, whose own efforts to secure Uganda for his country had vanished at the stroke of a pen, likened to, "two kingdoms in Africa bartered for a bathtub in the North Sea."

> Building of a railway from Mombasa to Lake Victoria had always been in the mind of Sir William Mackinnon and it became one of the Company's main objectives. *Permanent Way*

The Lugard mission was but one of IBEA's endeavours on behalf of the British Government. Whilst it was agreed by all that the surest way to introduce Western civilisation into the great interior of Africa as well as provide a speedy potential conduit for British troops to protect the Nile headwaters was the construction of railways from the coastal ports, this epic and expensive task was left by the British Government to IBEA's own devices. As George Blake in *BI Centenary* put it, "that the job was left to a company without subsidy is surely one of the sourest jokes in history." Yet IBEA took up the task and surveyed the route for the great Uganda Railway which would link Mombasa with Kisumu, on Lake Victoria.

The survey party, led by Captain J.R.L. MacDonald, Captain J.W. Pringle, Lt. Twining and Lt. H.H. Austin, Royal Engineers, arrived at Aden on 17 November 1891 where they transhipped to *Madura* and reached Mombasa seven days later. There they were joined by IBEA's F.J. Jackson. The monumental survey was completed on 23 September 1892.

Meanwhile, BI had continued to cast its net farther into the reaches of the Indian Ocean. Following a successful experimental voyage by *Booldana* (1880/2,823 grt) from Calcutta to Mauritius, via several Coromandel ports and Colombo during April-July 1887, a more frequent service was instituted early in January 1888 by *Warora* (1887/3,920 grt), her sister ship *Wardha*

(1887/3,917 grt) following her later the same month, with *Lindula* (1888/3,396 grt) also featuring in the sailing schedule by the middle of the year. After a number of voyages, the new service settled down to departures at six-weekly intervals, the return voyage being made via Bombay. A typical itinerary is listed in the 1890 *Handbook*:

21 May	sail CALCUTTA
30-31 May	call Colombo
10 June	arr. MAURITIUS
1 July	dep. MAURITIUS
11-12 July	call Colombo
16-21 July	call Bombay
31 July	arr. CALCUTTA

In the 1889 BI *Handbook* the new line was given the number 10; a year later it had become No. 9 and its frequency had been increased to four-weekly. *Lindula* was not the only "L" class ship on this run; they all made a handful of voyages each throughout the 'nineties; *Landaura* (1886/3,271 grt), *Lawada* (1885/3,269 grt), *Lalpoorla* (1885/3,269 grt) and *Loodiana* (1884/3,269 grt), the last-named presumed to have foundered in a cyclone shortly after leaving Mauritius for Colombo on 10 January 1910. The clipper-stemmed *Booldana* which had made the test run to Mauritius, returned there in 1904 and never left, being utilised as a cargo hulk for the next 17 years before she was sold to be broken up. *

Bhundara (1880/2,899 grt), found herself in the newspapers when she arrived at Mombasa from Bombay in 1888 with some of her deck passengers infected by bubonic plague. Refused permission to land there, Captain Stebbing found a similar reception at Zanzibar where officials ordered him to return to Bombay. After considerable wrangling between BI management and the Colonial Office in London, *Bhundara* proceeded to Prison Island (Changu), off Bombay, where her passengers were quarantined.

The extension of the Bombay East Africa line to Mozambique lasted for five years and after the 27 December 1888 sailing the 1889 *Handbook* deleted the southern ports from the itinerary:

24 January	sail BOMBAY
2-6 February	call Aden
15 February	call Lamu
16 February	call Mombasa
18-21 February	call Zanzibar
22 February	call Kilwa
23 February	arr. LINDI

Zanzibar became the new interchange point with Castle Line for southern ports.

An extension of the Colombo-Mauritius mail line was inaugurated on 24

46

October 1891 when *Coconada*, having just brought the mails from Colombo after a switch from the Tenasserim coast line, went on to Madagascar ports such as Tamatave and Vohemar and returned via Reunion. Though it was evident by May next year that the new branch line was running at a loss, *Coconada* continued to operate it until December 1892 when it was closed and she was able to return to her Rangoon-Mergui duties. *

Another of Mackinnon's ambitions was the establishment of a regular Home Line linking London, Zanzibar and Mombasa. In 1890 the Deutsche Öst-Afrika Linie (DÖAL) began regular sailings from Hamburg to East Africa under generous government subsidy. Another impetus was Messageries Maritimes' new direct service from Marseilles to Zanzibar en route to Madagascar, Mauritius and Reunion, whose negative effect on BI's service was commented on in the 1889 Annual Report:

> The trade on this line has been considerably hampered by the state of the southern Zanzibar coast and the future prospects are seriously menaced through the competition of highly subsidised foreign lines. One foreign company [Messageries Maritimes] which receives, it is believed, the largest amount paid by any Government as a mail subsidy, has already started a direct competing service between Marseilles and Zanzibar, offering both for goods and passengers the great advantage of through transit without transhipment, while the British India Company, with a line commencing at Aden, has to tranship both cargo and passengers, and the subsidy being based on a $7^1/2$ knot speed, the whole service is at great disadvantage as regards the foreign competition.

The London-Zanzibar via Naples mail service began in 1890 as Line No. 13 and partly replaced the India-Africa line, taking on its Aden to Zanzibar section, which could connect with the fortnightly BI London-Calcutta Home Line at Aden as well the P&O Bombay Mail.

Given the trial nature of the Home Line, no special tonnage was provided and the local Indian mail ships were considered suitable provided they were fast enough. The new route seems to have been tested first by *Arcot* (1871/1,782 grt), which sailed from London on 21 August 1883, and, after calling at Antwerp, Algiers, Jeddah and Hodeida, proceeded to Zanzibar and southern ports as far as Mozambique. The ship returned to London by practically the same route. In June 1888 *Madura* made a similar route-proving voyage, but instead of returning to England, went to Bombay and Calcutta for employment on the Indian coast. That September *Kistna* (1888/1,114 grt) was sent out to Zanzibar on her maiden voyage calling only at Malta, Port Said, Suez, Aden and Mombasa. From East Africa she went to Calcutta via Colombo. *Kistna* was also the ship that was used by Prince Albert Victor and

47

his staff from mid-December 1889 to 3 January 1890 when they were conveyed from Madras to Rangoon and thence Calcutta during the prince's Indian tour. *

The regular Home Line, which called at Naples instead of Malta, seems to have started with the departure from London of *Kavlana* (1889/1,125 grt) on 27 December 1889 which, like *Kistna* was on her maiden voyage out to India. The three-year-old *Kapurthala* (1887/1,122 grt) took the next sailing on 23 January 1890 as she happened to be back at her builders' yard not too long before. She came back again to London, leaving Zanzibar on 1 March, but that was her last appearance on the service and her next eastbound voyage was direct to India. *

From the 1890 *Handbook*, a sample Home Line itinerary:

4 April	sail LONDON
24-25 April	call Naples
29 April	call Port Said
30 April	call Suez
6-7 May	call Aden
13-14 May	call Lamu
15-16 May	call Mombasa
17 May	arr. ZANZIBAR

When *Africa* (1874/2,030 grt) left London for Zanzibar on 20 February 1890 she was starting an attachment to that line that lasted two years. Like her sister *Ethiopia* (1874/2,035 grt), she had been recently refitted at Denny's yard, the opportunity being taken to install electric lighting on board. Each ship could accommodate 35 First and 18 Second Class passengers as well as between 500 to 1,100 on deck. *Africa, Madura* and *Ethiopia* took all the Home Line sailings until early 1892 except for that of 20 March 1890 when *Malda* (1874/1,950 grt) sailed in lieu of *Madura*. The second half of 1892, however, saw the replacement of the trio with *Java* and *Mecca* on 6 June and 4 July. *

Today when it is fashionable to characterise the Empire as plundering the natural resources of its subject colonies, it is worth remembering that East Africa had only the barest of potential to warrant any commercial interest at all. Unlike India, this was wholly undeveloped country whose resources, both mineral and agricultural, were either undiscovered or yet to be introduced. It was first necessary to create the infrastructure, the railways, ports and trading posts, and then develop the export minerals and cash crops to pay for it.

Thus, like IBEA, BI's new African Home Line found it hard going. The principal problem, as so often with pioneering colonial routes, was the imbalance of full outbound cargo (rails, machinery, commercial goods, etc.) and marginal home cargo, largely bulky raw materials that often cost more to ship than they were worth. The DÖAL service had the same difficulty, but was compensated by substantial government subsidy. The British Government, however, remained unmoved in its reluctance to finance the commercial exploits of Britons overseas. If the BI service was partly conceived as a trial balloon to sway Whitehall, the results were perhaps marginal enough to further enforce the belief that taxpayer money should not follow private into East African adventures.

Having failed politically and commercially, BI had no choice but to terminate the Home Line, the 1891 Annual Report stating that the "service has not been remunerative, owing to the competition of more highly subsidised French, German and Portuguese lines." *Malda's* voyage from London on 24 October 1892, calling at Naples on 2 November before proceeding to Suez and Zanzibar, closed out the service. There was one more attempt to keep a direct Red Ensign route open to East Africa when beginning in 1893 Union Line sent some of its intermediate steamers up from the Cape as far as Zanzibar, but this ceased after only two years. As a result, DÖAL found itself employed by rival German and British colonists, a situation that Whitehall endorsed by patronising the line for the conveyance of British mails, cargo, passengers and even troops.

The BI Home Line was replaced with a resurrected Aden-Zanzibar branch service. This four-weekly mail service, under government contract, commenced from Zanzibar on 5 November 1892 and connected with the London mail service of the P&O via Brindisi, and passengers and cargo could also be transhipped at Aden where BI's London-Calcutta line touched every two weeks, the first such transfer being made with *Manora* which sailed from London on the 18th. For the first seven or eight months the Aden-Zanzibar line was worked by *Kola,* though the first mail connection at Aden was made by *Mecca* en route to India. *

An 1893 voyage by *Kola* is typical:

3 May	sail ADEN
10-11 May	call Mombasa
12 May	arr. ZANZIBAR
15 May	dep. ZANZIBAR
16-17 May	call Mombasa
24 May	arr. ADEN

This service proved shortlived as having arrived at Zanzibar from Aden on 13 June 1893, *Kola* sailed four days later for Aden (arriving on 29 June) and thence direct to Bombay.

The Bombay-Aden-Zanzibar-Mombasa line was revived in August 1893 and normally employed two 9-knot steamers:

20 January 1894	sail BOMBAY
28-31 January	call Aden
9-10 February	call Mombasa
11 February	arr. ZANZIBAR

Purulia (1878/1,554 grt) was one of the first vessels to be employed on the new service. Starting early in 1895 *Goa* (1874/1,902 grt) was regularly engaged on the line for over six years as well as *Culna* (1879/1,945 grt) and *Chindwara* (1879/1,983 grt) which could each accommodate 21 Saloon passengers in addition to deck travellers.

Meanwhile, IBEA was very close to following the Home Line into oblivion. In October 1892 Captain Lugard arrived in London and embarked on an extensive lobbying campaign on behalf of a continued British presence in East Africa. Amid the last gasps of the Salisbury Government, IBEA announced its intention to withdraw from Uganda by 31 December. The return of Liberals under Gladstone could have hardly encouraged IBEA's prospects except for presence of the new imperialist Foreign Secretary Lord Rosebery. He guaranteed the company's expenses until March 1893 and asked Mackinnon to advise him on the minimum amount of money required to maintain a presence in Uganda. IBEA was spending at least £40,000 a year there and Mackinnon replied with a £50,000 per annum figure. Stanley believed that whilst this was reasonable, Mackinnon had precluded any meaningful negotiation with so high a figure when half would have been sufficient to hold on. Stanley was with Mackinnon in London when Rosebery's reply arrived by messenger. There would be no money forthcoming from the government and thus cruelly ended Mackinnon's Imperial British East Africa Company.

Mackinnon's dream of a British East Africa did not die, however, for that November Rosebery prevailed upon the government to send a special commissioner, Sir George Portal, to Uganda to advise of the situation there. Shortly after his arrival he duly reported what Mackinnon and others had been saying for years, that IBEA's East African protectorate should be retained for the Crown for strategic and commercial reasons and that IBEA was in no position to continue alone and unaided its vital development role. On 1 April 1893 Uganda was declared a Crown Protectorate and the Foreign Office assumed the duties and responsibilities of IBEA.

> Mackinnon's soul was noble, his mind above all pettiness. His life was now bereft of its object, and the mainspring of effort had been removed, and so he visibly declined, and death came in kindness.
>
> H.M. Stanley

On 22 June 1893 Sir William Mackinnon died just short of his 70th year. Perhaps disappointed at the apparent failure of IBEA, his life's work was no less extraordinary in an era of remarkable Victorians. He had built a shipping line that held together an existing Empire and laid the foundations for another in East Africa.

Lord Rosebery became Prime Minister in March 1894 and on 1 July 1895

H.M. Government purchased for £250,000 IBEA's capital of £240,000, but declined to pay the company's £190,000 debt.

> With all its failings, it [IBEA] has been an honest concern, not a money-making one, and but for its works we should not now possess a footing in East Africa
>
> Sir John Kirk to Captain Lugard, 1895

The British East Africa Protectorate was proclaimed on 1 July 1895, incorporating the area (now known as Kenya) between the Zanzibar Protectorate and that in Uganda. When Seyyid Kahlid assumed the throne in 1896 and presumed to order the British out of his sultanate, British gunboats prevailed and he was deposed, and replaced by his more Anglophile heir. The Red Flag of the Sultanate continued to fly alongside the Union Jack, but the real power of the Sultans was gone forever.

In 1895 BI again revised its India to East Africa services by operating two distinct four-weekly lines between Bombay and Zanzibar; one went direct and also served Mozambique ports whilst the other was routed via Aden and Mombasa. It is recorded in *Permanent Way* that BI received an annual mail subsidy for the Bombay run of £8,000 whilst that given to DÖAL by the German Government was £45,000.

With the Messageries Maritimes mail steamers no longer calling at Mahé after the end of 1895 it was essential to give the Seychelles proper postal communications so arrangements were made for the BI steamers on the Bombay-Lourenço Marques line to call there in both directions under a £5,000 mail contract. This was inaugurated by *Kilwa* (1878/1,552 grt), at the beginning of 1896 or a few days earlier. *

The service now operated as follows:

18 January	sail BOMBAY
26 January	call Seychelles
30 January-3 February	call Zanzibar
6-7 February	call Mozambique
9-10 February	call Beira
11-12 February	call Inhambane
13 February	arr. LOURENÇO MARQUES

Sailings from Bombay were programmed for every fourth Saturday. In May 1897 Seychelles Governor Cockburn Stewart wrote that "the BI Company has been the salvation of the Seychelles as it gave them an opportunity of exporting the vanilla coconuts and coconut oil, while the Messagerie line only took the vanilla."

What steamships had begun, steam locomotives carried on into the vast interiors of East Africa In South Africa the Rand Gold Rush of 1886 spurred the construction of rail links into the hinterland. In 1894 the 57-mile railway from Lourenço Marques to Pretoria was completed and became an important independent link, which did not transit British Natal, to the Boer Republics. Much of the mineral wealth of the Transvaal (including copper ore and coal, the latter largely shipped to Bombay) began to flow from the once-sleepy anchorage at Lourenço Marques. The search for a port to serve Matabeleland and Mashonaland (Rhodesia) with its rich copper belt, led to a deserted sandspit at the mouth of the Pungwe and Busi Rivers, surrounded by mangrove swamps and teeming with mosquitoes. The Companhia de Moćambique was chartered in 1891, with largely British and Belgian capital, to develop the region and the port which was named Beira after a Portuguese province. The rail line, extending 374 circuitous miles to Salisbury, was completed in 1897.

> *The use of it, no one can conjecture,*
> *What it will carry there's none can define,*
> *An' in spite of George Curzon's superior lecture,*
> *It's clearly naught but a lunatic line.*

The IBEA's survey work for the great railway linking Mombasa with Lake Victoria was not in vain. The new Conservative government under Lord Salisbury went ahead with the epic project in 1896, one of the greatest construction feats of the age. George Whitehouse, the chief engineer of the project, arrived at Mombasa aboard BI's *Ethiopia* on 11 December 1895. As in other Empire enterprises, British engineering was accomplished by Indian labour; 32,000 indentured labourers from Gujarat had to be transported to East Africa when it was deemed that local labour was insufficient for the task. Construction began on Mombasa island in January 1896 using 2,000 Indian coolies. That year the first primitive port facilities at Mombasa were built in the form of a jetty; previously all equipment and stores had to be carried ashore by lighters and brought across the beaches. In May 1896 the first ship carrying Indian labourers arrived at Mombasa.

As well as the regular mailships, other BI vessels transported labourers, supplies and foodstuffs, especially rice from Burma. The East African authorities established a rigorous quarantine policy for incoming Indian labourers and to get round this delay, BI arranged for the ships to sail at a reduced 9-knot speed to stretch the passage to 16 days which satisfied the quarantine period.

That tragic turning point in the British Empire, the Boer War, saw BI contribute more than ever to Britain's aims in Africa with no fewer than 37 of its vessels employed in H.M. Service between 1899 and 1901. Among these were many ships that were or would be associated with the African run, including *Sirdhana, Booldana, Nerbudda, Nowshera, Lalpoorla, Lindula, Wardha, Warora, Golconda, Pundua, Palamcotta, Dunera* and *Dilwara.* Although most only made one or more trooping voyages between their normal services, their contributions were no less important and indeed, at the beginning of the war, vital. When war between Britain and the Boer republics of Transvaal and the Orange Free State seemed imminent in early June 1899 the situation in Natal was grave where the British forces were vastly outnumbered by the mobilising Boers. Twenty BI ships were requisitioned at once and such was the urgency that many had to land their passengers at the nearest port and race to India to collect badly needed troop reinforcements which were landed in Natal just 23 days later. Their timely arrival was believed to have saved the colony from certain invasion by the Boers.

Of all the BI ships to serve in the Boer War, none had a more adventurous time than *Fazilka* (1890/4,152 grt). As H.M. *Transport No. 30* (Captain G.J. Goss) she was on passage back from South Africa to Ceylon when she had the misfortune of breaking her screw shaft in two places on 6 February 1900 in the middle of the very lonely Indian Ocean. Thanks to the resourcefulness of her Chief Engineer, "Lachie" Brown, a very creditable jury sail rig was fitted using awnings for sails and roughly crafted spars. Had she been carrying a full complement of troops, the situation would have been perilous for lack of food and water, but unladen and undaunted *Fazilka* kept on course. Forty-eight days later, the ship and her plucky crew, long given up for lost, astonishingly arrived at Colombo harbour under sail. It was one of the most memorable acts of BI seamanship.

Overcoming difficulties of nature (the Great Rift Valley), beast (some 125 men consumed by the lions of Tsavo), insects, and man (hostile Nandi raiding parties), the Uganda Railway reached Lake Victoria on 19 December 1901. A waystop on the line which had not even existed before, Nairobi, became the new capital of the Protectorate six years later. It was fitting indeed that the final leg of the journey, across Lake Victoria from the railhead at Kisumu to Kampala, was made in the Uganda Government steamer *Sir William Mackinnon* which had been sent to Mombasa in component parts, carried the 600 miles inland on backs of porters to Kisumu and launched there on 4 June 1901, continuing in service until 1929.

It was once suggested that Britain's new African possessions be called Ibea, after the company that had laid the foundations. That name never stuck, but the more prosaically named British East Africa was, as the Victorian Age came to an end, finally just that. Along the sultry, spice-scented East African coast, Union Jack fluttered with BI burgee and Red Ensign in proud promise of Imperial progress.

4. MERGER AND MODERNISATION

P. and O. and British India ran the service in partnership, each a company of profound and crotchety character. Kipling said British India offered 'freedom and cockroaches', while P. and O. acted 'as though 'twere a favour to allow you to embark.'   James Morris, *Pax Britannica*

The Edwardian Era, a long halcyon summer before the darkness of the First World War, saw the British Empire reach its symbolic height with the Delhi Durbar of 1911 which proclaimed King George V and Queen Mary Emperor and Empress of India. For the British Merchant Navy, it too was a glorious age, its undisputed dominance on the world's sealanes exemplified by such legendary liners as *Mauretania, Olympic, Empress of Asia, Balmoral Castle, Ophir, Medina* and *Nevasa*. For British India, the period between the turn of the century and the First World War transformed it not only as regards the size and composition of its fleet, but also in the field of management and leadership.

This renewal was preceded by a difficult period for BI at the turn of the century, particularly on the African routes. The Home Line remained dormant and on the Indian Ocean field of competition BI found potent rivals among the German lines. What William Mackinnon had so long laboured for had been largely established politically, but commercially there remained far more sowing than reaping in British East Africa.   Conservative and jealous of his company's traditions, BI Chairman Duncan Mackinnon, steered a steady if well-worn course, but waiting impatiently in the wings was younger, more dynamic leadership.

The fate and fortune of BI's Indian Ocean services remained intertwined with those of the infant British East Africa Protectorate. Just as the Suez Canal had defined British interests in Egypt so did another fixed artery, the Uganda Railway, dictate policy in East Africa. Built with somewhat obscure strategic objectives, this last great engineering accomplishment of the Victorian Age had now to find some commercial role to justify its £7.7 million cost.   And Britain had to formulate a workable colonial policy for a large area that encompassed diverse native tribes, climates and terrains.

Under the enlightened administration of Hesketh Bell during the first decade of the 20th-century, Uganda was left an essentially African nation with its sophisticated Bugandan government intact under British guidance and its existing peasant-grown cotton industry encouraged, although the ginneries were firmly in Indian and European hands.

What is now Kenya presented more problems as there was no defined native political system upon which to establish Britain's preferred system of indirect rule and the nomadic cattle-grazing subsistence economy of the Masai and Nandi would hardly contribute its fair share towards developing the colony. Under the policies of Colonial Secretary Lord Elgin, Kenya was opened up to large-scale agricultural development to produce export cash crops. Such cultivation was centred on the highlands, an area of enormous fertility and pleasant climate, that had been evacuated by the local tribe after a smallpox outbreak. This apparently unwanted land was instead exploited by non-African settlers. From Whitehall came a welter of bizarre schemes to settle the highlands—a homeland for Jews being persecuted in Russia, a settlement of Finns or the Indians who built the Uganda Railway.

The Indian community remained the backbone of East African commerce. It has often but inaccurately been asserted that the Indians were mostly those who stayed on after building the Uganda Railway, but of the 31,983 labourers, only 6,794 elected to settle in East Africa and joined the already long-established Asian populace. In 1910, Sir John Kirk stated that were it not for the Indians, there would have been no European presence in East Africa at all, and for that matter there would have been no BI services there either. A wealthy Parsee, A.M. Jeevanjee, was the leading Indian merchant in Kenya and others controlled key aspects of the economy. In 1887 there were 6,345 Indians living in East Africa and in 25 years this population increased to 34,000. A vital component of BI's passenger traffic, the Indians were generally mistrusted by both the African and Europeans, but their contribution to the commercial development of East Africa proved invaluable.

It was finally decided that Kenya would be developed by a new breed of British Empire settler and become another White Colony along the lines of Canada, Australia, New Zealand, South Africa and Rhodesia. To encourage settlement a quarter of Kenya's arable acreage was set aside for whites at bargain prices.

Travelling out to British East Africa was no ocean holiday for the early settlers like Albert Boedeker and his family whose voyage to Mombasa by BI from Tilbury on 6 June 1896 was recalled in *The Kenya Pioneers:*

> They sailed on the s.s. *Goorkha,* a slow boat which called at every port for food and water. Sheep and cattle were bought in Mediterranean markets, taken aboard and slaughtered when required. At Aden, the Boedekers transhipped to the s.s. *Goa* when, after the excitement of seeing flying fish for the first time, 'a frightful passage ensued.' They were relieved to come ashore at Mombasa.

And so, the first settlers came to British East Africa, although up until the First World War, far more originated from South Africa rather than Britain. Led by the reckless aristocrat Lord Delamere, these were not typical colonial immigrants coming out in Steerage, but landed gentry travelling Saloon like Lord Hindlip, Lord Cranworth, Lord Enniskillen and American millionaire Northrup McMillan who had the financial resources to experiment with suitable crops. After disastrous failures, including Australian wheat, a successful mix of coffee, tea and sisal became the staple exports and there was a plentiful supply of cheap African labour. Nairobi was a frontier town in appearance and manners. British forces put down with unusual severity any recalcitrance from the native tribes whilst Indian aspirations for equality were denied. These were the policies and men who nevertheless created Kenya out of wilderness, a settler land with an export agricultural economy, that eventually ensured for BI's pioneer East African routes a prosperity and imperial place that Mackinnon had long strived for.

In step if not several paces ahead of imperial progress, BI rang in the 20th-century with a fresh commitment to its African and Indian Ocean routes by introducing a new route to Mauritius, extending the India-Africa run to Mozambique and Natal, providing a new East African coastal feeder service, and reviving the Home Line. Such was the pace of expansion, some of it admittedly initially unsuccessful and short-lived, that by 1903 BI was operating the following African services:

Line 16   Bombay-Zanzibar via Aden and Mombasa, four-weekly.
Line 17   Bombay-Durban via Marmagoa, Aden, East African ports
           and Lourenço Marques, four-weekly.
Line 18   Zanzibar-Lourenço Marques via Ibo, Pomba Bay,
           Mozambique and Beira, four-weekly.
Line 22   London-East African ports (direct), four-weekly.
Line 23   London-East African ports (transhipping at Aden),
           four-weekly.

In 1900 a new mail contract was awarded BI which provided a link between Mauritius and the Seychelles. A new circular four-weekly line went outward from Colombo to Port Louis (Mauritius) via Mahé (Seychelles) and returned via Mahé and Aden, whilst another four-weekly line ran a fortnight after the first direct from Colombo to Port Louis. *Warora* left Colombo on 4 February 1900 to inaugurate the new line via Mahé and *Wardha* sailed a fortnight later proceeding direct to Port Louis. *Booldana* followed *Warora* to the Seychelles on 4 March and *Merkara* (1875/2,971 grt) was the next direct ship to Port Louis; *Nuddea* (1883/2,964 grt) followed *Booldana* via Mahé and so on. *

At Port Louis, the service via Mahé connected with the Castle (later Union-Castle) Line's mailship to South Africa that left three days after the BI's scheduled arrival. In the other direction, however, the connection was a tight one for the Colombo steamer was timed to depart the day after the Cape Mail arrived; no wonder that BI timetables showed the next sailing four weeks later

56

as the "official connecting one" *

The first decade of the 20th century was one of bewildering change and confusion on BI's African routes owing to growing foreign competition and indecision and inter-company wrangling between the Calcutta headquarters of Mackinnon, Mackenzie and its Bombay agency. As a result, the story of the India-Africa routes between 1902 and 1906 is one of the most tangled of any British shipping service.

By the early 1900s, competition was becoming increasingly keen from several other companies, in particular DÖAL whose original eight-weekly service begun in the early 1890s was now increased to fortnightly sailings from Bombay (via Porebunder) to Mombasa and other East African ports. This was a regular and efficient service that connected with a branch line on the African coast and was rewarded by growing passenger trade. In 1900 BI continued to operate two distinct India-Africa routes as it had since 1896: Bombay to Zanzibar via Aden and Mombasa, and Bombay to Lourenço Marques via the Seychelles, Zanzibar, Mozambique and Beira. Whilst the long-established Zanzibar to Aden leg was profitable by virtue of being under mail contract, it also posed problems as the Bombay office wished to compete with DÖAL for the growing trade between India and Africa without having to detour to Aden.

In August 1901 Bombay proposed to combine a direct service to Zanzibar with the Aden to Zanzibar mail run:

Sat.	sail BOMBAY
Sun.	call Seychelles
Fri.-Sat.	call Zanzibar
Sun.-Mon.	call Mombasa
Tues.-Weds.	call Aden
Thurs.-Fri.	call Mombasa
Sat.-Sun.	call Zanzibar
Fri.	call Seychelles
Sat.	arr. BOMBAY

This four-week voyage cycle would be operated with *Palitana* (1886/2,998 grt) and *Putiala* (1886/3,305 grt) which had the required 10-knot speed. British India's ability to compete with other lines was adversely affected by a fleet largely designed for the lower, fixed-speed requirements of mail contracts, which lacked the flexibility to operate port-intensive itineraries whilst keeping to the established mail-contract frequency. As it was, BI assigned a hotchpotch of tonnage to the East Africa run and from July 1901 to June 1902 this numbered ten different vessels: *Canara, Goa, Katoria, Lawada, Nevasa, Nowshera, Palitana, Pemba, Putiala* and *Sirdhana*.

The combined itinerary proposal was not taken up as Calcutta wished to continue the direct Bombay to Aden link. Instead, it was announced on 10

January 1902 that the India-Africa line would be extended south from Lourenço Marques to Durban commencing with the 28 May sailing from Bombay. Durban calls had already commenced with *Scindia*'s (1879/2,680 grt) arrival on 4 January 1902 from Mauritius. The first sailing from Durban for Bombay via East Africa was by *Palitana* on 3 May via Lourenço Marques, Beira and Zanzibar followed by *Putiala* on 25 June which added Aden to the itinerary as an interchange port. Rounding out 1902's Durban-East Africa-Bombay sailings were *Nevasa* (1884/2,950 grt) on 22 August, *Canara* on 19 September and *Secundra* (1883/2,610 grt).

An announcement on 17 October 1902 stated that the Bombay to Aden connection had been cut and that the Aden to Zanzibar mail service would be maintained monthly by *Palitana* and *Putiala* running from Bombay to Zanzibar and thence to Mombasa and Aden. The Bombay, Zanzibar and South Africa line would be maintained by *Nerbudda*, *Nevasa* and *Nuddea*.

Typical timetables of the two services were:

BOMBAY-ZANZIBAR-SOUTH AFRICA, FOUR-WEEKLY

27 October	sail BOMBAY
10 November	call Mombasa
11-14 November	call Zanzibar
20 November	call Beira
24 November	call Lourenço Marques
27 November	call Durban
30 November	call East London
2 December	call Port Elizabeth
5 December	arr. CAPE TOWN

BOMBAY, ZANZIBAR AND ADEN, FOUR-WEEKLY

15 September	sail BOMBAY
30 September-2 October	call Zanzibar
3-5 October	call Mombasa
13-14 October	call ADEN
23-24 October	call Mombasa
25-27 October	call Zanzibar
5 November	arr. BOMBAY

As announced on 26 February 1903, from 28 March onwards the Calcutta to Mauritius line vessels would extend their voyages to Durban (which they had already in fact been doing) and Cape Town every four weeks.

In 1903 sailings from Durban to Bombay were undertaken by *Nuddea*, *Bancora* (1881/2,880 grt), *Dunera* (1891/5,413 grt), *Umballa* (1880/1,911 grt), *Nerbudda* (1882/2,977 grt), *Nevasa*, *Landaura*, *Nowshera* (1883/2,962 grt) and *Putiala* at four-weekly intervals. *Nuddea*'s 7 April sailing was the first which advertised "Passengers booked for Delagoa Bay [Lourenço

Marques], Beira, Zanzibar; also (with transhipment) for Inhambane, Chinde, Quelimane, Mozambique and Aden" in conjunction with BI's new East African coastal service of which more anon. The Mauritius route vessels proceeding to Durban that year comprised *Wardha, Shirala* (1901/5,238 grt), *Itria* (1901/5,267 grt) and *Surada* (1902/5,236 grt). By this time the Natal port was well caught up in the web of BI's inter-connecting routes; *Shirala's* 15 August arrival there, for example, carried transhipment cargo from *Nevasa, Warora, Culna* and *Okhla* (1885/5,288 grt), having arrived from Calcutta and Colombo and then setting off for Bombay via East Africa.

Yet there was already clear indication that BI was finding it hard going south of Durban. On 26 May 1903 Bombay advised Calcutta that it "will be best in Company's interests not to run beyond Durban now that the Calcutta steamers [on the Mauritius run] are available to take on passengers and any cargo on to southern ports." Instead it was recommended that a five-ship fortnightly service be established between Bombay and Durban via East Africa which would connect at Beira with the new feeder service for southern ports, and at Durban with the Mauritius steamers. "It will be better in Company's interests," the memorandum continued, "to run fortnightly with steamers more on par with the German boats, than try and cater for the trade with large monthly steamers while the Germans give fortnightly sailings."

The proposal from Bombay was accepted and fortnightly sailings to Durban commenced on 17 June 1903 with alternate trips calling at either Porebunder or Marmagoa and on the return at Aden. The separate Bombay-Zanzibar-Mombasa-Aden service was ended.

Fortnightly sailings on the Bombay-Durban run lasted only six months. The four-weekly pattern was resumed in 1904, operated by *Nuddea, Lindula, Nowshera, Nevasa, Nuddea, Loodiana* and *Lalpoorla.* An interesting one-off departure was that by the new *Waipara* (1904/5,505 grt) from Durban on 25 November to London via Cape Town. Sailings to Lourenço Marques continued every 14 days. The number of steamers was reduced to five and in July Bombay informed Calcutta that traffic to Lourenço Marques was much better than that to Durban. A new routing, Bombay-Marmagoa-Lourenço Marques-Beira-Zanzibar-Mombasa-Aden-Mombasa-Zanzibar-Bombay, was also proposed but never taken up. After the 21 May sailing from Calcutta, the Mauritius ships ceased to call at Durban.

The curtailment of service to South Africa occasioned this letter of 13 August 1904 to Calcutta from BI's Durban agents, Dunn & Co., complaining of:

[a] great loss in passenger business between this port and Bombay, through your steamer service on this coast as far as Durban being so irregular and infrequent.

We would like to point out that the German Line are doing all they can do to cultivate this business, and are securing the whole of it, not because the passengers prefer their steamers, rather the reverse, but they cannot help themselves. In fact the Indian passengers would much prefer to travel by the British India S.N. Co. steamers than any other line, and although we have numerous requests for passage, we are quite unable to secure any business owing to the uncertain movement of your steamers.

The German Line steamers always proceed direct to Bombay via Zanzibar while we are never certain that the BI steamer will adhere to the time-table.

The passenger statistics and vessel age for 1905 relative to the India-Africa services of DÖAL and BI show the unsatisfactory state of affairs.

British India ships (three employed at a time):

Loodiana	20 years old	*Nowshera*	22 years old
Nerbudda	23 years old	*Nuddea*	22 years old
Nevasa	21 years old	*Putiala*	19 years old
Sailings:	16 including some via Aden, others via Seychelles		
Carryings:	35 First Class		
	75 Second Class		
	895 deck		

Deutsche Öst-Afrika ships:

Bundesrath	15 years old	*Somali*	15 years old
Kaiser	14 years old	*Sultan*	14 years old
Reichstag	16 years old		
Sailings:	26 direct to Mombasa		
Carryings:	302 Cabin Class		
	4,992 deck		

Cargo carryings were more in BI's favour:

	Zanzibar	Mombasa	Lamu
British India	18,024 (tons)	4,255	745
DÖAL	8,128	4,323	290

Whereas the DÖAL passenger figures were reasonable, those for BI can only be described as miserable and would seem to illustrate that, marvellous as the company was on the Burma coast, in the Bay of Bengal and the Persian Gulf, it was still a pretty hopeless tangle on the African coast where only BI's oldest tonnage was deployed at that time. *

With losses on the African run for 1904 totalling some 2,640,000 rupees the Calcutta office's 20 June 1905 announcement that the India-Africa line would go no further south than Zanzibar came as no surprise. Instead a monthly service to Zanzibar and Mombasa in conjunction with the Aden-Zanzibar Mail was operated by *Putiala* and either *Nerbudda* or *Nuddea*. This was put into effect immediately with *Putiala*'s sailing of 27 June, which turned back at Zanzibar on 4 July, and *Nerbudda*, after taking the final Durban sailing in July, commenced the new schedule on the 22nd. A typical itinerary from 1906:

5 January	sail BOMBAY
16-18 January	call Zanzibar
19 January	call Mombasa
21 January	call Lamu
29 January	arr. ADEN
30 January	sail ADEN
8-9 February	call Mombasa
10 February	call Zanzibar
20 February	arr. BOMBAY

For 1906, the frequency was increased to fortnightly and effective with *Nuddea*'s 25 May sailing, every other voyage called at the Seychelles. When the unprofitable results of a *Putiala* sailing were brought to Bombay's attention by Calcutta, the reply of 6 December 1906 was somewhat caustic:

We are full well aware of the great loss there must be, but would remind you that we are working the East Africa Line under your orders and against our recommendations... The Aden traffic is not remunerative.

The London office intervened in the simmering dispute:

...the present working of the line is running steamers from Bombay to Mombasa and Zanzibar and then next to Aden and back to Zanzibar and thence to Bombay direct.

It would be advisable to endeavour to embrace in your arrangements a direct service from Bombay to Aden and a direct service from Bombay to Zanzibar such as was done in 1902, in this way you might be able to work in the mail service to and from the Seychelles now requested by the Colonial Office.

As a result the venerable *Africa* was back on the Aden-Zanzibar run starting in March 1907 whilst *Putiala* was running a five-week schedule from Bombay to East Africa via Aden.

By 1908 even Bombay was cut from the routing:

28 January	sail ADEN
6-7 February	call Mombasa
8 February	arr. ZANZIBAR
13 February	sail ZANZIBAR
14 February	call Mombasa
15 February	call Lamu
24 February	arr. ADEN

If BI's East Africa run had literally gone full circle and was back to its 1872 routine, efforts to establish a viable East African coastal service from

1902 to 1905 proved equally unsuccessful.

Concurrent with the extension of the India-Africa run to Durban and the revival of the Home Line was the creation of a new feeder service running south along the Mozambique coast to Mozambique, Beira, Lourenço Marques and smaller places like Ibo, Quelimane, Chiloane and Inhambane. The idea for this was first floated by Bombay in 1900 to cater to a demand for coastal passage north of Quelimane (the Aberdeen Line already ran a coastal service, but it did not go north) by Indian passengers and cargo, including copra and groundnuts from Quelimane as well cattle, the carriage of which in the Bombay-based liners with their largely Hindu passengers was precluded on religious grounds.

The first indication of a coastal service is found in the 1902 *Handbook* which listed a four-weekly Zanzibar-Lourenço Marques run that employed one unspecified vessel:

27 December 1901	sail ZANZIBAR
29-30 December	call Ibo
30-31 December	call Pomba
1 January 1902	call Mozambique
4 January	call Beira
6 January	arr. LOURENÇO MARQUES

When the Bombay service was extended south of Lourenço Marques, the feeder line was re-routed to start at that port and run south to Mozambique. This began in April 1902 and was operated by the trim little *Vasna* (1890/904 grt) and *Vita* (1890/904 grt), built for the Southern India-Ceylon ferry routes. *Vita* operated this typical voyage in 1903:

5 January	sail LOURENÇO MARQUES
6-7 January	call Inhambane
9-11 January	call Beira
12-13 January	call Chinde
14-15 January	call Quilimane
17 January	arr. MOZAMBIQUE

Originally, schedules in the BI *Handbook* listed fortnightly sailings every other Monday from Lourenço Marques and Friday-Saturday calls at Beira, these two ports being transfer points with the Bombay-Durban mailships. Smith, Mackenzie had to establish a network of port agents in the south and arrange for satisfactory bunkering en route; the "V"s usually coaled at Lourenço Marques. Initial results were uneven at best as indicated by records of these 1903 voyages:

Steamer	arr. Lourenço Marques	Earnings	Coal Cons.
Vasna	7 November	£1,000	263 tons
Vita	17 November	£560	185 tons
Vita	17 November	£560	184 tons

62

Vasna	7 December	£840	184	tons
Vasna	23 December	£296	86	tons
Vita	31 December	£1,000	311	tons

By the next year, *Vasna* maintained the now four-weekly service alone, reflecting the reduction in frequency on the Bombay-Durban run. The feeder run was dropped in April 1905 when the "V"s were sold to Japanese owners. On 7 April BI announced that arrangements had been made with DÖAL for the forward carriage of cargo from Bombay to Tanga, Ibo, Quilimane, Chinde, Mozambique, Inhambane, East London, Port Elizabeth and Cape Town.

Not all of BI's African enterprises were star-crossed early in the new century, which witnessed the successful rebirth of the Home Line between Britain and East Africa. The establishment of African colonies by the major European powers resulted in a sudden surfeit of services to East Africa DÖAL began the first round-Africa run in June 1901, a monthly operation using new vessels. In October 1902 Austrian Lloyd commenced a two-monthly Trieste-Durban via Suez run, two years later monthly sailings began. The Portuguese Empresa Nacional de Navegacao inaugurated a direct Lisbon-Mozambique line via the Cape in 1903. And the Messageries Maritimes' Marseilles-Mauritius route via Suez continued to call at East African ports. All of these services enjoyed the generous patronage of their respective governments, including substantial subsidies for carrying mail and, more importantly, "showing the flag."

One flag, however, was missing in the growing fleet of liners sailing direct to East Africa—that of Great Britain— from 1895 until 1902 when, in anticipation of another round of African railway construction, BI re-introduced its Home Line with the first sailing taken from London by *Swaledale* on 17 July. One of the principal cargoes was steel products, especially rails, and the revived service was based on Middlesbrough which was convenient to the Teesside steel and iron industry. The initial African calls were listed as Zanzibar, Beira and Lourenço Marques with four-weekly sailings.

This was essentially a cargo operation which did not employ BI tonnage; subsequent sailings that year were made by the chartered *Fullwell* (1902/3,824 grt/Tyzack & Branfoot S.S. Co.), *Clydesdale* (1895/3,565 grt/J.Laing), *Holywell* (1896/3,300 grt/Tyzack & Branfoot) and *Bodelewell* (1898/3,420 grt/Tyzack & Branfoot). In 1903 *Wensleydale* (1903/3,919 grt/J. Laing) and *Duke of Norfolk* (1889/3,819grt/Duke of Norfolk S.S. Co.) also joined the service.

None of the vessels operating on the revived Home Line carried more than 12 Saloon passengers, but the prospective East Africa traveller had several options. The transhipment facility at Aden with the Calcutta Home Line ships remained. Additionally, BI advertised an 18-day through connection to East Africa which entailed travelling from London to Brindisi by train where

P&O's marvellous little 22-knotter *Isis* or *Osiris* waited to speed one to Port Said in just 48 hours. There, one embarked on the P&O Bombay Mail steamer for the trans-Suez run to Aden to make a final connection with the BI feeder ship for Zanzibar or Mombasa.

In 1905 the Home Line, still maintained by the chartered "Dales", began to serve Mombasa. The next year Beira became the terminus and Port Sudan was added as a call with *Virawa*'s (1890/3,334 grt) 24 October sailing, the first in fact undertaken by a BI ship on the revived service.

A new succession of hired tonnage began to figure in BI's Home Line with the 8 January 1907 sailing of F.C. Strick & Co.'s *Baluchistan* (1897/2,746 grt), which was followed by *Turkistan* (1905/4,505 grt), *Bardistan* (1905/4,060 grt) and *Arabistan* (1893/3,194 grt). There was even a BI ship, *Berbera*, on the service, but she too was somewhat of a stranger having been built for Dale Line as *Nidderdale* in 1905. Under charter she had become a frequent caller at East African ports, making her first such trip in 24 March 1906. She passed to BI ownership in March 1908 and made her first sailing to East Africa as *Berbera* on 24 July. The 4,352-grt vessel could accommodate up to 25 Saloon passengers. Results were evidently marginal enough to warrant some experimental trips by *Berbera* and some of the Strick liners in 1909 whereby they called at East African ports en route from Britain to Madras and Chittagong.

The extension of the railway from Beira into Rhodesia's rich Northern Copper Belt in 1909 finally put the Britain-East Africa route on a firm footing when the engineering contractors, Paulings, contracted with BI and Union-Castle for the carriage of rails from Middlesbrough to East Africa.

There were gradual improvements to African ports. Steadfast dredging had reduced Durban's bar to the point that in 1904 Union-Castle's *Armadale Castle* became the first mailship to enter the harbour; the smaller BI steamers had done so from the beginning. Lourenço Marques' fine natural harbour was previously the only port north of Cape Town where large vessels could go alongside. The rest of the coast offered one wind-swept, bar-bound and treacherous tidal anchorage after another. Cargo at Beira was onloaded into lighters and deposited on the swampy shore of Chiveve Creek where the tidal range was 18 to 25 feet. When the swell was really up, landfall for passengers was often the most exciting, and for some terrifying, experience of the voyage—"the basket", the large wicker box holding four passengers that was lowered from the deck of the liner to a lighter or barge tossing ten or more feet with each swell and then an often wretched passage to the jetty where the basket would be hoisted up onto the quayside.

The progress from ship to shore at Mombasa circa 1903 is described in *The Kenya Pioneers:*

> After the anchor went down, the gang-side was quickly approached by hordes of small craft while, on the other side,

lighters moved in to unload baggage. Dug-outs bobbed about the rowing boats which were manned by Swahili oarsmen, smart in uniforms of white with red cummerbunds. All were clamouring for business. Passengers descended by a companion ladder pressed against the steep and rusting side of the ship. At the bottom they scrambled aboard a boat, sat upon white cushions and waited, under the protection of a scarlet-lined awning, for every seat to be filled.

It was Swahili custom to chant as they rowed; the lyrics were made up around each boatload and lent an air of festivity as the new arrivals were welcomed by song. Muscled Africans lifted them across the last few wavelets to the island; the impact of heat was fierce with neither breeze nor shade for relief.

Luggage was brought off by lighters which took packing cases and animals to a small wooden jetty nearby where it was unloaded by a hand-cranked crane.

Nairobi, the new capital of the Protectorate, rapidly grew from a haphazard collection of corrugated iron shacks along the Uganda Railway. The approach of the mailship towards Mombasa was heralded by flags flown from atop the Nairobi Post Office, a blue one signified that a vessel had left Aden, a red flag meant overseas post had arrived and a white flag indicated that citizens could call for their mail.

Sooner or later the provision of an adequate mail service to British East Africa, through the Suez Canal, will become a necessity, but up to the present the British India Company, which has been the British line largely interested in the trade, has not seen the way to provide a through service without more payment for mails than the Government now gives.

The Times, 7 February 1910

The Kenya settlers, whose political power, assumed and actual, far exceeded their numbers, lobbied ceaselessly for government sponsorship of a direct Britain-East Africa service via Suez. Acting independently and without subsidy, Union-Castle extended its Intermediate Service terminal from Lourenço Marques to Mombasa in January 1910. There was reluctance in some quarters to subsidise even the existing East African services and on 21 March 1910 a question was put in Parliament as to how much would be saved if instead of the BI service between Aden and Mombasa the mails were carried in French or German vessels or if Union-Castle could undertake a round-Africa service. The Government replied that BI was paid £9,000 per annum to maintain the Aden to Mombasa shuttle and if the mails were carried in foreign ships, a saving of £7,200 would be realised. It was further stated that Union-Castle was not prepared to undertake a round-Africa service.

At last convinced of the need to compete against the DÖAL and others, the British Government finally consented to a British service and whilst not granting any subsidy it promised to direct government freight and passengers to a Royal East African Service, London-Gibraltar-Marseilles-Naples-Port Said-Port Sudan-Aden-Mombasa, which commenced 13 September 1910 with the sailing of *Guelph*. This has sometimes been referred to as being a joint service between Union-Castle and BI, although it was not advertised as such and may have simply been a co-ordination of sailings, each line maintaining a four-weekly service employing four vessels.

Union-Castle detailed its *Guelph, Dunvegan Castle* and *Carisbrook Castle* to the East African service whilst BI's contribution was less impressive than some of what Union-Castle considered previously superfluous tonnage. In fact the pattern of BI sailings in 1910 and 1911 continued as before, alternating between the Aden transhipment with the Calcutta-bound vessels and the direct service, the latter still employing Strick ships. The failure of the original African Home Line in 1893 and that of the Queensland Royal Mail Line three years later focused BI's attention back to its traditional strength, localised services. The construction of larger Home Line vessels ceased, many of the bigger ships being taken up for the increasingly lucrative trooping trade and most London-Calcutta sailings from the 1890s onwards were made by freighters carrying only a handful of Saloon passengers. Thus the available fleet was perhaps not ideally suited to a revived East African Home Line.

With the Home Line now successfully back in place, BI revised once more its India-Africa service to include southern ports and terminate at Durban after a lapse of six years. First to arrive at the Natal port was *Pentakota* (1890/3,418 grt) on 20 April 1911 from Lourenço Marques, Zanzibar, Seychelles and Bombay. She was followed by *Pundua* (1888/3,305 grt), *Purnea* (1889/3,395 grt) and *Palamcotta* (1890/3,413 grt) and henceforth the "P"s faithfully maintained monthly sailings. All were products of A.&J. Inglis, had principal measurements of 350 ft. (*Palamcotta* was ten feet longer) by 42 ft. and had a service speed of 12 knots.

Prior to the First World War, the Home Line remained predominantly a cargo service and, from a passenger perspective, its tonnage was distinctly second rate compared to that of Union-Castle and DÖAL. In late 1910 BI had placed orders with Barclay, Curle for two 9,000-grt vessels possibly earmarked for the East Africa run. However, by the time they were launched on 12 September and 12 December 1912 as *Neuralia* and *Nevasa* respectively, BI had decided to considerably strengthen its Home Line to Calcutta and these ships were deployed on that service instead. In 1912 and 1913, BI sailing lists showed some departures by *Goth, Guelph* and *Gascon*, indicating some measure of co-operation with Union-Castle.

It was not until mid-1913 that the Aden transhipment gave way to a direct

BI four-weekly service beginning with *Berbera's* voyage of 23 July from London for Port Sudan, Zanzibar, Mombasa, Beira, Lourenço Marques and Durban. She commenced her northbound voyage on 11 September with calls listed as Lourenço Marques, Beira, Chinde, Mozambique, Port Amelia, Zanzibar, Mombasa, Aden, Port Sudan, Suez, Naples, Marseilles and Gibraltar. The last Strick ship, *Albistan*, made her final sailing on the route on 17 September and the former Calcutta Home Line steamers *Mombassa* and *Matiana* made their first voyages to Durban on 20 August (maiden arrival there on 7 October) and 15 October respectively.

The historic Aden to Zanzibar shuttle ended with the 7 July voyage with calls at Mombasa 10-17 July and returning to Zanzibar on the 18th.

The 1889-built *Mombassa*, 4,662 grt, could accommodate 35 First and 20 Second Class passengers. The five years newer 5,264-grt *Matiana* had berths for 34 First and 24 Second Class and both ships were good for about 11.5 knots. Writing in *BI News* of February 1956, W.L. Gordon, who started work for Gray, Dawes & Co. (BI's London agents) 51 years earlier, recalled, "these passenger ships were of pretty ancient vintage, with dining saloon running fore aft and passenger cabins leading off the saloon on both sides. There were long tables down the length of the saloon, and over each was one of the old but efficient punkahs operated by a punkah-wallah immediately outside the saloon."

In 1914, Union-Castle introduced its first ships specifically designed for the East African run, the 11,400-grt *Llandovery Castle* and *Llanstephan Castle* which were superior even to the Cape mailships in accommodation. British India could only respond by positioning the 27-year-old 5,878-grt *Golconda* on the Home Line on 1 April. She first called at Durban on 13 May. Built by Wm. Doxford, Sunderland, as a speculative venture for Guion Line or Canadian Pacific, she was instead purchased in October 1888 by BI and completed as its largest vessel, which she remained for 15 years. With her sweeping sheer, two funnels and four well-raked masts, she cut a dashing figure on the London-Calcutta run for 12 years. Operationally she was somewhat hindered by having a top speed of only 13 knots, a reputation for being a "roller" and a remarkably small passenger capacity of 78 First and 24 Second Class.

Irrespective of the relative merits of their tonnage, BI and Union-Castle fares were the same in First Class at £46 15s. and 6d. whilst BI surprisingly charged considerably more for Second Class at £34 10s. 10d compared to £20 15s. 9d. on Union-Castle.

A typical schedule from the 1914 Handbook:

LONDON-EAST/SOUTH AFRICA LINE NO. 21

R.M.S. *Matiana*

28 January	sail MIDDLESBROUGH
4 February	sail LONDON

12 February	call Marseilles
14 February	call Naples
18 February	call Port Said
19 February	call Suez
21 February	call Port Sudan
24 February	call Aden
3 March	call Mombasa
9 March	call Zanzibar
12 March	call Port Amelia
13 March	call Mozambique
14 March	call Chinde
15 March	call Beira
18 March	call Lourenço Marques
20 March	arr. DURBAN

Sailing northbound on 23 March, *Matiana* was not programmed to return, via the same ports, to London until 2 May.

British India was favoured by three extraordinary chairmen whose leadership proved invaluable to the company during trying and changing times—Mackinnon (1856-1893), Inchcape (1913-1932) and Currie (1938-1960)—and who left their distinctive stamp on not only the ships and services, fates and fortunes of the BI, but on the Merchant Navy as a whole. That last year of peace, 1913, found the Rt. Hon. The Earl of Inchcape, assuming the chairmanship in March, the apex of a brilliant career, and leading BI to its pinnacle.

Born at Arbroath, Angus, in 1852, James L. Mackay joined the Calcutta office of Mackinnon Mackenzie & Co. in 1874 and rose to prominence in the company when five years later he was sent to Bombay to sort out the mess following the collapse of the BI agents there, Nicol & Co. He also had an influential position with the Bengal Chamber of Commerce. As described by a colleague, the future Lord Inchcape "could think in millions with the same facility as he could discuss a working cost or an overhead charge worked out to decimals. He could not suffer fools, and he was ruthless towards inefficiency. He was hard, but it was with the hardness of one who never spared himself." (*BI Centenary*).

The Inchcape passion for detail, order and efficiency quickly manifested itself in the company's ships and services. There was an end of the often higgledy-piggledy jumble of incompatible ships on ever-changing services. The new chairman was keenly aware of the localised nature of BI's routes and services, hence the importance of consultation with the many agencies and ships' staffs. The rivalry between Bombay and Calcutta which had adversely affected the African trade was no longer tolerated. There was also an end of the see-saw relationship between BI's traditional local services and the Home

Lines in favour of a balance that complemented both.

British India under Inchcape's influence (which was felt long before he assumed the Chairmanship) did not tolerate competition lightly: it bought out the rival Bombay-Hedjaz Co. (Shah Line) lest it compete with BI's Persian Gulf service in 1910 and two years later the Apcar Line was absorbed and its services to the Straits, China and Japan incorporated into the BI network, the title still being retained and used for many years to come. In 1913 the Australian-based fleet of Archibald Currie came under BI ownership and in 1919 the F.C. Strick Co. fleet was purchased. An agreement was hammered out in 1923 to regulate competition with the fast-rising Scindia Company, one of the pioneer Indian-owned lines.

The Inchcape fleet (and it was just that considering BI had 99 vessels totalling 273,755 grt in 1896 and 158 vessels, virtually all newly built, totalling 915,852 grt in 1922) also showed a new sense of co-ordination. The traditional BI design creed of flexibility remained, but the newbuildings were now grouped into specific classes (starting with the "A", "B", "C", "E", "K" and "V"s) all with design features for their designated service, whether long distance "Home" voyaging, short distance, passenger-cargo or cargo only. Starting with *Neuralia* and *Nevasa*, the so-called Isherwood Cabin began to figure in the interior arrangement. Better known as the Bibby Cabin after the principal British line to Burma, this gave, by way of a narrow passage extending to the ship's side, natural light and air to inboard cabins. In deck passenger accommodation and facilities BI now set the standard for other companies.

The newbuilding programme got underway in 1910. In addition to the first of the famous "M" ships for the Indian Home Line (*Malda* which called at Port Sudan en route to Calcutta on her maiden voyage in May 1913), there were specially built vessels for the Indian-based routes. These included the "V" class quartet *Varela*, *Varsova*, *Vita* and *Vasna* for the Bombay-Gulf Mail and the first of three generations of "K" class vessels for the Bombay-Durban Mail.

Now a premier imperial link, the Bombay-Durban run deserved its own specially-built tonnage. In 1914, the monthly service was still being maintained by the 3,400-grt sister ships *Pundua*, *Palamcotta* and *Pentakota*, dating from 1888-90 and good for only 12 knots. As replacements, BI ordered from Swan Hunter's Newcastle yards the first specially designed ships for the service: the 7,000-grt *Karoa*, *Karunga* (delivered as *Karapara*), *Karagola* and *Khandalla*.

Before the advent of the "K"s, however, came two more wide-ranging and significant developments in 1914. In May was the announcement, which caught most by surprise, of the amalgamation of British India Steam Navigation Co. and the Peninsular & Oriental Steam Navigation Co. Such a merger had been first broached in 1901-02 by Inchcape and P&O's Sir Thomas Sutherland, but stifled by BI Chairman Duncan Mackinnon. Given the traditional co-operation of the two lines and the ideal networking of ships and services, such a merger was perhaps inevitable and negotiations began anew in March 1914, shortly after Lord Inchcape assumed chairmanship of British India.

In essence the amalgamation resulted in the union of giants boasting a combined capital of £15 million, a fleet of 201 vessels totalling more than a million gross tons and services which formed the very arteries of Imperial commerce and communication. Of the newly formed Joint Board of Directors, 12 came from P&O and eight from BI and the new Director was BI's Inchcape. That both lines retained fully their proud identities and established services demonstrated just how compatible they were.

In the great maritime junctions of the East, British all; at Aden, Bombay, Singapore, Sydney and Hong Kong, the ships of the BI and P&O, always united in purpose, went about their business as before until August 1914 when the tragedy of the First World War began. The contribution of the Merchant Navy and BI was incalculable. Many BI liners served as transports or hospital ships and all the essential mail and passenger services were maintained throughout the war as well. Both the Home Line and the Durban Mail continued, but with a variety of tonnage and irregular frequency. In 1916, for example, the Durban run was maintained by the sister ships *Dunera* and *Dilwara* and *Arratoon Apcar* (1896/4,510 grt), one of the clipper-stemmed former Apcar liners.

On 16th October 1914 a veritable armada of BI ships, 24 in all (the greatest assemblage of company tonnage in one place), sailed from Karachi and Bombay packed with Indian troops, most destined for France.

Having played a critical role in the initial development of British East Africa, it was all the more fitting that BI ships would figure in the conquest of German East Africa and thus ensure its eventual incorporation into the Empire. The pity was that unlike in 1877 when Britain could have had Tanganyika for the asking following the Sultan of Zanzibar's offer to Mackinnon, this now richly developed colony had to be secured by blood.

Operations against German East Africa began almost at once and were hastily and poorly planned. Four ships, *Barjora*, *Pentakota*, *Bharata* (1902/4,054 grt) and *Muttra* together with the P&O *Karmala*, transported Indian Expeditionary Force B to the landings at Tanga on 3 November. The Indian troops, unused to sea travel, fared poorly on the journey and were not fit to fight as a result. Considerable German resistance was encountered and six guns of the 28th Mountain Battery of the Royal Artillery, carried aboard *Bharata* for landing, were instead mounted on her Boat Deck and the plucky former Calcutta-Rangoon mailship joined H.M.S. *Fox* in bombarding Tanga whilst herself coming under fire from shoreside batteries. Continued resistance forced the re-embarkation of the troops and Captain O'Connor brought *Barjora* close enough to shore to cover the retreat with her guns. In all, 7,000 troops were safely evacuated from the beach using ship's lifeboats.

In later, successful landings on Mafia Island and Vanga, German East Africa, in January 1915, *Barjora* was also present and later continued to troop along the East African coast. Outnumbered ten to one, German General Lettow-Vorbeck's forces of native askaris conducted a brilliant campaign of guerrilla warfare in the hinterland which held down sizable numbers of Empire forces until the end of the war.

Progress continued apace on the "K" class ships, the first of which, *Karoa,* was launched at Swan Hunter in December, ran trials in March 1915 and was commissioned as a transport. She was soon followed by sister *Karapara* (originally ordered as *Karunga*) which was handed over on 21 August. British India immediately offered her as a hospital ship and agreed to bear all expenses for her operation. She was commissioned at Southampton as *Hospital Ship No. 17* on 21 February 1916 having been fitted with beds for 341 patients and carrying 200 medical staff. Resplendent in her white paint with green hull band and Red Cross markings, she was immediately sent to the grim shores of Gallipoli. Important research to combat sandfly fever and dysentery, which were claiming as many lives as the Turks, was conducted aboard.

Her sister ship *Karoa,* too, was at Gallipoli, but as a transport and found herself trapped in Suvla Bay with an enemy submarine outside the net defences and the target of a persistent if ineffective Turkish shore battery which fired some 30 rounds at the ship which could only raise anchor and sail defensively in circles. There were several close calls, but only one round struck home on the port side, doing only minor damage. After a day of torment, *Karoa* steamed out of the anchorage during that evening. In April 1916 *Karoa* was decommissioned and allocated to BI for service on her originally intended route.

The third "K", *Karagola,* also commissioned as a transport on 27 April 1917, found herself in the thick of action on her maiden voyage out East. On 19 May, 240 miles from Gibraltar, she encountered an enemy submarine on the surface and managed to get off two rounds with her deck gun until the U-boat submerged. A fortnight later, between Malta and Port Said, a periscope was spotted 900 yards off the port beam; Captain D.J. Chivas rang up to full revs and his ship passed out of range. For the duration of the war *Karoa* trooped in the Persian Gulf and Indian Ocean.

Whilst the "K"s weathered many a close call, the entire African Home Line fleet was lost to enemy action. *Golconda* was first to succumb, striking a U-boat-laid mine in the North Sea on 3 June 1916 en route to Calcutta and sinking with 19 of her complement. Before the year was out, *Mombassa* was torpedoed on 20 October by U-39 off Cape Corbelin, Algeria, whilst on her regular East Africa run. Of her crew and 19 passengers, only one life was lost. Just a day later, in the English Channel, her running mate, *Matiana*, successfully fended off a surfaced submarine. Her luck ran out when, after grounding on Keith Reef, Tunisia, she was torpedoed on 1 May 1918. A German torpedo also found *Berbera* on 25 March 1917 when the ship was nearing the Straits of Messina on passage from Bombay to Marseilles. It was a particularly dismal record and there can have been few lines which suffered the wholesale loss of an entire route's ships.

In all, BI lost 24 ships in the First World War. It was a heavy price, but one that prompted a post-war recovery which coincided with a final expansion of Empire that would see the company reach its pinnacle and reap what it had sown in East Africa.

The new *Coconada* was among the first to operate on BI's Aden-Zanzibar service, making her maiden African sailing on 27 December 1873.

A. Duncan collection, courtesy Charles Dragonette

Java and *Mecca* both served on BI's new Bombay-Africa run from 1880-1 and ten years later also plied the Africa Home Line. This is one of series of attractive (and accurate) paintings commissioned for new buildings by the line.

Laurence Dunn collection

The first BI ship with triple-expansion machinery, *Madura* achieved a measure of fame when she was chartered to carry H.M.Stanley's Emin Pasha relief expedition in 1887. Later she was a mainstay of the new U.K.-Africa Home Line circa 1890-92.

Laurence Dunn collection

Loodiana which called at Durban both from Bombay and as an extension to her normal Calcutta-Mauritius duties, was eventually lost with all hands in a cyclone en route from Mauritius to Ceylon in January 1910.

Laurence Dunn collection

True to her name, *Africa* was a faithful and familiar servant on BI's African routes, starting in 1890 on the new Home Line and 17 years later she resumed the Aden-Zanzibar shuttle.

Laurence Dunn collection

The "W"s, *Wardha* (above) and *Warora,* also figured in the Calcutta-Mauritius service and in 1900 inaugurated BI's new Mauritius-Seychelles run.

Laurence Dunn collection

75

When the Bombay-Aden-Zanzibar-Mombasa line was revived in 1893, *Purulia* was among the first to operate it.

Laurence Dunn collection

By the turn of the century the ever-changing India-Africa services were held down by a variety of ships including *Sirdhana* which was at 2,661 grt, BI's largest ship when completed in 1879.

Laurence Dunn collection

The "N" class was a mainstay of the India-Africa run in the early 1900s. The last of the quartet, *Nevasa* (above) joined the service in 1899.

Laurence Dunn collection

The first BI sailing from Durban to Bombay via East Africa was made by *Palitana* on 3 May 1902, but by that autumn she was put on the Bombay-Zanzibar-Aden run.

A. Duncan collection

After Boer War trooping (as pictured above), *Dunera* operated sporadically on the Bombay-Durban route. At 5,413 grt, *Dunera* and *Dilwara* were BI's largest ships on Indian Ocean service until the advent of the "K"s.

Laurence Dunn collection

After a decade fraught with change and upheaval on its India-Africa routes, BI settled down in 1911 to a regular monthly Bombay-Durban run maintained by the "P"s such as *Palamcotta*.

Laurence Dunn collection

In 1913 BI revived its African Home Line to which the former Calcutta mailships *Mombassa* and *Matiana* were assigned. *Mombassa* is shown above anchored in the Thames at Gravesend where passengers embarked by tender.

Charles Dragonette collection

With her rakish looks, *Golconda* looked the part of flagship of BI's African Home Line on which she began running in April 1914. In reality, she was not much competition to the new Union-Castle" Llans", being 16 years old and good for only 13 knots.

Laurence Dunn collection

79

Lead ship of the "K" class which were the first BI vessels built for the East Africa run, *Karoa* began Bombay-Durban sailings in November 1919. The photographer was tall enough to get a nice shot of *Karoa* over a passenger's sun umbrella!

A. Duncan collection

Ordered as *Karunga* and completed in 1915 as *Hospital Ship No. 17* (BI postcard, artist W.K. Rook), she had an adventurous war career (including the Gallipoli Campaign) before joining the Durban Mail as *Karapara* in August 1919.

Albert Watson III collection

British India Steam Navigation Co., Ltd.

R. M. S. KARAGOLA. *7,053 gross tons.*

Third of the "K"s, *Karagola* outran a U-boat on her maiden voyage in May 1917 as a transport. Making her first voyage on the Durban Mail in August 1919, *Karagola*, after a stint on the Straits run, resumed African sailings in January 1946. A BI postcard, artist unknown.   *Albert Watson III collection*

Nevasa (above) and *Neuralia*, first of the modern Home Line ships of the Inchcape programme, made the first of several voyages to East Africa in 1920 before being converted to full time trooping five years later.

A. Duncan collection

81

Beginning an enduring association between the "M"s and East Africa, *Margha* (b. 1917) was the first of this large group of similar BI liners to sail from the U.K. to Beira in July 1920.

A. Duncan collection, courtesy Charles Dragonette

In 1922 BI built two specially designed motor ships for East African coastal service, *Dwarka* and *Dumra* (above). Based at Mombasa, *Dumra* linked the small settlements along coasts of Kenya and Tanganyika.

A. Duncan collection, courtesy Charles Dragonette

Alongside at Marseilles in 1938, *Modasa* displays the cruiser stern that distinguished the five "M3"s that would serve the African Home Line for 30 years. Lead ship of the class, *Modasa* was the first "M" to make her maiden voyage to Africa in December 1921. *Marius Bar photo, Charles Dragonette collection*

It was not until 1923 that *Khandalla* (shown above on trials 31May) completed the quartet of "K"s on the Durban Mail. Shifted to the Straits run in 1932, she resumed Africa sailings in November 1940. A true stalwart of the service, she continued for another decade. *P&O*

Depicted at Aden (artist Frank H. Mason), *Mulbera,* last of the "M3"s, first sailed to East Africa in November 1924 carrying the Duke and Duchess of York (later King George VI and Queen Elizabeth) to Kenya. *author's collection*

In November 1927 *Ellora,* completed in 1911 for the Straits service, began Bombay-Mombasa sailings which continued through 1930. In this trials photo, with a bone in her teeth and a glorious plume of coal smoke, the 12-knot *Ellora* emulates an ocean greyhound. *A. Duncan collection*

British India rang in the troubled '30s with a flourish; the 9,890-grt *Kenya* and *Karanja* built for the Durban Mail. The imposing appearance of these superb ships is shown in this view of *Karanja* as delivered.

A. Duncan collection, courtesy Charles Dragonette

Kenya, glistening in the new white upperworks scheme adopted in 1935, manoeuvering in Kilindini Harbour. As the migrant ship *Castel Felice* she was not scrapped until 1970, outliving the post-war *Kenya* by a year.

A. Duncan collection, courtesy Charles Dragonette

85

Indian Ocean Greyhounds. The most impressive looking of all BI African liners were doubtless *Takliwa and Tairea* (above) of 1924 which joined the Bombay-Durban service in 1932. From the 1939 BI/P&O calendar (artist A.J. Burgess).

author's collection

On her first African voyage in July 1932, *Takliwa* was the first ship in 50 years to break the speed record between India and Africa, cutting 24 hours off the passage time. The "T"s were the smallest three-funnelled liners ever built.

A. Duncan collection

86

Unique in the fleet for her engines aft design, *Sofala* was built in 1937 to replace *Dwarka* on African coastal service. She was the first in a series of BI coastal and auxiliary vessels built at Leith by Henry Robb.

A. Duncan collection

One of three BI ships sunk on 6 April 1942, *Malda* was the only one of the "M3" class liners lost in the Second World War.

A. Duncan collection

KARANJA
Gr. Britain – LSI(L)
(KARANJA Class)
(1942)

Commissioned as H.M.S. *Karanja* in July 1941, the ship was one of five P&O Group vessels lost during the invasion of North Africa in November 1942.

Charles Dragonette collection

Tilawa joined the Durban Mail in November 1940 and was torpedoed and sunk on 23 November 1942 en route to Durban. BI postcard, artist Jack ("Jock") Spurling.

Richard Maxwell collection

5. WIDER AND WIDER STILL

The British Empire stands firm as a great force for good. It stands in the sweep of every wind, by the wash of every sea.   Stanley Baldwin

Although the political decline of the British Empire began after the First World War, the Treaty of Versailles expanded the bounds of the Empire to its widest scope. In Africa, particularly, Cecil Rhodes' coveted dream of an imperial swath, from Cape to Cairo, was finally realised with the mandate by the League of Nations of former German East Africa to Great Britain, becoming Tanganyika Territory.

Not coincidentally this apex of Empire found BI at its absolute peak of 161 ships in 1920 and the greatest-ever combined tonnage of 915,857 was reached two years later. British India had the largest merchant fleet in the world and one of the newest with the products of the pre-war newbuilding programme, like the "V"s and "K"s, finally on their intended services whilst an even more audacious building programme was undertaken that would renew both the Home and India-based routes.

Imperial progress, the lifeblood of the company, was to be found everywhere in what was loosely called "British East" and BI's African routes took on a new importance and profitability as exploitation of Africa's natural mineral wealth and development of non-indigenous cash crops found their stride.

That vital sector of BI's African passenger market, Indians, continued to greatly increase their numbers in East Africa after the war; the 34,000 residing there in 1914 rising to 54,434 by 1921. Just a decade later, the Indian population stood at 98,164.

In 1920 the Protectorate of British East Africa was annexed as Kenya Colony. Further white settlement was encouraged under the Soldier Settler Scheme which gave war veterans subsidised land in the Kenya Highlands. In November 1919 the first 1,500 new settlers sailed to Mombasa in *Garth Castle*. It was "officers to Kenya, N.C.O.s to Rhodesia", and Kenya attracted an extraordinary collection of retired colonels and aristocrats. The widely publicised antics of the Happy Valley Set were summed up by the popular joke, "Are you married or do you live in Kenya?" By 1920, 9,000 settlers lived in the colony and it would be unfair to dismiss them as dilettantes. There was much hard work and dedication which was reflected by booming inter-war East African trade:

1919	£16 mn.
1924	£29 mn.
1929	£35 mn.

Experimentation continued to find suitable cash crops to harvest and export successfully. In 1918 maize and wheat were widely planted in Kenya and in 1927 *Modasa* carried the first cargo of export maize to London. Far more successful, beyond sisal, was coffee and tea. An important mineral export was soda ash. So-called "insect flowers", the white blossoms of the pyrethrum, were widely harvested in Kenya for use as a nonpoisonous insecticide.

From Tanganyika, the most profitable export crop was sisal, used for the manufacture of cord and twine, which was introduced from the Yucatan, Mexico, in 1893. Dar-es-Salaam's predominance as the Territory's principal port was secured in 1914 when the railway was completed to Kigoma on Lake Tanganyika. This also was an important artery for trade to and from the Belgian Congo. German planters successfully introduced the cultivation of Arabica coffee. By 1935, 8,455 white settlers lived in the Territory.

In addition to coffee, a staple export crop of Uganda was cotton. In 1931 a through railway link was established from Kampala to Mombasa. Indians played a dominant role in the commercial development of the Protectorate, controlling 90 per cent of Uganda's trade. Most of the cotton gins were run by Indians and the whole of the crop exported to the textile mills of Bombay.

In 1923 Southern Rhodesia chose to become a self-governing colony instead of merging with South Africa. The 90,000 settlers owned 50 per cent of the land whose vast mineral resources were rapidly developed and became a major contribution to BI's homeward trade.

During the inter-war years BI's East African network became one of the most efficient of all Empire routes. Six years after its merger with P&O in 1914, BI ended the joint operation with Union-Castle and terminated the Home Line at Beira. The Bombay-Durban "K"s still connected with the homeward P&O and inbound Cape mailships.

Line No. 17, Bombay-Seychelles-East/South Africa, had maintained its fortnightly frequency during the war. With the lifting of wartime restrictions, the resumed newspaper shipping columns listed initial post-war Durban departures of *Taroba* (1902/6,309 grt) for Bombay via Lourenço Marques, Zanzibar and Mombasa on 30 November 1918 followed by *Khosrou* on 15 December and *Pundua* 10 days later. Into 1919, in addition to *Taroba* and *Pundua*, sailings from Durban were undertaken by *Coconada* (1910/3,958 grt) on 1 January, *Akbar* on 21 January and the former Apcar liner *Gregory Apcar* (1902/4,649 grt) on 31 May and 18 August. *Taroba* and sister ship *Tara* were built in 1902 for the Calcutta-Straits service. When completed, they had passenger certificates for 38 First, 32 Second and the extraordinary total of 5,691 deck. With their low freeboard, very long bows, deck cranes and large towering funnels, the "T"s were graceful and impressive-looking vessels.

The post-war future of the Durban Mail however lay in the restitution of the three virtually new "K" class ships which were still under the direction of the Shipping Controller. In this capacity, *Karagola* arrived at Accra from Bombay on 2 January 1919 and *Karoa* reached Plymouth on 16 July from Sydney. Completing her government service, *Karagola* docked at Bombay on 29 July and shortly thereafter began sailings to Durban, arriving there for the first time on 15 September. *Karapara*, after acting as a hospital ship at Istanbul and refitting, left London on 4 July and arrived at Bombay on the 21st. She made her first call at Durban on 7 September. Destined to join her sister, *Karoa* sailed from London on 11 September and reached Bombay on 6 October. Making her first departure from Durban for Bombay on 29 November, the *Natal Mercury* described *Karoa* as "being of such recent construction, her passenger accommodation has little to be desired."

Among the outstanding liners of the Inchcape newbuilding programme and the first designed specifically for the East African run, the "K"s were distinguished by their substantial superstructures, modern cruiser sterns and single funnel sited well forward of amidships. Measuring 425 ft. by 55.6 ft., the "K"s' service speed of 15.5 knots (17 knots maximum) came from two 5,800 ihp triple-expansion engines supplied by eight single-end Scotch boilers burning coal under forced draught and driving twin screws.

Karoa (6,631 grt) and *Karapara* (7,117 grt) each had accommodation for 44 First and 64 Second Class and as many as 1,490 deck passengers whilst the relative figures for the 7,053-grt *Karagola* were 58 First, 64 Second and 1,050 deck and for *Khandalla* (1924/7,018 grt), 60 First, 68 Second and 1,061 deck. Each had a crew of 197 officers and men. All First Class cabins were outside and had one, two or three berths. Public rooms comprised a music room, smoking room and entrance hall on Promenade Deck and a 64-seat dining saloon on Saloon Deck. In *Khandalla* (the décor was similar in the other "K"s), the dining saloon had white-painted panelling with gold-painted details, decorative mirrors over the sideboards, and dark oak furniture. The panelling of the music room was painted grey and the furniture and doors were polished dark mahogany. The smoke room, aft on Promenade Deck, featured fumed-oak panelling and two paintings by Frank H. Mason. Each ship had four holds of 274,000 cu. ft. capacity.

The three "K"s replaced *Pundua, Purnea* and *Gregory Apcar*, the latter two ships departing Durban for Bombay for the last time on 17 July and 18 August respectively. According to the *Natal Mercury, Gregory Apcar* "not only carried Indian passengers and general cargo, but her first-class accommodation was crowded to the utmost capacity. As a matter of fact, in several instances passengers desirous of travelling by her offered premiums for the quarters of the ship's officers. This line (the British India Line) is at present in great demand for berths and cargo. The *Gregory Apcar* also took 263 bags of mail for East Coast ports." Also on her last African voyage and ending the well-established association of the "P"s with the Durban Mail was *Pundua* whose

Durban sailing on 17 October received press notice mainly because theatrical star Miss Marie Tempest was among her passengers.

Like many commercial operations, the African Home Line had a somewhat fitful rebirth after the First World War, a result of not being particularly well established before the conflict. Cargo operations were resumed in 1919 with the London sailings of *Ormara* (1914/4,742 grt) on 20 January, *Japan* (1906/6,052 grt) on 12 March and *Gracchus* (1902/3,760 grt) on 30 April. Later departures were taken by the new *Homefield* (1919/5,324 grt) and *Cranfield* (1919/5,332 grt) which like their elder fleetmates were outbound to India and never sailed again to East Africa.

It was not until 1920 that the Home Line, now given No. 22 and initially routed Middlesbrough-London-Marseilles-Naples-Port Said-Suez-Aden-Mombasa-Zanzibar, was revived as a regular passenger line, independent of Union-Castle and no longer sailing to southern African ports. Among the hotchpotch of ships on the line that year were the new *Golconda* (1919/5,328 grt) and *Gairsoppa* (1919/5,237 grt), two of the 16 "B" type standard freighters purchased by BI, which left London on their delivery voyages on 24 February and 4 September respectively and called at East African ports en route to India.

More significant were the first East African sailings of *Neuralia* (1912/9,082 grt) on 27 February 1920 and *Nevasa* (1913/9,071 grt) on 19 October. These imposing 480.5 ft. by 58 ft. vessels, the largest yet built for BI, were also its first modern Home Line ships. Twin-screw and powered by 6,000 ihp quadruple expansion steam engines, they were good for 14.5 knots. Their passenger accommodation, for 128 First and 98 Second Class, was the most elaborate yet seen in a BI vessel. First Class had a dining saloon, drawing room, library, entrance hall, smoking room and veranda cafe. Yet they were destined to spend most of their careers as transports and made very few African voyages.

A more enduring association between East Africa and a long line of BI "M" class steamers began in 1920. If there was any group of British colonial vessels that could be characterised as ubiquitous it was the "M" class which held down all of the Home Line services during the inter-war period, and well into the post-war era as well. With their sturdy hulls topped by a substantial superstructure and single funnel, the "M"s were among the largest and most successful groups of British colonial liners. In the evocative Spurling and Dixon paintings of the period one of the "M"s was invariably portrayed together with a P&O mailship as partners in Imperial commerce.

Including variations and deviations, there were 23 "M"s, half of which had associations with Africa. They can be divided into three main groups referred to hereafter for convenience as M1, M2 and M3, the first comprising just a pair of ships with less midships accommodation than their successors and therefore not so high. Built by Barclay, Curle on the Clyde they were 450 ft. long by 58 ft., their twin screws being driven by triple-expansion engines to give a service speed of 13 knots and were named *Malda*, 7,884 grt, launched on 7 March 1913, and *Manora*, 7,875 grt, christened on 6 May 1913. Each could carry 45 First and 25 Second Class passengers, but more importantly, some 10,500 to 11,000 tons of cargo (498,000 cu. ft.) i.e. about half as much again as the Home Line's old *Matiana* of 1894.

The second or M2 group initially consisted of four more Barclay, Curle ships and two from Swan Hunter's on the Tyne. All had an extra deck amidships, this being a promenade deck above the open-sided bridge deck thereby increasing their passenger capacity to 89 First and 40 Second Class. Since 23 berths were interchangeable these figures could be varied according to voyage requirements. The First Class music room and smoking room were forward on Promenade Deck and the Second Class lounge and smoking room aft on the same deck. On Bridge Deck were found the 86-seat First Class dining saloon forward and that for Second Class aft with staterooms in between and on Upper Deck amidships. *

The Clyde-built vessels were:

> *Mashobra* (8,173 grt), launched 30 December 1913
> *Merkara* (8,228 grt), launched 7 September 1914
> *Mandala* (8,246 grt), launched 1 June 1915
> *Mantola* (8,246 grt), launched March 1916

whilst those from Tyneside were:

> *Mongara* (8,203 grt), launched 11 February 1914
> *Morvada* (8,193 grt), launched 23 July 1914

and characterised by their distinctly taller and slimmer funnels and lattice-girder type derrick booms. This group was especially hard-hit by the First World War, *Malda*, *Mashobra* and *Mongara* being lost.

Two further ships of the M class were taken over by the Admiralty prior to completion and converted for use as oilers, *Margha* becoming *Boxleaf* in 1915 and *Masula* the *Limeleaf* a year later. Neither ran for BI. A new *Margha* (8,278 grt) however joined the company fleet in 1917. Though having the same dimensions she had initially a quite different profile with a squat funnel and only a single mast which was stepped amidships. Only after hostilities were over was she altered to conform to the general appearance of the others. *

Masula (1919/7,261 grt) and *Mundra* (1920/7,275 grt), a pair of "M"s laid down during the First World War as future M2s, were never completed as such due to shipyard strikes at Barclay, Curle's and emerged as 12-passenger freighters.

Still two more counter-sterned Barclay Curle-built M2's, both passenger ships and having the same dimensions as their sisters were to join the fleet after the war, *Mashobra* launched on 14 July 1920 and *Manela* (8,303 grt) christened 9 October. The former had the well-tried triple-expansion machinery, but *Manela* was distinguished by being the first BI ship powered by double reduction geared turbines. Both carried their lifeboats above deck. Their accommodation was for 67 First and 38 Second Class. *Mashobra* began her maiden voyage from London to Bombay and Karachi on 12 November 1920 and *Manela* left London for Bombay on 28 May 1921.

The "M"s could be described as London's answer to the expanding and much improved Mersey and Clyde based passenger-cargo services of the Anchor and Ellerman's City and Hall Lines and others. They were intended for use on India's two Home Lines, Bombay and Karachi now enjoying a separate service from the Calcutta one following the transfer of the imperial capital to Delhi, but several of the M1 and M2 ships made individual voyages between London and East Africa. * *Margha* was the first to do this when she sailed on 17 July 1920 with *Merkara* and *Mandala* being similarly employed a few years later, the former leaving London on 21 January 1926 and the latter on two occasions in 1923 (12 July and 6 September) and again on 13 May 1926. It was not until 8 March 1923 that *Mashobra* left London for East Africa whilst *Manela's* first African voyage commenced on 21 January 1925. *Morvada* was another of the M2 series to make individual East African voyages, 17 April 1925 and 8 July 1926, but she spent almost her entire life on the Indian Home Line.

Additionally, both *Margha* and *Mandala* made Indian Mail voyages to and from Bombay for P&O in 1920 whilst in 1921 *Manela* went to the Far East carrying the mails and also filling a gap in the P&O schedule. Similar mail voyages were undertaken by other BI vessels including *Nevasa* and *Angora* (1911/4,299 grt), but none of these went beyond Bombay. *

Within three years of the Armistice came a new series of improved "M"s, the M3 series of six ships all with cruiser sterns and slightly larger than their M2 predecessors with dimensions of 465 ft. by 58 ft. and gross tonnages of nearly 9,000 tons— *Madura* (1921/8,975 grt), *Modasa* (1921/9,070 grt), *Mantola* (1921/8,963 grt), *Malda* (1922/8,965 grt), *Matiana* (1922/8,965 grt) and *Mulbera* (1922/9,100 grt)— which would spend most of their long lives on the East African run.

By continuing the system of interchangeable First/Second Class two-berth cabins, all except *Mulbera* could initially accommodate either 103 First and 41 Second (45 for *Modasa*) or 67 First and 77 Second (81 for *Modasa*), but heavy demand for First Class berths to East Africa caused the company to fit 15 extra two-berth cabins in *Modasa* in 1925 and 12 more in each of the four Barclay Curle ships in 1927 giving totals therefore for the latter of 127 First and 41 Second or 91 First and 77 Second. *Modasa's* capacity was 133 First and 45 Second or 97 First and 81 Second whilst *Mulbera* needed no modification and carry 114 First and 44 Second or 78 First and 80 Second Class. In 1933 when a one-class system was introduced passenger capacities varied between 168 and 180 and following the Second World War there were further minor changes in some cases. *

The cabins, on Bridge and Promenade Decks, were one- to three-berth in First and one- to four-berth in Second. The two dining saloons were on Bridge Deck separated by the galley and cabins whilst the First Class music room, smoking room and foyer and Second Class smoking room were on Promenade Deck. These latest "M"s were fitted with four superheated oil-fired boilers and two sets of Brown-Curtiss double-reduction geared 4,320 shp turbines giving 13 knots. *Malda* made 14 knots on trials. There were variations within the class, *Modasa* having Metropolitan-Vickers Rateau-type turbines whilst *Mulbera* and *Matiana* had Parsons machinery. Good earners, each had five cargo holds of 467,000 cu. ft. (11,080 dwt) capacity worked by three sets of samson posts.

The Swan Hunter-built *Modasa* was the first of this series to be launched, on Christmas Eve 1920, followed by the christening at Barclay, Curle's Whiteinch yards of *Madura* on 28 September 1921, *Mantola* on 15 October 1921, *Malda* on 28 December 1921 and *Matiana* on 26 January 1922. The last of the "M"s and the only one built by Alexander Stephen was launched at Linthouse as *Mulbera* on 14 February 1922. Not only was she a larger ship with a gross tonnage of 9,100, but her profile was noticeably different in that the foremast was further aft and the mainmast moved forward, thereby giving her a somewhat unbalanced appearance. Like all other post-war "M"s she was equipped with two heavy-lift derricks, a 30-ton one at the foremast and a 20-ton at the mainmast. Even her stern was slightly differently shaped than that of the others. *

Indicative of their lasting importance to East Africa, the second of the M3s, *Modasa*, was the first "M" to make her maiden voyage, from London on 30 December 1921, to East Africa and she stayed pretty much on this route. The others commenced their careers running to India and were shifted about on all the Home Lines. *Madura's* maiden voyage was from London on 16 December 1921 to Bombay with her first trip to Africa beginning on 8 February 1923. The third of the series, *Mantola*, was nearly lost on her maiden voyage which began from London on 6 January 1922 for Calcutta where fire broke out simultaneously in her three after holds; arson was indicated but never proved and the vessel returned to Newcastle for extensive repairs. Her first deployment on the East African run began on 27 December 1923.

Destined to become the only war casualty of the M3s when she was sunk by the Japanese in the Bay of Bengal on 6 April 1942, *Malda* entered service almost 20 years earlier to the day (from London to Calcutta on 13 April 1922) and first sailed to East Africa on 20 February 1924. The new *Matiana* left London for Calcutta on 26 May 1922 with her maiden African voyage commencing on 29 October 1924. Completing a memorable sextet, *Mulbera* entered service upon her London departure for Bombay on 8 July 1922, beginning her long association with the African Home Line on 26 November 1924.

The "M"s and their officers and crew immediately figured in the life and times of East Africa— Captain Claud Feller's 13 years at *Mantola's* helm, a record for the line; *Mulbera's* first master, Captain Walter Royston Steadman, an amateur boxer who organised bouts at Beira between runs, and that ship's Fifth Engineer, the Hon. Victoria Drummond, goddaughter of Queen Victoria, who in 1926 became the first woman engineer in the Merchant Navy.

There remained two final "M"s, the first launched as *Megvana* at Whiteinch on 24 December 1920, followed by *Melma* which was laid down in March 1923. Whereas BI had the reputation for conservatism in ship design, it did help initially to pioneer the motor ship, making the bold decision to fit *Megvana* with a pair of North British four-stroke diesels instead of steam turbines. Otherwise she was structurally identical to her "M" fleetmates except for the curious regression to a counter stern of the M2s. Adopting a new "D" (for diesel) nomenclature for motor ships, BI renamed her *Domala*. The first liner powered by British-designed diesels, *Domala* began her maiden voyage from London to Bombay on 30 December 1921. It was claimed that she could maintain 13.5 knots on less than 20 tons of oil a day and carry sufficient fuel for a round voyage. Sister ship *Dumana* followed on 11 April 1923; both "D"s stayed on the Indian Home Line and never sailed to East Africa.

British India's network of local feeder services continued to carry flag and trade to some of the Empire's more remote backwaters. Calling at such exotic locales as Ibo, Lamu, Kilwa Kivenge and Mikindani, BI's East African coastal service was one of the most intriguing. After an unsuccessful initial operation between 1902 and 1905, this route was revived after the First World War when sisal and coconut plantations were established along Kenya's remote northern coast, most so isolated from road and rail that apart from the BI service, their only outside contact was by native runners.

Two specially designed vessels were commissioned for the East African feeder run (assigned No. 43), the 2,304-grt *Dumra* and the 2,328-grt *Dwarka*, both built at Bristol by Charles Hill & Co. *Dwarka* was launched on 8 September 1922 and *Dumra* on 16 November. The price of these small vessels even considering post-war inflation seems quite high, *Dwarka* costing £260,199 and *Dumra* £282,499. Measuring 280 ft. by 43.5 ft., the twin-screw vessels were the first motor ships regularly employed along the East African coast. Each was powered by a pair of six-cylinder North British four-cycle, air-injection diesels developing 1,000 bhp at 165 rpm. Accommodation was for 20 First, 24 Second Saloon and 300 deck passengers. Three holds had a

123,000 cu. ft. (2,030 dwt) capacity.

The "D"s proved busy and successful ships, providing a connecting feeder service to the Home Line vessels and also linking the Kenyan, Tanganyikan and Portuguese East African coastal ports. Prior to commencing her service, *Dwarka* arrived at Durban on 17 May 1923 for drydocking after her delivery voyage from Britain and sailed for Lourenço Marques in ballast on 12 June.

Two itineraries circa 1931 are representative of the "D"s' voyage patterns:

NORTHERN FEEDER SERVICE - *DUMRA*

9 April	sail MOMBASA
10 April	call Tanga
10-11 April	call Zanzibar
11 April	call Dar-es-Salaam
12-13 April	call Lindi
13 April	call Mikindini
14-15 April	call Ibo
16-17 April	call Mocimboa
18-19 April	call Lindi
19 April	call Ruvu Bay
20 April	call Dar-es-Salaam
21 April	call Tanga
21 April	arr. MOMBASA

SOUTHERN FEEDER SERVICE- *DWARKA*

4 May	sail LOURENÇO MARQUES
6-7 May	call Inhambane
9 May	call Beira
10-12 May	call Quelimane
15 May	call Mozambique
16 May	call Port Amelia
17 May	call Ibo
21-23 May	call Beira
25-26 May	call Inhambane
27 May	arr. LOURENÇO MARQUES

Chief Officer R.D. Macfadyen contributed this description of his *Dumra* (*Dwarka* was identical) and her coastal service to *BI News*:

she was a closed shelterdeck ship, without tonnage openings. Her raised bridge-deck space contained saloon passenger accommodation, and on the bridge deck her Officers were all accommodated in comfortable outboard cabins.

There was a broad alleyway between the cabins and the engine room casing, and as the boat deck had an overhang on each side of about 30 inches, they [the cabins] were reasonably cool. The passenger cabins compared favourably with those in the

Company's "M" class vessels with which *Dumra* co-operated. The forward part of the bridge deck, about 50 ft. in fore and aft length, was entirely clear from side to side, except for the saloon companionway at the after part, and varnished wood pipe-trunk and two stanchions in the centre line. For a vessel of her small dimensions this was a remarkably good passenger promenade deck, but it must be remembered that, apart from the two dining saloons, she had no public rooms. Within the companion-house were two settees, and the panelling of the companionway and the saloon entrance was of fine, rich, red mahogany.

At the time the Home Line service to East Africa was a four-weekly one, and *Dumra's* time-table was arranged so that she did two voyages in that time. On the "A" voyage she loaded a small amount of general cargo at Mombasa and awaited the arrival of the outward "M", sailing as soon as the   passengers for Tanganyika ports had been transferred to her. The itinerary was: Tanga, Zanzibar, Dar-es-Salaam,   Kilwa Kivenge, Lindi and Mikindani, and at each of these ports some passengers left the ship and were replaced by local passengers, very largely officials and their families on transfer. A certain amount of cargo was also loaded at Dar-es-Salaam, but it was mostly "grocer-stores", with the occasional motor car, and very occasionally machinery or components of which, I remember, "Corona Parts" figured frequently on the manifest.   The "Corona" in this case was not a typewriter as I discovered after expressing amazement at the size of the first cases, but a machine for decorticating sisal.

On the northward passage the Kilwa call was omitted, and the cargo loaded was mostly sisal. This was carried in the vessel for a round trip, and was added to on voyage "B".   The idea of this was to allow the sisal factories to clear their godowns [sheds], and also to ensure that the cargo did finally travel to Europe in a BI bottom. I should add that sisal was at that time almost a drag on the market, fetching only between £9 and £13 per ton; freights were correspondingly low. A seasonal cargo was cashew nuts, and on the "B" voyage we loaded bales of tobacco which had been introduced as a crop to Tanganyika by the "White Fathers", in the mission at Songea.

The "A" voyage ended when the vessel arrived in Mombasa, and when she had discharged her small amount of cargo she went off to anchor near the Kilindini cliffs beacons for about four to five days, whilst the ship's engineers "fettled" her engines. These were a pair of six cylinder North British Diesels. They were prone to cracked cylinder heads, were never sure at starting, and at the very best gave the vessel only 8 1/2 knots, when clean off the slip. Incidentally, she had only two generators, and as both were required when manoeuvering it was considered prudent to conserve them by shutting down after 10 p.m., when there were no passengers aboard. This was very unpleasant in hot weather, and we usually slept on deck on those occasions.

"B" voyage began with a trip to Lamu. Only a few small amount of general cargo, groceries mostly, was carried, but there was generally a good muster of deck passengers. Many of these were Somali "ladies of the town", and northbound they usually carried with them their brass-knobbed bedsteads.

Saloon business on this trip was practically non-existent. Once or twice we had a honeymoon couple for the round trip; the Provincial Commissioner made an annual safari of inspection of the Lamu area, and a missionary priest once travelled to Lamu with us. But apart from these our saloon was usually completely empty between Mombasa and Lamu.

The Lamu call lasted only from 0700 to 1600 hours of the same day, and during that time about 200 bullocks and 1,000 goats were loaded. These were for Zanzibar's butchers, and the cattle were brought alongside in two large pontoons, which were propelled by a steam launch, lashed alongside. The cattle were hoisted aboard in bellybands and impounded in temporary stalls erected in No. 3 shelter deck, whilst the goats were passed in through the shelter-deck door by hand, from rowing boats lying alongside.

Apart from livestock, Lamu afforded very little cargo. Dunnage mats formed the bulk of it, with some copra and some cane chairs, both shipped by a type named Coconut Charlie. Charlie's sole topic of conversation was the departures and routes of mainline trains out of London. One supposes that his only reading was "Bradshaw". I think that the District Commissioner and Charlie at the time comprised the whole European population of Lamu.

The southward call at Mombasa was a brief one, just long enough to load a small amount of "groceries", sometimes with cased kerosene or petrol on deck, for the carriage of which with passengers we had a special dispensation, as there was not sufficient alternative tonnage available. Except that the Kilwa call was omitted the southbound "B" voyage was the same as the previous one, but on the northbound a call was made at Ruvu Bay.

Ruvu Bay is a mere dent in the Tanganyika Coast, about eight miles north of the entrance of the Lukuledi River, on which Lindi stands. The Mto Kera runs into the sea there, and just off the break in the coastal reef there is a bank with 30 fathoms of water on it.

The reef is only a mile from the 100-fathom line. The call was made for the purpose of lifting the sisal from Mkos Shamba (plantation), a coastal plantation which was connected to the loading point on Mto Kera by a 12-mile Decauville-track railway. Our method of approach to this anchorage was to steam in slowly on a pair of hardly visible leading marks which the plantation manager had set up, with our starboard anchor trailing at 30 fathoms outside the hawse-pipe. As soon as I, as Chief Officer, heard the anchor touch bottom, the windlass brake would be thrown open, and the vessel would be brought up to four shackles on deck. When she swung round the vessel's stern was within biscuit toss of the reef. A very unpleasant anchorage, and we always endeavoured to get away before the afternoon breeze freshened.

Dwarka's Southern Feeder Service called at Lourenço Marques, Inhambane, Chinde, Quelimane, Beira (connecting there with the Home Line mailship), Angoche, Mocimboa, Port Amelia and Mozambique. Of the two coastal runs, this was evidently the less important for every November-December when *Dumra* went to Durban for drydocking, *Dwarka* took her place for one or two voyages on the Northern Feeder Service. One of *Dwarka's* masters, Captain H. Foskett, recalled in *BI News* the potential perils of the southern ports:

Quelimane, Chinde and Angoche have very dangerous Bars with a maximum of 16 feet of water at High Spring Tide with a constant heavy swell... which will reduce your depth of water 18 inches in anything like boisterous weather. The channels are constantly changing and much is left to be desired in the way of frequent surveys. The soundings on the inward passage, are the final factor on deciding your final loaded draft on the outward passage. From this it will be seen that much depends on the man on the spot.

Exemption from Pilotage was necessary in most ports. It was always delightful to everyone on board to tie-up alongside our Home Line steamers in the main ports and tranship our cargoes direct. We got all the latest "Gup", saw old friends and anyone going home on privilege leave had only to step from one ship to the other.

The *Dumra* and *Dwarka* were very happy ships and applications for transfers were seldom known. Up and down the Coast Agents and friends were exceptionally kind and hospitable and all the "Clubs" welcomed us as honorary members. Sports, Picnics, and Dances were easily arranged when time and freedom from duty permitted. I remember at one time in the *Dwarka*, by some curious incidence, every Officer (Deck and Engineer) happened to be a musician and each specialised in a different sort of instrument, thus we had a very fine ship's Band and in some small measure we were able to return much hospitality by giving an occasional dance with Jazz, or a Concert with classical music.

Finishing the impressive post-war newbuilding programme for the African routes was a vessel of pre-war design, *Khandalla*, which completed the quartet of "K"s for the Bombay-Durban run nine years after the first such vessel was introduced. Illustrative of the great increase in shipbuilding costs after the war, she cost £283,581 compared to *Karagola's* £158,426 price. Launched at Swan Hunter's Wallsend yard on 16 February 1923, *Khandalla* ran trials on 31 May (reaching 17 knots) and sailed from London for Bombay on 7 June— pretty fast going, but perhaps making up for lost time! Arriving at Bombay on 1 July, her maiden voyage to Durban concluded on 29 August.

Replaced by *Khandalla*, *Taroba* left Durban on her last voyage on 1 October 1923 for Lourenço Marques, Mozambique, Zanzibar, Mombasa, Seychelles, Marmagoa and Bombay, and was sold to Italian breakers the following year. Finally, the Durban Mail was maintained four-weekly by *Khandalla*, *Karagola*, *Karapara* and *Karoa*, a perfectly matched foursome whose comfort and reliability established a lasting reputation on the Indian Ocean.

On 19 May 1923 *Karapara* arrived at Bombay with a fire in one hold which ruined 500 bales of Kenyan cotton, but caused no serious damage to the vessel. *Malda* had an exciting time the next year, arriving at Plymouth on 11 January 1924 none the worse for wear after being hove-to for more than 24 hours in the Bay of Biscay in a winter gale and unsuccessfully searching without success for missing crew members of the Italian steamer *Tasmania* which foundered in the same storm. The lost vessel was none other than the former BI *Cooeyanna* (1902/3,922 grt) which had been sold to D.L. Pittaluga, Genoa, only 13 months before. In another slice of adventure, *Malda* arrived at Marseilles on 3 May with *Treneglos* in tow after that ship had lost her screw. Upon leaving Lourenço Marques on 23 December 1925 *Karagola* collided at the harbour entrance with the British freighter *Kosmo* lying at anchor off the pilot boat. The BI liner sustained only minor damage to deck fittings whilst *Kosmo* was more seriously damaged.

One of the more memorable voyages was that by *Mulbera*, which on her first trip to East Africa, conveyed the Duke and Duchess of York, later King George VI and Queen Elizabeth, to Mombasa in 1924 for an official visit to British East Africa. Like most passengers, the Royal Party took the overland route, leaving Victoria Station on 1 December for Marseilles by Channel steamer and train. Their Royal Highnesses, accompanied by Viscount and Viscountess Broom, embarked in *Mulbera* four days later. Royal travellers were much in evidence upon arrival at Port Said on the 11th where *Mulbera* was joined by the P&O *Caledonia* with Prince and Princess Arthur of Connaught aboard, bound for India.

The Times described the enthusiastic reception at Mombasa upon *Mulbera's* arrival on 22 December 1924:

> The landing stage at Kilindini was a mass of flags and palms, with the royal standard as the centrepiece, and at the pierhead was a flagstaff flying a flag inscribed 'Welcome to Kenya,' when the Duke of York in white naval uniform accompanied by the Duchess, wearing a cream costume and a neat white helmet stepped out of their launch. A crowd of thousands of Africans, Arabs, Somalis and Indians greeted the visitors with hoarse cheering. The Duke inspected the Guard of Honour, composed of Native Police, and afterwards a number of loyal and affectionate addresses of welcome were presented by Arabs, Natives and Goanese, who all expressed their happiness and contentment.

It was added that the Duke and Duchess "greatly enjoyed their voyage" and Her Royal Highness penned a letter of appreciation to Lord Inchcape:

Government House
Nairobi, Kenya Colony
5th February 1925

Dear Lord Inchcape,

I am writing to thank you so very much for having arranged such comfortable accommodation for us in the *Mulbera*. Everything was so well done, and we had an excellent voyage out to Mombasa.

The Captain and officers were so helpful, and my husband, having been in the Navy, was much struck by the way the ship was run, and by the discipline and punctuality maintained on board.

With so many thanks for all the trouble you have taken,

I am

Yours sincerely,

(signed) Elizabeth

After a highly successful visit of Kenya, Uganda and Tanganyika, the Royal Party returned in the P&O *Maloja* via Suez.

The Home Line was reassigned No. 23 in 1926 by which time its routing was Middlesbrough-London-Marseilles-Port Said-Suez-Aden-Mombasa-Zanzibar-Dar-es-Salaam-Beira. There was some experimentation with Continental ports with some voyages commencing at Antwerp from 1920 onwards and from Hamburg starting with *Neuralia* on 28 January 1922, and continuing through 1923.

After only four East African voyages, *Neuralia* began her final such trip on 19 October 1923, with *Nevasa's* last Beira-bound voyage commencing on 18 February 1925; both ships were then converted to permanent BI-managed troop transports. Thereafter, the route belonged to the "M"s of which BI assigned a bewildering number and variety, peaking in 1925 and 1926 when no fewer than nine different ships were responsible for the monthly sailings per year:

1925: *Manela, Malda, Morvada, Madura, Modasa* (2), *Mulbera* (2), *Mashobra, Mantola* and *Matiana.*

1926: *Merkara, Manela, Modasa* (3), *Mulbera* (3), *Mandala, Mantola, Morvada, Madura, Matiana*

In 1927, the six newest "M"s, *Madura, Mantola, Modasa, Mulbera, Matiana* and *Malda*, maintained the Home Line. Whilst only a few voyages began from Antwerp in 1925-27, all did so from 1928 onwards by which time *Mulbera* had been switched to the Indian Home Line as was *Mantola* the next year. Thereafter *Madura, Matiana, Malda* and *Modasa* held down the East African service exclusively with no more alternating on the Indian routes.

Supplemental tonnage was occasionally added to the Durban Mail. On 16 August 1926 *Takliwa* (1924/7,936 grt) called at Dar-es-Salaam en route to Durban from Bombay whilst on 15 November 1927 *Ellora* (1911/5,206 grt), one of the seven "E"s normally on the Straits run, made her first visit to Dar-es-Salaam. This vessel maintained a monthly Bombay-Mombasa service from 1928 to 1930.

Khandalla made herself unwelcome upon arrival at Mombasa from Bombay on 14 January 1928 when it was discovered that some of her passengers were infected with smallpox. The ship was immediately fumigated and sent to Zanzibar for quarantine. Inbound from Beira, *Matiana* collided with, and sank, the ballast-laden sailing barge *Alice Laws* in the Thames off Gallions Reach on 6 June. Arriving at Beira on 11 October, *Malda* collided with the quarantine hulk *Charles Racine* and fouled her port screw with a cable, requiring an inspection by a diver.

The earlier part of *Malda's* September 1928 outbound voyage was considerably more newsworthy when she became the second "M" to participate in a Royal visit to East Africa, conveying the Prince of Wales (later King Edward VIII and finally the Duke of Windsor) and his brother, the Duke of Gloucester, to Kenya. For the voyage, six of the ship's First Class staterooms were converted into two large bedrooms with a private sitting room for the Royals who had travelled by the P&O Overland Express to Marseilles, leaving London on 6 September 1928 and embarking on P&O's *Kaisar-i-Hind* for Port Said where, after two days in Egypt, they boarded *Malda* at Ismailia at 2.30 p.m. on the 14th. According to *The Times*, *Malda's* transit of the Canal attracted a curious escort: "Along the dusty road, for the first few miles, all manner of transport, including solitary Camel Corp riflemen on rocking mounts, engineers on bicycles, parties in cars and occasional natives on donkeys with their womenfolk behind, kept pace with the ship."

After calling at Port Sudan on 18 September 1928, *Malda* and her passengers, regular and royal, proceeded through a sweltering Red Sea and the arrival at Aden, two days later, "was welcomed with general relief by those on board, since it meant the close of the most trying Red Sea passage within the memory of most East Africans. The heat caused a complete stagnation of shipboard life." (*The Times*) After rounding Cape Guardafui, weather conditions became "most pleasant" and the Prince of Wales "spent an hour in the engine room showing an extreme knowledge of the subject, and also in the radio room, where he was attracted by the auto alarm device." On the 26th the Duke of Gloucester was among the 20 initiates for the Crossing the Line ceremony, being "charged with trying to undermine the foundations of the Suez Canal by playing golf, not visiting East Africa until 1924, and, finally, with being one of two first-class sportsmen aboard." The other "first-class sportsmen", the Prince of Wales, acted as the barber's assistant and "wielding a large distemper brush, which he thrust into a bucket of so-called 'soap', he lathered the new subjects of the Sea King, including the Duke of Gloucester."

The Times' on board correspondent described the arrival at Kenya:
"The *Malda*... made an impressive entrance into Mombasa Harbour this morning [28 September 1928]. While the flags of welcome, including the Prince of Wales's special code flag, were flying from the signal station, a group of small yachts of the Mombasa Yacht Club manoeuvring near the harbour entrance, spread out in perfect formation, and passed the *Malda*, dipping their flags. The *Malda* acknowledged this spontaneous

104

addition to the official programme of welcome, and as she steamed into the harbour, the small craft doubled back and streamed out behind."

Disembarking into a launch of the cruiser H.M.S. *Enterprise* at 10.00 a.m., the Princes were met on the pontoon by Sir Edward Grigg, Governor of Kenya Colony, as a Royal Salute was fired by the warship and the National Anthem rendered by the band of the King's African Rifles. Ahead lay a long holiday trip visiting British East Africa and travelling by motorcar south via the caravan routes to Rhodesia and South Africa.

Beira was devastated on 1 February 1929 by a cyclone with winds of 84 mph which dumped five and a half inches of rain in six hours. Railway sheds, houses and telegraph poles were uprooted and sections of the Rhodesia Railway washed-out. In the harbour, *Karagola*, *Malda* and the Portuguese liner *Mocambique* were swept from their moorings and blown aground. Although *Karagola* was refloated on the next day's flood tide and sailed for Lourenço Marques on the 3rd, *Mocambique* remained fast for several more days and *Malda*, her stern embedded in five feet of sand, proved the hardest to refloat. In the meantime other liners arrived at the port, disembarking would-be Rhodesia-bound travellers who were stranded by the still-closed Rhodesia Railway; some opted to continue in other ships to Lourenço Marques. Finally on the 8th *Malda* was refloated on the afternoon flood tide, loaded cargo and sailed for England the next day.

In 1929, the Home Line began northbound calls at Plymouth which proved a popular time saver for both passengers and the mails. Trade boomed as evidenced by cargo handled at Beira which totalled 507,511 tons in 1923 and by 1927 had risen by 60 per cent to 820,624 tons.

Two of the "K"s found themselves in trouble later in 1929 and 1930. In another outbreak of smallpox among Indian passengers, the Mombasa-bound *Karoa* was diverted instead on 4 September 1929 to Zanzibar for quarantine. On 25 March 1930 *Karagola* was reported at Lourenço Marques with a fire in one of her cross bunkers. Surveyors ordered 500 tons of coal removed from the vessel which was delayed for four days. *Malda* again figured in the shipping columns when on 11 May she had to return to Mombasa to effect repairs to her refrigeration plant; this completed she proceeded to London.

An undated incident to *Khandalla* was recalled in "BI News" by her then master, Captain G. Harley:

> one of my ports of call was Seychelles, sometimes called "The Gem of the Indian Ocean", and a very good name for it.
>
> On this occasion I entered the port and proceeded to what is sometimes called the "Pool or Inner Harbour". This is not very large, and there is room for about one large vessel.
>
> When I was on my "Marks" I told the Chief Officer to "Let

105

go. Starboard Anchor". This he did and there was a roar and "Crash". He called out "Cable parted Sir". After getting the ship back on her marks, the port anchor was let go and the cargo work commenced.

There was of course an anchor Buoy on the lost anchor. The Agents were informed and asked to do what they could to recover it.

On my next call I asked them what had been done, and they said "nothing". It appears that a passing fisherman had seen the buoy and had cut the rope as low as possible.

After about eight months, I entered the "Pool" as usual and anchored on the "Marks". I only stayed the night there, and the next morning at daylight the Chief Officer started to "Heave up". I noticed that the Windlass was doing some heavy work, and asked the Chief Officer what was wrong. He replied "I think have hooked something". When the anchor broke surface, he called out "I have hooked another anchor".

I proceeded to the Outer Harbour and anchored. A derrick was rigged and the anchor hove inboard. After we had got away, I went along to have a "look-see", and I also took the anchor certificate with me. On comparing the number on the anchor with the one on the certificate I found that it was my missing anchor. On arrival in Bombay the spare anchor was sent to the Dock, and the Marine Superintendent informed, and the old anchor was placed in position and continued to do its work after its long rest in the sea bottom.

Reunited with her wayward anchor, *Khandalla* and her sister "K"s continued to faithfully ply to and fro' across the Indian Ocean as the prosperous 'twenties gave way to the tumultuous 'thirties. Within two years the "K"s were supplanted by a brace of new ships in whose wake would follow the trials of the Depression and another world war.

6. HOPE AND GLORY

. . . the ships now setting forth along 'the wet road heaving, shining' in all the strength and comeliness of youth will carry within them, beneath the Company's flag, not only the goods and products by the export of which this country must rebuild her strength, but also a tradition of devotion, endurance and faith which is above the peculiar treasure of kings.

Valiant Voyaging

As the gloom of the Depression set in on world trade routes, the inter-Empire lines felt the effects later and less severely and indeed were strengthened by a new generation of mailship. The first of P&O's famous "Straths" and the latest in the dynasty of "K" class liners for BI's African routes represented a final flourish for the East of Suez services before the advent of the Second World War.

The Bombay-Durban Mail Line assumed new importance on 24 August 1930 when, at Alexander Stephen & Sons' Linthouse yards, the first of two magnificent new mailships was launched as *Kenya.* Her sister *Karanja,* named after the large island in Bombay Harbour, was finally christened on 18 December eight days late owing to bad weather. These 9,890-grt, 487 ft. by 64 ft. vessels were dimensionally the largest commissioned for BI commercial service during the inter-war period.

With their single funnel, high freeboard and cruiser sterns, the new "K"s somewhat resembled their smaller predecessors. Faster than those ships, *Kenya* and *Karanja* achieved 18.5 knots on trials and maintained a 16-knot service speed from two sets of 8,800 shp Parsons single reduction geared turbines driving twin screws at 120 rpm. Steam was supplied at 250 psi/600 degs. F. from seven single-end superheated Scotch boilers. All installations and auxiliaries were electrical and supplied by three Atlas Polar diesel generators.

Each ship had a cargo capacity of 448,000 cu. ft. and 13,800 cu. ft. reefer in five holds worked by mast-mounted derricks and a pair of samson posts immediately forward of the superstructure. Life-saving equipment, given the considerable numbers carried aboard, was extensive, comprising 20 double-banked boats carried at luffing davits on the Boat Deck, another four carried on the poop, two forward, and two accident boats in gravity davits abaft the bridge.

Accommodation was for 66 First Class, 180 Second Class and 1,981 deck passengers. That for First was the best yet fitted in a BI ship having a music room, lounge, smoking room and veranda on the Promenade Deck and 30 single-berth, 18 two-berth and four de luxe cabins with private bath and a 77-

seat dining saloon on Bridge Deck.

As described in *Fairplay,* the "accommodation and its decoration have been designed for Indian Ocean and hot weather conditions with large opening windows, light panelling and cool upholstery" with the *Natal Mercury* adding, "the public rooms have an air of spaciousness and coolness. This has been obtained mostly by the use of clean, subdued colours; and the exclusion of any unnecessary drapery and hangings. Chairs and tables are provided in abundance, but even though extremely comfortable, have an absence of fussy decoration that might impart any feeling of 'hotness'." The dining saloon was in Georgian style with ivory-coloured panelling, the music room featured a Wedgewood blue scheme and the polished oak-panelled smoking room was distinguished by Elizabethan style lattice windows.

Second class public rooms consisted of a 130-seat dining saloon and smoking room whilst the cabins had two, three or four berths. Deck class facilities on Lower and Main Decks, including separate galleys for Hindu and Moslem faiths, ample sanitary arrangements and Thermotank forced-draught ventilation, were the best of any India-based liners.

After running trials from 18-19 December 1930, *Kenya* (Captain W.E. Grant) was handed over, her final cost being quoted at £407,535. On her delivery voyage to Bombay from Middlesbrough on 6 January 1931, *Kenya* called en route at London (16), Antwerp (18), Southampton (20), Port Said (31), Suez (1 February), Aden (6) and reached Bombay on 11 February. Her maiden voyage to Durban commenced one month later. Her docking at Durban on 1 April was not without incident for as she was being swung into her berth at C Shed by a tug at 2.30 p.m., *Kenya's* stern brushed against *Armadale Castle's* bow, the Union-Castle mailship being tied up at the adjoining pier. The BI liner's aft docking bridge was slightly damaged as was *Armadale Castle's* foredeck railing. *Kenya* was visited by Durban's European citizens on the 4th and by the Indian community the next day. Her maiden voyage to Bombay via Lourenço Marques, Dar-es-Salaam, Zanzibar, Mombasa, Seychelles and Marmagoa began on the 6th. On her next voyage *Kenya* grounded briefly on 25 May whilst on passage between Zanzibar and Dar-es-Salaam, but was refloated without serious damage.

The subsidiary Bombay-Mombasa service was operated four-weekly throughout 1930 again by *Ellora,* but this proved to be its final year with the last sailing occurring on 16 January 1931.

Upon her arrival at Bombay on 28 March 1931 *Karapara* was withdrawn from the Durban Mail and re-assigned to the Calcutta-Straits run.

Karanja (Captain D.C. Fitz-Herbert) ran trials on 11 March 1931 and sailed on the 26th from Cardiff with cargo but no passengers for Bombay where she docked on 15 April. Commencing her BI service with two sailings direct to Mombasa and Zanzibar on 23 April and 15 May, *Karanja* carried one

108

class Saloon passengers on these instead of two classes. Durban-bound for the first time, *Karanja* sailed on 17 June and made her maiden arrival at the Natal port on 8 July. The northbound voyage began five days later and called at Lourenço Marques, Beira, Dar-es-Salaam, Zanzibar and Mombasa.

Thus relieved, *Karoa* (Captain F. Dolton) concluded her final African voyage at Bombay on 4 July 1931 with 39 Saloon and 501 deck passengers. With general cargo she sailed on the 17th for Colombo, Madras and Calcutta, her new home port as she joined *Karapara* on the Straits service.

Although the overseas colonial routes suffered less from the Depression than did the North Atlantic run, East African trade still declined:

Cargo handled (tons)	1929	1930	1931
Mombasa	890,193	837,771	706,708
Dar-es-Salaam	261,183	240,347	178,214

The price for Kenyan coffee vanished and with it the carefree heyday of Happy Valley. There were bright moments however as in early 1931 when BI's *Hatarana* (1917/7,522 grt) loaded 23,995 bales of cotton at Mombasa for India, the largest single export of Kenyan cotton to date. Marking an upturn in the spice trade, *Karoa* landed 325 bales of cloves at Bombay in early February.

In the first of several efforts to spur sales during the slump, BI announced that with *Matiana's* 8 May sailing from Britain and homewards from Beira on 24 June that all First Class "C" grade three-berth cabins on Bridge Deck of the "M"s would henceforth be graded as "D" to give more minimum priced accommodation in First.

There were two minor collisions involving BI ships at Mombasa in 1931. On 7 August a tug struck *Karagola* on the starboard bow above the waterline, denting two plates and bending two frames, but she was able to continue her voyage. The DÖAL liner *Njassa*, approaching the Kilindini quays, hit *Madura* alongside and both vessels sustained superficial damage to their upperworks. *Matiana* got no farther than the harbour entrance upon sailing from Dar-es-Salaam on 14 February in heavy wind conditions, but it was a jammed anchor chain that detained her until early evening and not the weather.

Mantola's 5 May 1932 sailing from London called at Tangier en route to Africa for the first time. The North African port then figured in summer outbound Home Line sailings. A number of homeward sailings called at Rotterdam from 1932 onwards.

In 1932 *Tairea* and *Takliwa* (1924/7,934 grt), the smallest ocean-going three stackers ever built (466 ft. overall by 60 ft.), were displaced from the Calcutta-Japan run because of Japanese incursions into China and it was announced on 6 June that they would replace *Karagola* and *Khandalla* on the Bombay-Durban service to make it an all-oil fuel one. The third of the T-class, *Talamba* (1924/8,018 grt), remained on her original designated route and the two "K"s went on the India-Straits run.

The "T"s were quite new ships; *Tairea*, launched at Whiteinch on 6 March 1924, made her maiden sailing from London for Calcutta on 20 June with *Takliwa* following on 15 August. Designed to impress Chinese passengers who, like European emigrants a generation before, judged a vessel's size and speed by the number of its funnels, the third stacks of *Tairea* and *Takliwa* were dummies. The profile was more pleasing than the twin-funnelled *Talma* (1923/10,000 grt) and *Tilawa* (1924/10,006 grt). And the three-stacked "T"s, true to Oriental expectations, were indeed faster; powered by 7,700 ihp triple-expansion engines driving twin screws, they were good for 16 knots and *Tairea* made 17.5 knots on trials, becoming the fastest ship in the BI fleet. Steam was supplied by seven single-end oil-fired Scotch boilers working at 215 deg. psi.

Each was certified to carry as many as 3,262 deck passengers, but on the Durban Mail, the capacity was "only" 1,700 in addition to 56 First and 80 Second Class in excellent all-outside accommodation (one-, two- and three-berth in First and four-berth in Second) on Bridge and Promenade Decks. First Class had a music room, smoking room and dining saloon whilst the Second Class was situated aft on Bridge Deck and provided with a dining saloon and smoking room.

In speed and appointments, the "T"s made a good match with the "K"s and fortunately their Indian passengers were less funnel-conscious than their Asian counterparts otherwise the newer, but single-stack "K"s might not have proved so successful. Prior to joining the Durban Mail, *Tairea* and *Takliwa* were refitted and their refrigerated cargo space extended to carry 300 tons of South African fruit.

Captain D.M. Gill brought *Tairea* into Bombay Harbour from Calcutta on 22 June 1932. Five days later she sailed on her maiden voyage to Durban under Captain A.G. Fishley and the vessel docked on 20 July. As reported in the *Tanganyika Standard* 16 July, the first departure from Dar-es-Salaam was newsworthy for other reasons:

> The British India liner s.s. *Tairea*, on leaving the harbour at 12.45 yesterday, was the first ship on this occasion, to have the opportunity of thus saluting H.M.S. *Effingham* [flagship of the visiting East Indies Squadron]. As the *Tairea* drew near to crossing the flagship's bows her Red Ensign fluttered down, and as it did so did the *Effingham*'s White Ensign— with Navy promptness— dip in answering salute.

Tairea's introduction also marked the first offering of a new 1st Saloon Excursion Fare, 900 rupees return from Bombay to Durban within a three-month period or 500 rupees return to Mombasa. *Takliwa* (Captain V.O. Bannehr) arrived at Bombay from Calcutta on 20 July and commanded by

Captain A.E. Carter she began her first voyage to Durban seven days later. Sweeping past the Bluff at 7.00 a.m. on 17 August, *Takliwa* had cut 18 to 24 hours off the old schedule, which the *Natal Mercury* noted, was a "feat [that] will be the only one of its kind in the 50 odd years of the operation of the mail contract between the two countries." Once slotted into the service, both "T"s called at Mozambique en route to Durban whilst *Takliwa* assumed the Seychelles call.

Encountering the full force of a 50 mph gale off St. Lucia, Natal, on 7 June 1932, *Karanja* was forced to reduce speed and was consequently five hours late arriving at Durban the next day.

After another rough monsoon voyage, *Karagola* (Captain A.G. Fishley) which left Durban on 30 May 1932 finished her last African run at Bombay on 18 June where she disembarked 54 Saloon and 146 deck passengers. Eight days later, commanded by Captain D.M. Gill, she left for Calcutta and new duty on the Straits run. "For ten years this steamer has carried his Majesty's Mail from Bombay to Durban and back, and for ten years it has faithfully abided by the contract," so the *Natal Mercury* summed up the career of *Khandalla*, last of the original "K"s on the route, as she arrived at Durban for the last time on 22 June. Religious riots in Bombay had forced her to leave behind much of her cargo and some 50 deck passengers. Sailing from Durban on the 27th, *Khandalla* (Captain A.E. Carter) completed her 59th East African voyage and landed 50 Saloon and 333 deck passengers at Bombay on 15 July. Fourteen days later she departed for Calcutta via Pondicherry on the 29th under Captain V.O. Bannehr.

Margha left London on 10 March 1933 on her first African voyage since 1920 and this was also her last such trip for she together with the older coal-burning "M"s *Manora*, *Merkara*, *Mandala* and *Morvada* were sold for scrap between 1932-1934, victims of the shipping slump more than superannuation.

On 20 May 1933 another fare reduction scheme was announced whereby First Class "B" accommodation would be offered on the "K"s and "T"s. This comprised a block of superior Second Class cabins now offered at the lower "B" rate which also permitted a cheaper Second Class tariff.

This was followed by the 10 June 1933 announcement that upon *Matiana's* 28 July sailing from London, the "M"s would carry one combined Saloon Class for approximately 158 passengers. The ships would also benefit from refurbishment and accommodation enhancements as reported in the *Tanganyika Standard*, "In addition to the usual public rooms there will be added an attractive cafe lounge [created out of the former Second Class smoking room and music room aft]. There will also be provided on each ship a bright and well-furnished nursery on similar lines to those on the Calcutta Line motor vessels *Domala* and *Dumana* where they have already proved so popular with parents." The nursery occupied the port side of the former

Second Class dining saloon.   Additionally, deck chairs would now be provided free of charge and fares were cut across the board.   Now the "M"s offered six grades of cabins "P" at £83 one-way to Mombasa, "Q" at £76, "R" at £69, "S" at £62, "T" at £55 and "V" at £48.   The *Tanganyika Standard* noted, "it is sure that, in view of the depressing financial conditions we are all experiencing, the company's actions will receive from the public the support it deserves."

By 1933, passage to Dar-es-Salaam cost from £51 to £86 and BI further reduced fares on the Durban Mail, with return excursion fares from Dar-es-Salaam and other B.E.A. ports to Durban and back for £28 First Class "A", £20 15 s. First Class "B" and £18 7 s. Second Class.

Dumra was featured in a bit of unaccustomed publicity when she and her officers were featured in a *Tanganyika Standard* article, "The East Coast's Chummy Ship", 13 January 1934:

> Probably the best known vessel seen frequently in East Coast ports during the last twelve years and a familiar sight in the larger ports such as Dar-es-Salaam, Tanga and Mombasa, the *Dumra* receives the greatest welcome in the other towns to the south, Kilwa, Lindi and Mikindini, where her advent is an occasion of the greatest importance.   Her mails are looked forward to, and the comfort which a visiting ship can bring to some of the more lonely stations.
>
> She is very well-fitted and comfortably equipped.   Under the happy conditions of a short cruise, one may learn a great many things.   It is to be realised what a close knowledge her officers have of the hinterland and of the residents of East Africa, both official and non-official.   They know not only the coast but are up-to-date with information on such attractions as Kakemega and the Lupa, and have a vast number of friends up-country.
>
> When there is time for a chat, a passenger gains much information of great variety. He meets officers who sailed (and had to work) with a woman engineer.   The real reason why invitations to see the engine room are timed for 7.00a.m. is that is the only way the enthusiasts have of an insight into the machinery— and time is not wasted on idle triflers.
>
> The man behind the *Dumra's* power— the Chief Engineer— Mr. J. Steel is happiest when the ship is 'fairly skelpin' along'.
>
> Whether on coastal voyages or on longer runs with other BI ships, the officers of the *Dumra* have a lot of friends throughout the length and breadth of East Africa, and they are true

112

comrades of all those whose tasks lie on land.

Normally to have sailed from Bombay on 7 February 1934, *Takliwa*'s departure was advanced to the 3rd so that she could proceed, without calling at Porebunder, direct to Aden with the English Mails for transhipment, and then continued to East African ports as per her original timetable. A call at Beira was added to the itinerary of both "T"s on northbound voyages commencing with *Takliwa* from Durban on 25 June.

Suspected propeller trouble caused the outbound *Mantola* to turn about and anchor off Gravesend on 28 July 1934. Returning to her berth at Tilbury, a diver was then sent down to inspect her screws. Found to be undamaged, *Mantola* resumed her voyage the next day.

"Can you send doctor aboard? Four men's throats cut. One dead... another dying.", was the dramatic message received by *Malda*, three days out of Mombasa, homeward-bound in February 1935 from the Ellerman liner *City of Batavia* which had sailed from Mombasa for Britain on 9 February. Upon reaching the Ellerman ship, *Malda*'s surgeon Dr. E.R. Mumford was rowed out in very rough seas in one of the ship's boats. Aboard *City of Batavia* he found two dead Malays, one wounded and another, with his own throat cut and holding a straight razor, in the forecastle. He was taken into custody and transferred to *Malda*.

Two of the great perils of the East African coast are the dangerous bars and heavy swell to which remarkably few BI ships fell victim, at least prior to 2 August 1935 when *Dwarka* (Captain C.H.D. Clark) came to grief on the Chinde bar in heavy weather. Heavily laden with 600 tons of copra, groundnuts, maize and sugar, she remained fast on the sandy bottom, but stayed dry. A tug and lighter were dispatched, but on the 4th *Dwarka* was reported to be straining badly in a heavy swell. Four days later it was advised that if she was to be refloated on the next tide, most of cargo would have to be jettisoned. Finally on the 16th she was refloated and, with the tug *Rio Tejo* in attendance, *Dwarka* sailed for Beira, managing seven knots on one screw, the other being inoperable. Upon examination at Beira she was found to be heavily damaged, but seaworthy. Durban-bound for drydocking she sailed on the 26th and arrived five days later. With the graving dock there occupied, she was moored to buoys in the harbour as work on six Antarctic whaling ships was rushed to clear the dock. *Dwarka* was finally drydocked on 21 September where she remained for some nine days.

Few ships, no matter how well found, can survive such a grounding followed by 12 days of pounding in a heavy swell. With many of her hull plates badly distorted, *Dwarka* was damaged beyond economic repair. Leaving Durban on 21 October 1935 for Bombay, *Dwarka* was laid up there until sold to local breakers on 4 January 1937.

Kenya, too, went aground in the treacherous waters off Mozambique when

113

coming into Beira on 21 September 1935 she got stuck in a mudbank at 11.08 p.m. whilst navigating the entrance channel. *Kenya* and her 133 passengers had to wait 12 hours until the midday tide when she refloated and was able to continue on her way.

Kenya's commander, Captain J.H. Longhurst, appeared in court in Mombasa on 21 February 1936, charged with disregarding a harbour signal and entering the harbour without a pilot. He pleaded not guilty to the first count and guilty to the second charge. Coming into Mombasa closely behind the Japanese vessel *Kifuku Maru*, the black ball signal was hoisted just as *Kifuku Maru* turned the buoy and entered the harbour and Captain Longhurst was of the opinion that the signal advising him not to follow was hoisted too late and it was imprudent for him to try to turn and anchor his ship. Further he stated he presumed the pilot boat coming out to meet the two incoming ships would have two pilots and when the only one aboard boarded *Kifuku Maru* he decided to come in alone. The Court acquitted him on the first charge and fined him £5 for the second.

With *Dumra* filling-in for *Dwarka, Barjora* (Captain R.W. O'Beirne) operated on the Northern Feeder Service, sailing from Dar-es-Salaam for Lindi and Mikindini on 8 October 1936. She continued to ply the route until her departure from Dar-es-Salaam on 4 December 1937 and *Dumra* resumed her run three days later.

A replacement for *Dwarka* was immediately ordered from Henry Robb Ltd. This was *Sofala,* launched at Leith on 25 August 1937, and named after the port across the Pungwe River delta from Beira, once believed to have been ancient Orphir. As of 1991, she is, as *Sincere Orient*, the only former BI East African ship still in commercial service. *Sofala* was handed over in October 1937 to Captain J.L. Ruddiman. This remarkably handsome £53,234 coastal motor vessel was the first in a series of BI coastal and auxiliary ships built by Henry Robb. A tropicalised version of Robb's basic *Ocean Coast* design, *Sofala* was quite different from *Dwarka* in that she carried no passengers and was also the first BI liner with machinery aft. The experience with the underpowered "D"s saw the new ship capable of 12 knots from two Polar Atlas diesels developing 725 bhp at 250 rpms. The 1,031-grt *Sofala* measured 244.7 ft. by 37.2 ft. and had a cargo capacity of 8,320 cu. ft.

A machinery defect caused the outbound *Malda* to anchor off Gravesend on 26 June 1937 to effect repairs after which she was on her way the next morning. The two remaining counter stern "M"s, *Manela* and *Mashobra*, which had been absent from African waters for some 13 years, returned for one voyage each, the former sailing from London on 1 May 1937 and the latter on 25 June 1938. The newer *Mulbera* which had not sailed to Africa in ten years, made a similar one-off voyage beginning on 14 August 1937. Otherwise the faithful quartet of *Malda, Madura, Matiana* and *Mantola* maintained the Home Line from 1934 to 1939.

In June 1937 Imperial Airways commenced its service from Britain to East and South Africa using the splendid 220 mph "Empire" flying boats which could make the passage in six and a half days to Durban. To service the aircraft during their call at Lindi, an all-steel, 46-foot tanker launch for Shell Co. of E.A. Ltd. was shipped from Dar-es-Salaam to its base aboard *Matiana* on 22 September.

By 1938 a 2,712-foot-long deep water quay had finally been constructed along the Pungwe River at Beira which could handle five ships at a time. That year the port handled 1.2 million tons of cargo, some 70 per cent of which was to and from the Rhodesias.

Early in 1939 *Dumra* added Kilifi, on Kenya's northern coast, to her Northern Feeder Service. This was to load sisal and occasionally cashew nuts from Lilywhite's plantation. The service was formerly provided by the African Wharfage Company's tugs *Kifaru* and *Ndovu* and the lighter *Changu*. This latter vessel was transferred to BI, based at Kilifi, and towed by *Dumra's* motor launch.

With what was initially reported as a slight fire in her No. 3 hold, *Mantola* put into Alexandria on 12 May 1939. Upon arrival there the next day, however, she was described as being badly on fire on the starboard side of the lower No. 3 hold which had to be flooded. With harbour firefloats and tugs also attacking the blaze, it was soon extinguished, but not before it damaged 40 tons of cargo and some motorcars carried in the 'tween decks. After the salvaged cargo was reloaded on deck, *Mantola* proceeded to East Africa.

In 1932 Earl Inchcape died and was succeeded as chairman by his son-in-law, Alexander Shaw. Inchcape left a BI fleet entirely renewed and in reasonably good stead to weather the Depression. Yet things stagnated under Shaw and not a single newbuilding for commercial service was contracted during his six-year directorship. It was all in marked contrast to Union-Castle which under the new and dynamic leadership of Sir Vernon Thomson embarked on an unprecedented newbuilding programme which included two 15-knot, 15,000-grt and two 17-knot, 17,000-grt intermediates for the "Round-Africa" run. Holland-Africa and DÖAL also renewed their fleets. British India's "M"s, if reliable and well-loved, were completely outclassed by this new tonnage, but before the competition got too keen, the Second World War intervened.

> Those who plan their journey to include a series of voyages by BI vessels will be richly rewarded. The ever romantic appeal of places off the beaten track can here be satisfied to the full; and the departure from great cities, where life flows on in modern style, does not imply any loss of comfort to the passenger, for the ships have a reputation that has eighty years of experience behind it.
> BI brochure, circa 1936

115

A pre-war BI timetable was a marvel of interconnecting ships and lines, a complex web of services and schedules that was more than just a welter of sailings and ships, but the very sinews of an Empire both at its height and near its end. Before war clouds thicken, time perhaps to pause, peruse a copy of the May 1937 *Official Steamship & Airways Guide* and BI African Lines, No. 1, March 1937, and plan one last great Imperial progress by BI to British East:

HOME LINE OUTBOUND

R.M.S. *Malda*	26 June	sail LONDON (Tilbury)
	1 July	call Tangier
	3 July	call Marseilles
	10 July	arr. Port Said
		transit Suez Canal
	11 July	arr. Suez
	14 July	call Port Sudan
	16 July	call Aden (bunkers)
	23 July	arr. MOMBASA

Notes: sailings were programmed to depart London on Saturdays and from Marseilles on the following Sunday.

NORTHERN FEEDER SERVICE CONNECTION (FOR B.E.A. PORTS)

m.v. *Dumra*	23 July	sail MOMBASA
	24 July	call Tanga
	24-25 July	call Zanzibar
	25 July	call Dar-es-Salaam
	26 July	call Kilwa
	27 July	call Lindi
	27-28 July	call MIKINDINI

Notes: used by passengers to travel to the more remote northern Kenyan ports, but mostly to save time to B.E.A. ports south of Mombasa where the Home Line steamer worked cargo for five days, e.g. Dar-es-Salaam reached on 25 July in *Dumra* as opposed to 31 July in *Malda*.

DURBAN MAIL (NORTHBOUND) (FOR SEYCHELLES & BOMBAY)

R.M.S. *Takliwa*	28 July	sail MOMBASA
	31 July	call Seychelles
	7 August	arr. BOMBAY

Notes: whilst P&O's Bombay Mail was obviously the fastest route to the Indian port, the Seychelles could be reached only by BI's Durban Mail either from Mombasa in five days or from Bombay in six, or by K.P.M.'s Orient-Java-Africa Line whose tickets were interchangeable with those of BI.

DURBAN MAIL (SOUTHBOUND) (FOR MOZAMBIQUE AND S. AFRICA)

R.M.S. *Tairea*	31 July	sail MOMBASA
	2 August	call Zanzibar
	2 August	call Dar-es-Salaam
	4 August	call Mozambique
	7 August	call Beira
	10 August	call Lourenço Marques
	11 August	arr. DURBAN

Notes: although BI quoted a through fare to Durban using the Mombasa transhipment, this was not an entirely satisfactory arrangement as the Durban mailship left three days after the Home Line steamer proceeded south, entailing an eight-day sojourn at Mombasa. In any event, it was far faster to travel to Natal via Union-Castle's Cape Mail.

HOME LINE EAST AFRICAN COASTAL (SOUTHBOUND)

R.M.S. *Malda*	28 July	sail MOMBASA
	29 July	call Tanga
	30 July	call Zanzibar
	31 July	call Dar-es-Salaam
	4 August	arr. BEIRA

Notes: continuation of the southbound voyage, mainly for cargo working (see Northern Feeder Service above).

SOUTHERN FEEDER SERVICE SOUTHBOUND (CARGO ONLY)
s.s. *Barjora*, and later
m.v. *Sofala*

SOUTHBOUND

sail BEIRA
call Quelimane
call Chinde
call Inhambane
call LOURENÇO MARQUES

NORTHBOUND

sail BEIRA
call Angoche
call Mocimboa
call Ibo
call Port Amelia
call MOZAMBIQUE

HOME LINE (NORTHBOUND)

| R.M.S. *Malda* | 18 August | sail BEIRA |
| | 22 August | call Dar-es-Salaam |

117

23 August	call Zanzibar
24 August	call Tanga
25 August	call MOMBASA

BOMBAY MAIL (NORTHBOUND) (FROM DURBAN)

R.M.S. *Tairea*	16 August	sail DURBAN
	17 August	call Lourenço Marques
	20 August	call Mozambique
	23 August	call Dar-es-Salaam
	23 August	call Zanzibar
	25 August	arr MOMBASA

Notes: the northbound connection from Durban to the Home Line mailship at Mombasa was usually tighter than the southbound, but there was usually a several day gap. Another possible connection point was Beira.

HOME LINE (NORTHBOUND) CONT'D

R.M.S. *Malda*	28 August	sail MOMBASA
	3 September	call Aden (bunkers)
	6 September	call Port Sudan
	9 September	sail Suez
		transit Suez Canal
	10 September	arr. Port Said
	16 September	call Marseilles
	23 September	call Plymouth
	24 September	arr. LONDON
		(Royal Albert Dock)

Notes: during the summer, a call would also be made homewards at Tangier, three days out from Marseilles. The Plymouth call was solely for passenger disembarkation and landing of mails, permitting a rail connection via the GWR to London and thus saving a day. *Malda* would not sail again from London until 16 October, having loaded cargo beforehand at Middlesbrough, Antwerp or Rotterdam before coming round to London. The mails and many passengers travelled via the faster overland route by special train to Marseilles to join the ship there, cutting six days off the journey.

The off-season outbound on the Home Line was May, June and July and from Africa, September, October and November. During this period BI offered fare reductions as well as special Excursion Return Tickets from Africa e.g £82 to London and return from Mombasa, valid for one-year. The same fare was available for the annual Special Christmas Excursion offered, in 1937, outbound to England in *Mantola* in November and back by the same steamer in January or *Malda* in February.

BI's East African Home Line was just one of several services on that route.

Well loved and thoroughly reliable, the "M"s were nevertheless always in the shade of their larger, faster and more palatial lavender-hulled Union-Castle "Llan" competitors: *Llanstephan Castle* (1914/11,293 grt), *Llandaff Castle* (1926/10,786 grt), *Llandovery Castle* (1925/10,640 grt) and the motor ship *Llangibby Castle* (1929/11,951 grt), three of which maintained the via Suez leg of the "Round-Africa" route in direct competition to BI.

The Union-Castle intermediates were a knot faster than the "M"s and a prospective Mombasa-bound First Class passenger would reach his destination from Britain by BI in 26 days and pay £48 (in 1937) or pay Union-Castle an extra £9 and save two days. The U-C ships also offered the facility of Tourist Class passage which at £36 was certainly good value for money. Still, there were many old Africa hands who would travel only in their "M" boats, often one particular vessel. Many preferred the one-class atmosphere and the Goanese service that the BI ships offered. Even so competition between the two lines was more congenial than cut-throat and tickets between BI and U-C were interchangeable for passage between ports common to both.

Foreign flag competition on the Europe-East Africa run was considerable. Although stripped of her African colonies, Germany's DÖAL and its new post-war fleet rivalled that of the British lines in ships and services. Whilst the magnificent new (1936) 16,662-grt *Pretoria* and *Windhuk*, routed via the Cape, went only as far as Lourenço Marques and occasionally Beira, DÖAL operated a comprehensive round-Africa service with *Usaramo*, *Ussakuma* and *Wangoni*, 7,775-tonners dating from 1920; *Adolph Woermann*, *Usambara* and *Njassa* of 8,600 grt and built 1922-24; and *Watussi* and *Ubena*, 9,500 grt of 1928. These maintained four-weekly sailings via the West and East Coast and offered a direct Southampton-Mombasa via Suez passage in as little as 25 days for £57 First and £33 Tourist.

That long-standing rival of both P&O and BI, Messageries Maritimes, remained an attractive choice for passage to East Africa, especially for those Britons who, to save time and avoid the Bay of Biscay, travelled the overland route to Marseilles to embark on the Africa-bound steamer. Maintained in 1937 by *Ville de Verdun*, *Bernardin de Saint Pierre*, *General Metzinger*, *Explorateur Grandidier*, *Angers*, *Chenonceaux* and *Leconte de Lisle*, the Marseilles to Mombasa leg of the twice-monthly Madagascar Mail took 17 days, three days shorter than by the "M"s on the same route.

British India tickets were interchangeable with those of Holland Africa Line which maintained monthly sailings from Hamburg, Amsterdam, Antwerp and Marseilles to the principal East African ports via Suez in *Springfontien*, *Randfontein*, *Klipfontein*, *Meliskerk* and *Heemskerk*, in addition to a separate service via the Cape. This comprehensive interchange permitted a round-Africa routing with BI outbound via Suez and Holland-Africa homewards via the Cape. Another interchange via the Cape was available in conjunction with the Blue Funnel-White Star-Aberdeen Line joint service on the Liverpool-Cape Town-Durban and v.v. leg of this Australian run.

These ships, running under Mail contract, enjoy a most enviable reputation up and down the African coast for their clockwork regularity.

BI brochure, circa 1936

The Durban Mail offered its own transhipment facilities beyond those with the Home Line. *Kenya, Karanja, Tairea* and *Takliwa* maintained fortnightly sailings from Bombay every other Wednesday to Mombasa, Zanzibar, Dar-es-Salaam, Beira, Lourenço Marques and Durban whence northbound trips commenced every other Monday. During the southwest Monsoon off-season period (May-August), the additional monthly calls outbound at Porebunder by *Tairea* and *Takliwa* and at Marmagoa by *Kenya* and *Karanja* ceased whilst the monthly Mozambique calls by the "T"s were augmented by the "K"s and assumed fortnightly frequency from August through October. Southbound, the "K"s called monthly at the Seychelles year-round. Northbound, only the "K"s served Beira monthly whereas the "T"s exclusively called at Mozambique. Outside of May through July, the Seychelles were only served once every two months by the "K"s. Very infrequent calls were made northbound at Marmagoa by the "K"s and at Porebunder by the "T"s.

Whilst there was no longer any formal co-ordination of sailings with Union-Castle, it was still possible to sail outbound by the Cape Mail from Southampton to Durban and connect with the BI mailship to Bombay with a one- to six-day layover in the Natal port. There was a same-day connection at Bombay with the P&O London-bound mailship. Here is an example of a typical transhipment with both services:

UNION-CASTLE CAPE MAIL
R.M.M.V. *Winchester Castle* – 11 June   sail SOUTHAMPTON
Via the Cape and intermed. ports
4 July   arr. DURBAN

BI DURBAN MAIL

R.M.S. *Karanja*		
5 July	sail DURBAN
6 July	call Lourenço Marques
9 July	call Beira
13 July	call Dar-es-Salaam
13 July	call Zanzibar
15 July	call Mombasa
18 July	call Seychelles
24 July	arr. BOMBAY

P&O BOMBAY MAIL
R.M.S. *Carthage*   24 July   sail BOMBAY
                    via Suez and intermed. ports
                    6 August   call Marseilles
                    12 August   call Plymouth
                    13 August   arr. LONDON

Notes: the fortnightly P&O and BI services always made a same day connection at Bombay. Additionally, the Saturday arrivals of the BI Durban mailship at Bombay connected the same day with the weekly BI Kathiawar Service to Porebunder, Dwarka, Cutchmanvie, Port Okha and Karachi (Monday arrivals). However, one could not make a satisfactory Persian Gulf connection as the Gulf Mail was programmed for weekly Thursday sailings from Bombay. Every other Saturday found BI's Gulf Mail (weekly) and Durban Mail (fortnightly) both arriving in Bombay in time to connect with the homebound P&O steamer. Finally, there was a monthly two-day connection at Bombay between the Durban Mail and the P&O Far East service to Colombo, Penang, Singapore, Hong Kong, Shanghai, Kobe and Yokohama. These ports could also be reached by BI's Apcar and Straits services, but from Calcutta.

In less than a decade, those noble names that filled the pages of Cook's and Bradshaws—Imperial Indian Mail Train, Royal Mail Ship *Takliwa* and the Bombay-Durban Mail—were merely evocative of a vanished age.

British India served Queen and country from the Indian Mutiny to the Falklands, but nowhere was the contribution or cost greater than in the Second World War. On 3 September 1939 the fleet comprised 103 vessels totalling 801,343 grt. By 15 August 1945, 51 ships (351,756 grt) had been lost. Tonnage could be replaced, but not the 1,083 officers and men who died with their ships nor for that matter the Raj itself for India was now ripe for independence.

The eve of war found BI's African ships scattered about on their regular runs plying their lawful occasions. Of the Home Line "M"s, *Malda* was at Middlesbrough, the outbound *Madura* at Marseilles, the homeward *Mantola* at Port Said and *Matiana* at Beira with *Sofala*. *Nevasa* was at Mombasa on a trooping run and *Dumra* and *Tairea* were off the East African coast. *Kenya* was in the middle of the Indian Ocean and *Karanja* and *Takliwa* at Bombay. There was no immediate requisition of vessels operating essential mail services which were now maintained under the direction of the Ministry of Shipping.

The "M"s had a varied and extensive mixture of commercial and war service. Homeward on a regular East African voyage, *Madura* was diverted to Bordeaux on 17 June 1940 to embark 1,300 refugees fleeing the German advance into France. These included the British Ambassador to Spain, the dramatist Henri Bernstein and Mlle. Eve Curie. Despite the mass of humanity aboard (added to which was a full list of regular passengers), everyone praised the "sheer generosity" of the officers and crew including Purser H.W. Cooper who compared the appearance of the public rooms to the "London tube air-raid shelters, for there were all sorts and conditions of men, women and children sleeping huddled up together with not an inch to spare" (*Valiant Voyaging*). The *Madura* safely reached Falmouth two days later.

The same ship participated in another evacuation, this time from Singapore, where she arrived on 15 January 1942 with Japanese infantry advancing only 100 miles from the north and Keppel Harbour under near constant air attack. Fifteen days later a bombing raid scored several hits on *Madura* and set part of the vessel and the quayside godowns ablaze. Fires extinguished, she was anchored in the roadstead to await cargo, rather an extraordinary bit of normalcy given the situation. On 2 February she went alongside and embarked instead 200 Chinese and European refugees, sailing for Java the next day. During the evening of the 3rd whilst in the Dempo Strait, off Sumatra, *Madura* was again hit by Japanese aircraft, killing five crew members and injuring 13 others as well as destroying the hospital. The injured were landed at Palembang and *Madura* safely reached Calcutta. For the remainder of the war, she trooped mainly between India and Australia.

Not to survive the evacuation of Burma was *Malda,* one of three BI ships sunk on 6 April 1942. Recently refitted as a transport, she was in the Bay of Bengal bound for Colombo when a Japanese seaplane spotted her convoy. Soon afterwards a Japanese squadron, including two cruisers and a destroyer, came up and attacked the hapless merchantmen. Blue Funnel's *Autolycus* was sunk and then *Malda* took numerous direct hits and was quickly set afire. Her Chief Steward, W.H. Walters, poignantly described *Malda's* loss in *Valiant Voyaging*:

> As she listed to starboard, before taking the final plunge, I turned my back to her for I could not bear to watch her death agony any longer. As every seaman knows, a feeling of sadness comes over one... when watching the end of a ship, especially if one had been in her, as I had, for some fourteen years. I shall always remember her, sailing gaily along, swaying like a graceful lady, to the song of the turbines...

Mantola and *Mulbera,* whilst never requisitioned as troopships, did carry soldiers between India, East Africa and the Middle East in addition to passenger and cargo sailings under the MoWT's Liner Division. *Matiana,* after narrowly escaping a direct bomb hit during a raid on Liverpool, served in the Indian Ocean and the Far East as a depot ship for the Royal Marine Engineers for the construction of base facilities.

Of the Durban mailships, *Tairea* was converted by the Magazon Dockyard, Bombay, during August 1940 into *Hospital Ship No. 35* with a capacity of 506 bed patients and 120 medical staff. Glistening in white, with a red cross on each of her three funnels, she was surely the most elegant looking hospital ship and doubly a welcome sight to her patients. Her first action was at Kismayu and Mogadishu where she took off wounded from the beaches using her own lifeboats. She then participated in the landings at Diego Suarez and Madagascar and served as a hospital transport carrying wounded British and Italian POWs between Alexandria and Izmir in 1942. Together with the BI hospital ships *Talamba, Amra* and *Vita, Tairea* was at the landings on Salerno in July 1943 where all four came under constant German air attack despite being clearly marked and illuminated. *Talamba* was struck by one bomb at 10.05 p.m., 10 July and sank, with sister ship *Tairea* rescuing the survivors; all 400 patients were saved but five crew members lost their lives. *Tairea* concluded her war service repatriating POWs from Hong Kong to India.

Takliwa spent the war in the drab paint of Admiralty grey after being taken up as a transport in 1940. January 1942 found her assisting in the evacuation of Singapore and later that year she was at the invasion of Madagascar. She participated with *Rohna* (1926/8,602 grt) and *Rajula* (1926/8,478 grt) in the landings at Siracusa and Augusta, Sicily, in July 1943. Joining *Tairea* in summer 1945 repatriating POWs from Hong Kong to India, *Takliwa* survived the war only to run aground and burn out on Car Nicobar, South Nicobar Island, in the Andamans, on 15 October 1945.

Kenya remained on the Durban Mail until May 1940 when she and *Karanja* were requisitioned for conversion into transports and sailed together in convoy to Britain. As H.M.T. *Kenya* and fitted with four landing craft and 11 of her original lifeboats, she participated in the unsuccessful landings at Dakar later that year. When the war entered the offensive phase for the Allies, she and *Karanja* were converted into a Landing Ship Infantry (Large) or LSI(L) in 1941. To avoid confusion with the cruiser H.M.S. *Kenya*, she was commissioned on 23 July 1941 as H.M.S. *Hydra*. In October she was further converted to serve as a Landing Ship Headquarters (Large) or LSH(L) with additional communications equipment in addition to carrying nine LCA, one LCS(M), two LCP(L) and two LCM landing craft hung outside from her existing davits. Her name was altered to *Keren*, after the recently won pivotal battle against the Italians in Eritrea. She could now carry 1,296 troops and was armed with one six inch and one three-inch gun in addition to eight 40 mm and 14 20 mm anti-aircraft guns. Participating in the 5 May 1942 landings at Diego Suarez, Madagascar, she later won battle honours for the operations at Algiers, Sicily, Southern France and Burma.

Karanja was bound for England, carrying a battalion of the Royal Ulster Rifles, and conversion into a transport, steaming in convoy between Bombay and Durban with *Kenya, Talamba, Rajula* and *Rohna* destined for the same purpose. On 10 June 1940 fire broke out in her main baggage hold which had to be flooded to extinguish the blaze which was believed to have been caused by a home-made time bomb.

After serving as a transport, *Karanja* was commissioned on 24 July 1941 as a LSI(L) (Landing Ship Infantry Large) with capacity for 1,500 troops, carrying nine LCP(L), two LCS(M) and two LCM landing craft, and armed with one six-inch and one three-inch gun. Conversion complete she was based at Inveraray in Loch Fyne for working up and training exercises followed by a six-week refit at Liverpool. In March 1942 she sailed for Durban where she joined up with the invasion convoy for Madagascar which left on 28 April. She sailed for the Clyde, arriving on 18 September.

Bound for the invasion of North Africa, *Karanja* left the Clyde on 26 October 1942 and successfully completed the landing at Sidi Ferruch, near Algiers. Next she sailed for Bougie, 130 miles away, where after her landing craft had departed, she came under resolute air attack by *Luftwaffe* Ju.88 bombers on 11 November which hit and sank *Awatea* and *Cathay*. *Karanja's* turn came early the next morning when she caught a stick of bombs— "By God, those were close" remarked the Captain on the bridge, to which an officer replied, "Yes, sir, they are in the engine room" (*Valiant Voyaging*)— and the ship was soon ablaze and later sank. Several of her engine room staff were lost, but the ship was successfully abandoned and her survivors rescued by *Strathnaver*. This was a particularly black period for the P&O Group which lost *Viceroy of India*, *Ettrick* and *Strathallan* in addition to *Cathay* during the North African operations. That month alone, BI lost *Tilawa*, *Hatimura*, *Cranfield* and *Karanja*.

Even the little African coasters had their wartime adventures. *Dumra* served from mid 1940 through May 1941 as a Commodore ship and supply vessel for the operations at Kismayu, Somaliland. Fitted with four anti-aircraft guns and carrying 200 stevedores, she did yeoman service supplying the advance against Italian East Africa and later moved on to Merka and Mogadishu. On passage Madagascar to Durban on 5 June 1943, she was torpedoed by *U-198*. She withstood the first hit, but a second torpedo was fatal to 25 of her crew, including Captain W.C. Cripps. Of the survivors in lifeboats, the *U-198* took Chief Engineer H.T. Graham prisoner who later died in captivity. The others, towed by *Dumra's* motorboat, safely landed at St. Lucia lighthouse.

The almost new *Sofala* spent 1940 through May 1941 in company with *Dumra* on the Mombasa to Somaliland supply route after which she became a cased petrol carrier on the famous Mediterranean "Bomb Alley" run and had the distinction of being the first British ship to enter Benghazi after its surrender. Based on Alexandria, she continued to ply the North African coastal route. Her gunnery officer later commented on her main initial armament, a four-inch gun (all that was available at the time): "When it was fired we jumped from about 11½ knots to 14 as a result of the recoil. A kick in the pants from a giant could not have produced a more pronounced effect."

After November 1940, a limited Bombay-Durban service was maintained by *Khandalla*, back on her old run, and *Shirala* (1925/7,745 grt), a fine ship of the three-strong "S" class built for the India-Far East route. Measuring 436.1 ft. by 57.8 ft. and powered by twin-screw, triple-expansion machinery, *Shirala* had a service speed of 13 knots. Saloon accommodation was for 42 First and 80 Second class. Another addition was *Tilawa* which with sister ship *Talma* were the first BI ships to reach the 10,000-grt mark (451 ft. by 59.03 ft.) and were built by Hawthorn Leslie, Newcastle, for the Calcutta-Japan Apcar run. Otherwise handsome vessels, their profiles were spoilt by two thin, very closely spaced funnels. But their accommodation, for 62 First, 74 Second and a maximum of 3,136 deck, was among the best in the fleet. First Class had a music room, a oak-panelled Jacobian style smoking room and dining saloon whilst Second was provided with a lounge and dining saloon. *Tilawa* was hindered by her remarkably slow speed (12 knots) from single-screw, quadruple-expansion machinery and proved short-lived on the Durban Mail.

En route from Bombay to Durban via Mombasa *Tilawa* was torpedoed on a clear moonlit night on 23 November 1942 by the Japanese submarine *I-29*. The 912 deck passengers panicked and 252 jumped overboard and were drowned, although the ship remained afloat until hit by a second torpedo. The behaviour of her officers and crew was of the highest order; the First Radio Officer E.B. Duncan transmitted SOS messages until he was drowned and Captain F. Robinson and the Chief Officer remained on the bridge until washed overboard; both were saved and went on to help injured passengers in the lifeboats. After a wretched day in shark-infested waters, the 661 survivors were picked up by H.M.S. *Birmingham* and landed at Bombay on 27 November.

British India ships and crews had once again paid a heavy price for a victory that proved in some respects hollow. Having won the war, the peace was harder to determine as India, Burma, Malaya, Ceylon and other parts of Britain's empire experienced political unrest and sought immediate independence. The well-ordered world that BI had helped to create, maintain and had profited by and thrived on was, like so many fine BI vessels and men, ultimately no less a casualty of the war.

7. POST-WAR PROGRESS

Thanks to the turn of post-war politics, indeed, the East African territories under British control are a happier hunting-ground for a British-owned shipping concern than independent India. BI Centenary, 1856-1956

Trade did follow flag and before the Second World War the combination of Red Duster and BI burgee had been a potent and profitable one on the inter-Empire routes. Peace brought myriad new flags and disrupted trade patterns. As colonies achieved their independence, BI's market share declined or was re-oriented. In an extreme example, Burma, trade was almost wiped out as that once prosperous colony entered a repressive and regressive era from which it has yet to emerge. Once independent, India reserved her lucrative coastal trade for Indian tonnage. In most places, however, it was a more paced and peaceful transition and regardless of their changing political status, these emerging nations were still well served by a resourceful and resilient BI.

Wisely, BI staked its post-war fortunes away from the Bay of Bengal and westwards to the Indian Ocean and East Africa where 75 years previously William Mackinnon planted the seeds of Imperial progress. Here there was no rush for independence; British East Africa had been spared the physical scars of war and its mineral and agricultural wealth had proved invaluable to the Allies. Having conceded India and Burma, the Colonial Office turned its attention to strengthening Britain's African possessions, and for the first time, BI's routes there were to assume dominance.

Even before final victory, BI was resolutely planning for resumption of its African services and the building of a new fleet, encouraged by the post-war future of South and East Africa. The mineral resources of the two Rhodesias seemed boundless, emigration to South Africa boomed and in British East, hoped-for prosperity was summed up in one word: groundnuts. Intended to supply Britain with badly needed vegetable oil and fodder and to spur a new generation of settlers, the ill-fated but promising programme for the cultivation of peanuts in Tanganyika began in 1947. Initially planned by the Colonial Office, but entrusted to the newly created Overseas Food Corporation, this fantastic scheme envisaged putting three million acres of land into cultivation with highly mechanised farms of 30,000 acres each. Expectations of turning Tanganyika into a Commonwealth vegetable patch were very high and so was the estimated £25 million cost of the project. Another £4.5 million was earmarked for a new deep water port (Mtwara) in southern Tanganyika and a new connecting railway.

The Labour Government's largesse towards the once neglected East African colonies also included the £4.8 million Owen Falls hydro-electric scheme in Uganda which was begun in 1948 and completed in 1954.

By 1948 Kenya's non-African population included 24,000 Arabs, 90,500 Indians and 46,500 Europeans; that of Tanganyika 24,000 Indians and 17,000 Europeans, and Uganda, 35,215 Indians and 3,448 Europeans. By 1952 the rate of immigration to Kenya was three times greater than the period 1937 through 1939. Whilst the number of European arrivals by air had doubled between 1949 and 1952, there was plenty of traffic to share with the steamship. A substantial increase in the Indian population in East Africa after the war (104,697 in 1939 rising to 366,013 by 1962) ensured a prosperous future for the Bombay-Africa run.

The last hopes of Empire were fixed upon East Africa and here, too, were hinged the post-war aspirations of BI whose ambitious newbuilding programme comprised two "K" mailships for the Bombay-Durban run, two "M" East African coastal liners, three "S" ships for the Calcutta-Yokohama service, four "D" vessels for the Bombay-Gulf route and nine additional "C" class cargo liners. In August 1946, BI had 18 ships on order and by 1949 had invested over £13 million in new tonnage, partially funded out of war risk insurance.

Resumption of principal services with existing tonnage began within a few months after V-J Day. Despite severe war losses, BI was fortunate to have five of the six "M3" class ships (*Madura, Modasa, Mantola, Matiana* and *Mulbera*) with which to resume the Home Line services as soon as the vessels were released from government duty and reconditioned.

As refitted, *Mantola*, for example, had one-class berths for 173 passengers. There were 12 twin-bedded cabins on Boat Deck, four single-, 18 two- and 20 three-berth on Bridge Deck, one single-, six two-, seven three- and three four-berth cabins, all outside with washbasin, on Upper Deck. The music room and smoking room were forward on Promenade Deck and the cafe lounge and bar aft. The 166-seat dining saloon was forward on Upper Deck whilst the space occupied by the former Second Class saloon aft was now the hospital. Not modern, speedy or palatial after 25 years hard service, the "M"s in their dotage nevertheless assumed a vital role in BI's post-war recovery.

Reopening the African Home Line, *Mantola* sailed from Liverpool on 21 March 1946 for Mombasa (arriving on 16 April), Dar-es-Salaam (26) and Beira. En route to Bombay, *Madura* called at Mombasa on 3 June, but was then assigned to a new Calcutta/Bombay-Melbourne-Sydney run that September partnered with *Mulbera* which had started the service a year previously. The new cargo vessel *Urlana* (1946/6,834 grt) departed London for Beira the same month. *Modasa* left Hull on 17 July, reached Mombasa on 15 August and continued to Tanga, Zanzibar and Dar-es-Salaam. Initial

127

homeward sailings from Kenya were by *Mantola* on 15 May and *Modasa* on 4 September and these two vessels for a time maintained the Home Line service on their own augmented by occasional freighters.

Among the cargo vessels resuming sailings to Africa were *Gazana* (1919/5,284 grt), one of the only three remaining "B" type First World War standard ships in the fleet, which arrived at Durban on 16 March 1946 with 2,000 tons of cargo and thereafter made several voyages to the Mediterranean and Adriatic, and *Ozarda* (1940/6,895 grt) which on 28 January 1947 discharged the first large (41,600 cases) of dates at the Natal port since the war. Making the first of many such trips, the new *Landaura* (1946/7,829 grt) sailed from London on 5 October 1946 and docked at Beira on 19 November.

British India elected not to recommission *Keren*, ex-*Kenya*, which was sold on 3 April 1946 to the Admiralty and later became Sitmar's very successful emigrant ship *Castel Felice*. Thus it was left to the first generation of "K"s, *Karagola* and *Khandalla*, along with *Shirala*, to continue the Durban Mail into the post-war period, augmented by a variety of chartered or government-owned tonnage. *Kutsang* (1922/5,869 grt/Indo-China S.N. Co.) made the first advertised arrival at Durban from Bombay via Mombasa and Beira on 20 November 1945 followed by *Karagola* on 3 December and the elderly *Hong Kheng* (1903/6,167 grt/Ho Hong S.S. Co.) on 15 December. *Karagola* sailed from Bombay for Mombasa, Beira and Durban on 11 January 1946 with 825 passengers followed by *Shirala* on 26 February for Mombasa, Lourenço Marques and Durban with 31 Saloon and 1,162 deck passengers. After a voyage from Bombay beginning 20 February to East African ports only, *Khandalla*, with 170 Saloon and 859 deck passengers, left Bombay for Durban on 26 April. Revival of the call at Veraval, India, by *Karagola* on 12 March en route to Africa was cause enough for a celebration there attended by Khan Bahadur Abdul Kad, Dewan of Junagadh State.

Vasna (1917/5,767 grt), one of the famous Gulf line "V"s, was a newcomer to Africa. Concluding her final voyage as a hospital ship at Bombay on 17 March 1946, and after refitting, she inaugurated a new direct Bombay-East Africa service upon her sailing for Mombasa on 10 June with 59 Saloon and 731 deck passengers. A heartening sign that things were gradually returning to normal, *Vasna* and *Urlana* were berthed together at Mombasa in 26 July. Taking a break from her African duties *Shirala*, which arrived at Bombay from Durban on 12 October, was chartered to the Indian Government for a single voyage to Jeddah for that year's Haj and she left eight days later with 1,050 pilgrims.

Planning of BI's first post-war liner dated to November 1944 and the contract with Alexander Stephen & Sons was signed on 18 December 1944, the 21st ship built by Stephens for the line. Laid down in October 1945, she was to have been launched on 10 December 1946 by Lady Currie at the

128

Linthouse yards of Alexander Stephen & Sons as *Kampala,* the first BI ship named after the capital of Uganda, and among the spectators was Mutesa II, Kabaka (King) of Buganda. Instead dense fog made the launching impossible and Lady Currie had to be content to christen the immobile hull which was successfully sent down the ways without ceremony the next day.

After *Vasna* was diverted to the Madras-Singapore run, she was replaced by Mogul Line's *Rizwani* (1930/5,447 grt) for two Bombay-Dar-es-Salaam voyages, 24 January-1 March and 13 March-14 April 1947. Part of the P&O Group, Mogul Line would contribute chartered tonnage to BI's African routes on a fairly regular basis after the war, outside of the annual Haj or Moslem pilgrimage season which was Mogul's principal trade.

Nothing symbolised more the post-war importance of the African routes in BI's future than the re-assignment of the company's newest vessels away from the once premier Calcutta-Rangoon run. So diminished was post-war Burmese trade that Rangoon, once busy BI hub, was reduced to a mere waystop on the Calcutta-Yokohama run. The crack Burma mailship *Amra* and her sister *Aronda,* completed as a transport, would instead serve on the Bombay-Durban run after being restored to peacetime standards. Originally a trio (*Aska* (1939/8,322 grt) was sunk in 1940), the Swan Hunter-built *Amra* (1938/8,314 grt) and *Aronda* (1941/8,396 grt) were splendid looking ships with their well-proportioned cowled funnels and trim lines. *Amra* was distinguished by a magnificent varnished teak bridge, the wartime-built *Aronda* having an armoured steel wheelhouse.

Launched by Lady Willingdon on 29 April 1938 *Amra* sailed from London on 18 November on her delivery voyage to Calcutta to begin her brief career as a Burma mailship. Commissioned as *Hospital Ship No. 41* in December 1940, she operated between Durban, Mombasa and Somaliland. Completing her 27th voyage repatriating South African troops from the Middle East, *Amra* arrived at Durban on 18 March 1946 and then sailed for Britain for refitting.

Amra originally carried three saloon classes; 45 First (one de luxe stateroom, 12 single- and 15 two-berth cabins) having a lounge, smoke room and dining saloon, 78 Second "A" (15 four-berth and six three-berth) with a lounge and dining saloon, and 40 Second "B" with 10 four-berth cabins and a 50-seat dining saloon. The attractive *moderne* decor, by A. McInnes Gardner, was the first of its kind in a BI ship. The lounge had panelling of figured weathered sycamore and the smoking room was lined in Indian silver grey wood. As many as 2,327 deck passengers could be carried.

As initially refitted for the Durban Mail, *Amra* had 154 Saloon Class berths in one twin-bedded special cabin with private bath, and single, two-, three- and four-berth cabins, all outside and with washbasin, on Bridge and Shelter Decks. The public rooms comprised the lounge, music room and smoking room forward on Promenade Deck and another lounge aft. The dining saloon was forward on Bridge Deck. An Intermediate Class, with four eight-berth and two four-berth cabins, was forward on A Deck.

Powered by two sets of Parsons single reduction geared turbines (8,000 shp) driving twin screws at 130 rpm at 16 knots, the "A"s were among the last coal-fired liners built and had three Babcock & Wilcox boilers with Erith Roe mechanical stokers. Each had a deadweight capacity of some 6,000 tons and four holds worked by four sets of samson posts.

Returning to Bombay from Southampton on 18 July 1946 *Amra*, after additional refurbishment, first sailed for Durban via Marmagoa and the Seychelles on 9 February 1947 commanded by Captain K.G. Mace, with 121 Saloon and 835 deck passengers. At Durban on 6 March she disembarked 91 Saloon and 557 deck passengers.

To resume the fortnightly Mombasa-Tanga-Zanzibar-Dar-es-Salaam-Lindi-Mikindani service, BI took the unusual step of looking to the second-hand market for a replacement for the lost *Dumra*. In October 1946 China Navigation Co.'s *Kiungchow* (1921/2,653 grt) was purchased for £77,214 from the MoWT. The single-screw turbine steamer was good for 11 knots and accommodated 11 First Saloon, 18 Second Saloon and 350 deck passengers. Renamed *Kilwa* (Captain P.G. Allerton) on 19 February 1947 she sailed from Bombay on 10 March for Port Okha and Porebunder and thence to Dar-es-Salaam where she arrived on the 31st with a cargo of cement. Her coastal service commenced on 3 April.

Among those disembarking from *Amra* at Mombasa on 27 May 1947 were 50 Europeans quitting soon to be independent India to settle in East and South Africa, including a Scots tea planter who was quoted in the *East African Standard*, "India as a country is fine, but we are completely disgusted with the people. There is no management, and when the British go, there will be chaos."

Matiana (Captain J. A. Cleese) sailed from Bombay on 20 February 1947 for Mombasa and Beira via Port Okra with 138 Saloon passengers. Calling at Dar-es-Salaam, northbound, on 27 March she proceeded to London where she arrived on 29 April. Upon her 14 June departure for Beira *Matiana* joined sisters *Modasa* and *Mantola* on the Home Line.

New to BI African routes was an infrequent cargo service from Australian ports which commenced with *Palikonda*'s (1945/7,434 grt) departure from Sydney on 7 May 1947 for Mombasa. She was followed by sister ship *Pemba* (1945/7,449 grt) on 8 August.

Back on her pre-war run, *Tairea* (Captain H.M. MacDonald) sailed from Bombay on 27 June 1947 and reached Durban on 23 July with 91 Saloon and 142 deck passengers. "Fezzes and multi-coloured silks predominated at the Point yesterday afternoon where large numbers of Durban Indians thronged the quay at A Shed to welcome friends and relations returning from India on the BI liner *Tairea*. Immigration officials worked till nearly midnight checking and clearing the 140 Indians aboard." *(Natal Mercury)*

Also resuming her peacetime duties was *Sofala* upon her 14 July 1947 sailing from Dar-es-Salaam for Mikindani. Unlike in pre-war days, she stayed mainly on the Northern Feeder Service and did not normally call at southern ports.

The Durban Mail, already strengthened by *Amra* and *Tairea,* was further enhanced by the addition of the "new" (in so far as commercial service was concerned) *Aronda*. Launched at Swan Hunter on 5 August 1940 and commissioned as H.M.T. *Aronda* on 17 March 1941, the ship did yeoman service as a transport during the war. On her final voyage on H.M. Service she sailed from Bombay in November 1946 carrying Italian POWs to Naples and on to Newcastle where she arrived on 3 December. There she was refitted with her originally intended accommodation which included 155 Saloon berths. *Aronda* (Captain W.H. Brown) departed Tyneside on 5 June 1947 and after calls at Mombasa and Zanzibar (28 June) docked at Bombay on 6 July with 107 passengers. With 1,137 aboard, she sailed on her maiden mailship voyage to Durban on the 26th and arrived at the Natal port on 16 August.

About to be relieved by *Aronda, Karagola* (Captain D.R.P. Gun-Cunninghame) left Bombay on 23 July 1947 with 579 passengers on her last voyage to Durban via East Africa and returned on 18 September with 278 aboard. After a cargo-only trip to Rangoon, she began a regular Bombay-Karachi run under Indian Government charter carrying capacity loads of Hindu and Moslem refugees between newly independent India and Pakistan. This important work completed, *Karagola* left Calcutta on 10 March 1948 and arrived in London 11 April. On 3 June she was sold to British breakers.

The first of the new "S" class for the Calcutta-Yokohama run was christened *Sangola* by Mrs. Liddle, wife of BI's Marine Superintendent, at Barclay, Curle on 23 December 1946. Commissioned on 6 June 1947 by Captain R.H.A. Bond, *Sangola* carried passengers from London to Mombasa on her delivery voyage beginning on the 28th. At Dar-es-Salaam on 23 July she discharged 2,000 tons of cargo and returned to Mombasa for 68 Saloon passengers and 4,000 tons of cotton and soda ash for Bombay where she arrived on 20 August. Unlike her sister ships, she never returned to East Africa.

Also destined never again to call at African ports, *Shirala* (Captain F. Robinson), sailed from Bombay on 6 August 1947 with 828 passengers for Dar-es-Salaam via Bedibunder, Mombasa and Zanzibar. Back at Bombay on 16 September with 1,005 passengers, she joined *Karapara* on the Bombay-Karachi repatriation run and was later assigned to a new BI Karachi-Chittagong service linking West and East Pakistan. *Shirala* was finally sold for scrap on 3 May 1951. Bound for the breaker's yard at Blyth, she sailed on her 146th and final voyage from Chittagong to Plymouth on 7 March and arrived on 15 April.

Final fitting-out of the £1,104,000 *Kampala* included two cat mascots, Blackie and Ginger, presented to the ship by Alex. Stephen's yard canteen girls. The ship left Glasgow on 28 August 1947 for her acceptance trials on which she made 18.5 knots. Commanded by Captain W.H. Cleese, BI's first post-war African mailship sailed from Tilbury on 13 September 1947 and arrived at Mombasa on 2 October. Among those disembarking at Dar-es-Salaam six days later was 84-year-old Robert Scott, from Herefordshire, en route to his son-in-law's farm in the Southern Highlands and who was the oldest immigrant to Tanganyika. Very much the celebrity of the voyage, he told the *Tanganyika Standard*: "We had a really enjoyable trip all the way. The food was excellent, we had a fine crowd of people on board, and the service and accommodation were very good. We stopped at only three places on the way out and considering we were a week at Mombasa and we left England on September 13, that's not bad going." It was added that Mr. Scott won the ship's tote four times, three times in succession.

With 195 passengers and 3,500 tons of cargo including two giraffes for the former Maharaja of Mysore's zoo, *Kampala* reached Bombay on the evening of 25 October 1947. On her first Bombay-Africa voyage, she called at Dar-es-Salaam on 25 November and made her maiden call at Durban on 3 December after a 22-day passage. The next day the ship hosted a celebratory luncheon attended by Durban Mayor L.C. Boyd.

Replaced by *Kampala, Khandalla* left Durban for the last time on 1 December 1947 and went on the Bombay-East Africa run effective with her 7 January 1948 sailing via Karachi.

Launched at Swan, Hunter by Mrs. Duncan, wife of BI's Superintendent Engineer, on 8 January 1947, the second of the "S" class, *Sirdhana* (Captain H.E. Evans), called at Mombasa on 28 January 1948 with passengers on her delivery voyage from the Tyne and London. She arrived at Bombay on 6 February with 6,345 tons of cargo and proceeded to Calcutta to join *Sangola* on the Yokohama run.

Making her first voyage on the Home Line was *Garbeta* which left London on 23 February 1948 and augmented the regular cargo sailings of *Landaura* and one trip by *Durenda*. On the Australia-East Africa run that year were *Palikonda, Pemba, Pentakota* and *Okhla*.

Chartered to the Indian Government, *Kampala* left Bombay on 9 March 1948, for Karachi with 1,618 Muslim evacuees and returned on the 17th with 2,317 Hindu refugees. On 14 April she went on the Bombay-East Africa run. Karachi was added on India-bound trips beginning with her stop there on 3 July.

A sister ship of *Kampala, Karanja* (II), had been ordered from Stephens on

31 January 1946. She was launched by Mrs. J.F. Stephen, deputising for Lady Inchcape, at Linthouse on 10 March 1948. Entering dry dock on 23 September, *Karanja* ran trials the next week and was handed over at 8.30 p.m. on 1 October. Commanded by Captain J.W. Milne, the liner left Tilbury on the 16th for Mombasa with 300 passengers where she called 6-7 November and reached Bombay via Karachi on the 18th. Her maiden voyage from Bombay to Durban, with 1,131 passengers, was from 7-28 December. The following day she was joined alongside by the new Union-Castle *Edinburgh Castle* also on her maiden voyage.

The 10,304-grt *Kampala* and 10,294-grt *Karanja* (507 ft. by 66.3 ft.) were the largest British liners ever built for an India-based route. Traditionally designed for an unchanged service, the new "K"s were modestly updated versions of the pre-war pair with flared bows, sharply raked stems and pear-shaped funnel instead of round. Otherwise, the cruiser sterns and large open superstructures topped by a double-banked row of lifeboats were practically indistinguishable from the old ships.

Depending on allotment of interchangeable cabins, there were berths for either 60 or 102 First Class passengers in two de luxe single-bed cabins with private bath, 14 single-berth and 21 twin-bedded cabins, all outside and with washbasin, on Bridge Deck. On Shelter Deck forward were two single- or double-berth cabins and 20 double or four-berth cabins which were interchangeable between First Class (when only the lower berths were utilised) and Second Class when the upper berths were also sold. The Second Class had either 180 berths or 116 without these interchangeable cabins. Permanent Second Class accommodation comprised eight two-berth, 12 three-berth and 12 four-berth rooms (outside with washbasin) on Shelter Deck and 4 four-berth cabins on Main Deck.

The Boat Deck had officers' accommodation, on the Promenade Deck were the First Class lounge forward, foyer, smoking room, bar and cardroom, dancing/cinema space, and aft were the Second Class smoking room, foyer and lounge. Decorated by A. McInnes Gardner, Glasgow, at a cost of £50,000 per vessel, the public rooms were panelled in African mahogany, Nigerian cherry, Australian maple, sycamore and cedrona, and the patterned linoleum flooring was in complementary tones. A wide promenade was glazed forward and arranged with wicker furniture. On Bridge Deck forward was the 114-seat First Class dining saloon whilst that for Second Class, seating 120, was aft on Shelter Deck.

Unique to *Karanja* was the 68-berth Intermediate Class aft on Lower Deck which had two eight-berth, two six-berth and four 10-berth outside cabins with an adjoining public room. Unberthed passengers' space was forward and aft on the Main Deck and forward on Lower Deck with separate galleys amidships for Hindu and Moslem faiths.

Good for 16 knots, the "K"s were powered by two sets of Parsons turbines developing 9,700 shp and single-reduction geared to twin screws at 125 rpm and supplied by three Babcock & Wilcox boilers. The five holds had a 367,340 cu. ft. (*Kampala*), 375,070 cu. ft. (*Karanja*) capacity plus 10,468 cu. ft. "reefer". Befitting ships with deck passenger certificates of 2,441, no fewer than 26 lifeboats and two motor launches were carried at Welin davits.

To join *Kilwa* on the busy Mombasa-Mikindani coastal run, *Kola* (1924/1,538 grt), with 18 passenger berths and provision to carry cattle, arrived at Dar-es-Salaam from Singapore on 29 July 1948. Built for the Singapore-Bangkok feeder service, *Kola* and *Kistna* (1924/1,466 grt) were BI's first single-screw motor ships.

Both new and old BI ships made one-off East African voyages in 1948. *Dara* (1948/4,867 grt), on her delivery trip from London beginning on 15 July, called at Mombasa on 7 August, and the old *Talma*, long a stalwart of the Far East run but since the war used between Calcutta and Australia, left Melbourne on 12 October for Mauritius (9 November), Beira (30) and Mombasa. She arrived at Bombay on 21 December.

A reorganisation of the India-Africa services was announced on 13 February 1949. Destined to revert to her original Calcutta-Yokohama route, *Tairea* sailed from Durban on 29 January on her final voyage via Lourenço Marques, Beira, Dar-es-Salaam, Zanzibar, Mombasa, Seychelles and Marmagoa to Bombay where she arrived on 28 February. *Khandalla* resumed her six-weekly Bombay-East Africa service on 12 March after a single cargo voyage to Rangoon and Colombo. *Kampala* rejoined *Karanja* on the Bombay-Durban run effective 14 February. *Amra* and *Aronda* went on a new Durban-Lourenço Marques-Beira-Mozambique (southbound)-Dar-es-Salaam (north)-Zanzibar-Tanga (south)-Mombasa route. The 31-day voyage had five days turnaround in Durban and sailings were programmed from the Natal port on the 18th and 26th of every month. *Amra* left Bombay on 10 March and sailed from Mombasa for Durban nine days later to begin the service whereas *Aronda* arrived at Durban on 21 April from Mombasa via India and received a thorough cleaning and painting before joining the new service. British India now offered three sailings a month from Durban.

The groundnut scheme put enormous pressure on the existing and inadequate East African ports, especially in Tanganyika, causing lengthy and costly delays for ships awaiting a berth. Lighterage and coastal services thus assumed a new importance. In 1948 the new *Julyvanda*, built by the Suez Canal Lighterage Co. at Port Said for Rene Zarb & R.H. Elkington, was purchased to join *Sofala* on the East African coastal run. Renamed *Tabora*, the diminutive 390-grt, 157 ft. by 27 ft. ship was described in *BI News:*

Built on typical coaster lines, she had her accommodation, engine room and bridge aft, and was powered by a four cylinder

Ruston & Hornsby Diesel engine, capable of driving her at the theoretical speed of 8.7 knots. In practice, under ideal conditions she seldom exceeded a speed of 7 knots at sea. Two large hatches with a combined capacity of 22,700 cubic ft., a net tonnage of 276 tons, gross of 390 tons, and there you have the *Tabora*. While, undoubtedly, an ideal vessel for service on rivers or canals, those who had the misfortune or otherwise to sail in her will be the first to admit that even in very moderate weather she behaved in anything but a ladylike manner.

The next year BI purchased the tug *Empire Minnow* (1943/262 grt), renamed her *Thika* and based her at Mombasa with three 20,000 cu. ft. capacity Thames barges to operate as far south as Ibo, Tanganyika, and north to Mogadishu, Somalia, in addition to harbour and local duties.

The 31-year-old First World War standard "C" type freighter *Warina* (1918/3,120 grt) played out her BI career along the East Africa coast. Arriving at Mombasa from Cochin on 19 April 1949 she made several coastal voyages before proceeding south to Durban where she docked on 13 September. She left Mombasa for Bombay on 24 October where she was broken up in January 1950. On her first such voyage, *Ozarda* (1940/6,895 grt) arrived at Durban on 18 April from Wallaroo, Australia, with 3,000 tons of bagged wheat.

Beginning to make periodic forays south of Beira, *Kilwa* called at Lourenço Marques for the first time on 9 April 1949 en route to Durban from Mombasa.

Khandalla survived a seven-hour-long fire in her No. 3 hold, filled with 300 bales of cotton, at Mombasa on 7 April 1949, delaying her departure for the Seychelles and Bombay for six days. The next month, 340 Indian deck passengers signed a petition complaining of overcrowded and unsatisfactory conditions aboard, prompting an Indian Government investigation.

The Home Line finally reverted to its pre-war monthly frequency when *Mulbera* and *Madura* joined the other "M"s on the service. Owing to extended calls in port due to harbour congestion and the diminished speed of the ageing "M"s, five vessels were now required to maintain the service whereas before the war four were sufficient. Ending the India-Australia passenger run *Mulbera* left Melbourne on 25 June 1948. She sailed from Calcutta on 25 August and underwent a refit upon her London arrival on 14 October. Beira-bound, she departed from London on 25 March 1949 and reached Mombasa on 20 April. *Madura*, whose final sailing for Australia was in March 1948, left Calcutta on 12 October 1948 and, after refurbishment, joined the East Africa run upon her 9 April 1949 London departure. She arrived at Mombasa on 3 May. By this time successive refits at different times had resulted in a wide variance of Saloon berths on the "M"s: *Madura* (170), *Mantola* (189), *Matiana* (163), *Modasa* (177) and *Mulbera* (158).

Having all five "M"s on the East Africa run reduced the need for periodic voyages from London by cargo vessels. In 1949 these were confined to three, one by *Goalpara* (1943/7,278 grt), another by *Obra* (1946/5,695 grt) and the first of the post-war "C" class ships, *Carpentaria* (1949/7,268 grt), which left Middlesbrough on her maiden voyage on 29 April and London on 14 May for Mombasa (7 June) and Lindi (5 July) and thence to Bombay. She was not the first of the "C" class to visit East Africa as the wartime-built *Chyebassa* (1942/7,043 grt) called at Beira on 16 January from Australia. Other ships on the Australian run that year included *Ozarda* and *Pemba*. Bound for Scottish breakers after a quarter of century service, *Queda* (1925/7,766 grt) called at Mombasa on 13 October from Mauritius and Australia.

For a special Haj voyage direct from East Africa, *Vasna* arrived at Mombasa from Bombay on 27 August 1949 and sailed for Jeddah on 3 September. Returning to Mombasa on 2 November via Bombay, she made an additional East African voyage from Bombay on 8 February, calling at Mombasa and returning to India on the 20th.

With her Saloon berths increased from 116 to 152, additional public bathrooms and other accommodation improvements, *Khandalla* resumed six-weekly Bombay-East Africa service on 5 October 1949.

The coal-burning "A"s proved a nuisance on the East African coast where the fuel was full of clinker and difficult to obtain. When Durban closed its coaling facilities, *Amra* and *Aronda* bunkered at Lourenço Marques where the coal ports were inacessible from the quay at low tide and had to be labourously bunkered by coolies one basket at a time. On 26 August 1949 the *Natal Mercury* reported that BI was planning to convert both ships to oil-firing and had already sent engineers to survey *Aronda*'s engine room and bunkers whilst the ship was at Lourenço Marques as the bunkers were always half-filled and inaccessible during Durban turnrounds. The conversion was expected to commence with *Aronda* in January 1950 and prefabrication of much of the new exhaust pipe fittings already completed. This "scoop" proved correct when in September a £250,000 contract was let to James Brown, Durban, to convert both to oil fuel, the largest such job carried out in a South African yard.

Aronda sailed from Mombasa for Durban and drydocking on 13 March 1950. The *Natal Mercury* of the 30th reported that work in stripping *Aronda*'s coal handling apparatus was already well underway and the mechanical stokers removed. It was added, "The famed Black Hole of Calcutta has nothing on *Aronda*'s boiler room and stokehold... At one point it was proposed to remove the funnel and pass the new parts down through the opening, but because Durban has no cranes of sufficient height, the new equipment will be passed through the stokehold via one of the hatches and then through the bulkhead."

The post-war sponsored passage scheme whereby intending passengers

136

from Britain had to be endorsed by the Colonial Office and those from India by the Kenya authorities, ended on 27 January 1950, and BI resumed normal commercial trading.

The Britain-bound *Madura* made an unscheduled call at Malta in late January 1950 to land a suspected appendicitis case and make minor engine repairs. The venerable *Vasna* left Bombay on her last East African voyage on 30 January, bidding farewell to Mombasa on 20 February. After a spell back on the Madras-Singapore run, *Vasna* was sold to BISCO (British Iron & Steel Co.) for scrap on 2 April 1951 and broken up at Blyth after completing no fewer than 431 voyages.

On 25 March 1950 fire broke out in a cargo of hay aboard *Kola* at Mombasa causing minor damage.

From March 1950 onwards, *Kampala* resumed the direct Bombay-East African run partnered with *Khandalla*. Now alone on the Durban Mail, *Karanja* was programmed to leave Bombay on the 8th of even-numbered months and call at Marmagoa on the 9th (except June and August), Seychelles (14th), Mombasa (17-19th), Zanzibar (20th), Dar-es-Salaam (21st), Mozambique (23rd), Beira (25-26th), Lourenço Marques (28-29th) and arriving at Durban on the 30th. Northbound, she would sail from Durban on the 5th of odd-numbered months and call at Lourenço Marques (6th), Beira (8-9th), Mozambique (11th), Dar-es-Salaam (13th), Zanzibar (14th), Mombasa (14-17th), Seychelles (20th), Marmagoa (26th, except for May, July and September) and arrive at Bombay on the 26th or 27th.

The first of two East African coastal liners was launched by Mrs. W.J. Gordon, wife of the Director of Gray Dawes, BI's British agents, on 21 October 1949, at Henry Robb & Co.'s Leith yard as *Mombasa*. This 2,213-grt pocket-sized liner carried eight First Saloon (three double and two single cabins) with a sycamore-panelled lounge and dining saloon, lined in Australian Eucalyptus, shared by the officers, 16 Second Saloon (four 4-berth cabins) with a dining saloon, and 250 deck passengers. Three cargo holds, two forward worked by booms and one aft served by a pair of samson posts, had a capacity of 87,000 cu. ft. plus 1,873 cu. ft. reefer. Powered by two five-cylinder British Polar diesels of 1,600 bhp, the twin-screw *Mombasa* had a service speed of 12.5 knots and made 13.8 on trials. Her contract price of £295,297 represented good value considering the 1922-built *Dumra* cost only £12,798 less.

With her rigging coated with icicles and carrying a cargo of motorcars and cement, *Mombasa* (Captain Robert Trimble) sailed from London on 2 February 1950. A Force 9-10 gale in the Bay of Biscay on the 5th forced her to heave to off Ushant for 28 hours. Another blow was encountered south of the Red Sea, but she still averaged 11.2 knots out. Her maiden call at Dar-es-Salaam from Mombasa was on 16 March.

Making her first call at Lourenço Marques on 30 June 1950, *Kola* began to sail to Durban from Mombasa in between her Kenyan coastal runs and occasionally even farther afield; on 19 September she arrived at Durban from Matadi. Making what may have been her only East African voyage, *Masula*, the only survivor of the two cargo only "M"s, called at Lourenço Marques on 28 September en route from East Africa to Australia. *Kola*, which arrived at Bombay from Mombasa on 12 February 1951, was transferred to a Chittagong-Penang run and sold in 1952.

"The weather was comparatively calm and I was sitting in my stateroom reading. Suddenly the ship seemed to stop, shudder and lift up and down violently. It was so violent that I was almost sick, but very soon the liner settled down again." So a passenger described *Karanja*'s encounter with what the *Natal Mercury* called "a miniature tidal wave" on 28 August 1950 whilst on passage between Lourenço Marques and Durban. Undamaged the vessel then underwent her periodic fumigation upon arrival which entailed the ship's company going ashore, but instead of being put up in hotels as before, the officers were quartered aboard the still refitting *Aronda* at the adjoining quay.

East African port congestion made it difficult even for the five "M"s to maintain the monthly Home Line service and prompted the chartering of the new Bibby liner *Leicestershire*. Homewards on her maiden voyage from Rangoon, she had collided with the British tanker *Regent Jaguar* in the Suez Canal and reached Liverpool on 11 April 1950 with her bows stove in. Repaired, she entered BI service making her maiden call at Mombasa on 9 September. The 8,922-grt, 14.5-knot ship carried 76 one-class passengers in one-, two- and three-berth cabins and two special staterooms with private bath. Among her amenities was an open-air swimming pool, the only one in the BI fleet at the time. Unfortunately, as she did not carry the minimum 100 passengers required for priority berthing, *Leicestershire* was herself often held up for weeks, especially at Mombasa.

> "South African history was made yesterday [6 September 1950] when oil was pumped into the *Aronda*, the first ship to be converted from coal to oil-burning in a Union port. Standing by was Mr. D.S. Beattie, engineer superintendent of the British India Line, who flew from India last month, when the conversion started. 'Durban engineers have done a fine job of work, which could not be bettered anywhere'.
>
> *(Natal Mercury)*

Shortly after 9.15 a.m. on 13 September *Aronda* left port for engine trials. A fault in the oil feed system resulted in the vessel having to stop just after clearing the harbour, but this was soon corrected. For the balance of the day *Aronda* ran her paces one mile off the Durban coast, chalking up 50 miles altogether. However when the ship was ready to return to her berth, the weather began to deteriorate and a 40 mph wind came up. *Aronda's* berth at M Shed had been taken temporarily by *Nelson Star*, but as that ship's engines were shut down and port officials did not want to risk moving her by tugs in the wind, the BI liner was forced to spend the night riding the storm outside the harbour.

Aronda resumed Durban-Mombasa sailings on 21 September 1950 and had some condenser trouble, unrelated to her conversion, upon leaving Lourenço Marques. *Amra*, after her final voyage burning coal, 20 August-3 September, arrived at the James Brown shipyard on the 15th for drydocking and conversion to oil fuel.

The last of the original "K"s, *Khandalla* made her final Bombay-East Africa trip from 15 December 1950-16 January 1951. A true Indian Ocean stalwart after 229 voyages, she left Calcutta on 26 October and reached London on 4 December. Sold to BISCO nine days later, *Khandalla* was broken up at Troon.

Santhia (Captain C. J. Feller), the third and final vessel of the "S" class, launched on 1 June 1950 at Barclay, Curle, by Mrs. J.B. Currie, carried passengers from London to Mombasa and cargo on to Bombay on her delivery trip that November. Although it had been planned to have *Tairea* return for one African trip, *Santhia* instead made two voyages from Bombay to Dar-es-Salaam, 23 January and 4 March 1951, before joining the Calcutta-Yokohama service.

The Durban-Mombasa run proved short-lived and the "A"s were reassigned. *Aronda* returned to Durban from Mombasa on 18 February 1951 and she sailed for Bombay on the 23rd via Lourenço Marques, Beira, Mozambique, Dar-es-Salaam, Zanzibar, Mombasa, Seychelles and Marmagoa. She then replaced *Shirala* on the Karachi-Chittagong berth on which she carried 126 Saloon passengers.

Leaving Durban on 31 March 1951, after conversion to oil and now with 210 Saloon berths, *Amra* commenced fortnightly Bombay-Dar-es-Salaam service on 27 April. All this rather spoiled the plans of two of *Amra's* engineers, Edwin Dent and Michael McAnespie, whose wives had only just arrived from England to resettle in Durban to be close to their husbands. "It cost us about every spare penny we had to bring our wives out. Now we have to find the fares back to England and in any case, they cannot get passage for several weeks", lamented one of the officers.

There remained a demand for a Durban-Mombasa cargo service, however, and after a refit in India, *Sofala* arrived at Durban on 10 March 1951 and began to ply the coastal run in place of the "A"s. Her first arrival at Durban from Mombasa was on 18 April.

A cyclone off the East African coast caused *Karanja* to be six hours late in arriving at Durban on 2 March 1951 and was also encountered by *Aronda* en route to Beira where it was too rough to embark the pilot.

Kampala rejoined the Bombay-Durban run effective 9 August 1951. Henceforth the "K"s sailed from Bombay on the 8th or 9th of every alternating month, taking 21 days to Durban via Mombasa, Zanzibar, Dar-es-Salaam, Mozambique, Beira and Lourenço Marques. The Indian ports of Mormugao and Porebunder were served during the September/May fair season and Bedibunder during the monsoon. *Kampala* also called at Karachi and *Karanja* at the Seychelles.

The Colonial Office's high hopes for the groundnut scheme in Tanganyika literally turned to dust in the sun-baked soil of the territory's southern region which proved unsuitable for large-scale mechanised cultivation. By 1949 the project was threatening to exhaust the finances of the Overseas Food Corporation and the next year the scheme was shelved in favour of a more realistic six-year £6 million programme. The construction of the deep-water port at Mtwara and the connecting railway would continue under the auspices of the East African Railways and Harbours Administration.

From the perspective of BI and other lines, the cancellation of the groundnut scheme was in large measure welcome. The project had over-taxed the already inadequate port and rail facilities of East Africa and the ensuing harbour congestion cost lines an enormous sum in idle ships riding at anchor awaiting a berth. In planning schedules, BI programmed 28 days for working cargo along the East African coast and often even this proved inadequate. Fortunately for BI, the renewal and expansion of its African fleet ultimately paid off due to the continued expansion of the more well-established East African exports. Still, the project's collapse came at an awkward time when the company's newbuilding programme was just hitting its stride and ironically the vessel named after the "Groundnut Port" would be the most effected by events.

Mombasa's intended running mate, the 2,629-grt, 298 ft. (oa) by 46 ft. *Mtwara*, was launched by Mrs. P.G. Knott at Henry Robb's yard on 29 August 1950. After averaging 15.31 knots on trials in the Firth of Forth, the ship was commissioned on 14 February 1951 under Captain F. A. Spenceley. A twin-screw vessel, *Mtwara* was powered by a pair of Kincaid-Polar diesels developing 4,000 shp. The 26 First Saloon passengers were accommodated in 10 two-berth and two three-berth cabins on Bridge Deck amidships with the English walnut-panelled lounge forward and dining saloon below on Upper Deck. The 40 Second Saloon passengers had 10 four-berth cabins on Upper Deck and their dining saloon aft Bridge Deck and lounge aft on Upper Deck. As many as 250 deck passengers were sheltered in No. 1 and No. 2 'tween decks. Two forward holds and one aft had a 85,646 cu. ft. capacity.

Unfortunately, the failed groundnut scheme left the largest and finest East African coastal liner ever built without a trade. Instead *Mtwara* operated Karachi-Muscat-Bundar Abbas-Shahjah-Dubai (starting 31 March 1951) and

140

on Bay of Bengal services in between spells of inactivity at Calcutta until sold in March 1953 to Denis Freres, Saigon, for French Indo-China coastal runs for which she was renamed *Ville de Haiphong*. The vessel changed hands again three years later, becoming *Navarino* of Empresa Maritima del Estado for Valparaiso-based services. In 1991 she was still in service with the Chilean Navy.

Recalling her war service, *Mantola*, whilst on passage from Aden to Port Sudan on 25 September 1951, was invited to take up convoy station with the Royal Netherlands Navy 1st Minesweeping Flotilla on an exercise, her lady passengers lounging on the Promenade Deck providing an unexpected diversion for the Dutch sailors.

As a replacement for *Thika*, the 346-grt, 121 ft. by 33.5 ft. tug *Arusha* was launched by Mrs. G.G. Robertson at Henry Robb on 17 August 1951. Two days after arriving at Mombasa on 2 December, *Arusha* was commissioned. Powered by a triple expansion reciprocating engine (built by Messrs. White Engineering Co. Ltd.) developing 800 ihp at 180 rpm supplied by a single oil-fired boiler, *Arusha* achieved 12 knots on trials, but at 130 rpms and towing a loaded lighter, the normal speed was 6.5 knots.

Arusha was joined by four new 10,000 cu. ft. capacity, 148-grt, 110 ft. long barges, *Taa, Taza, Tenga,* and *Tewa*, built in sections by J.S. Watson and assembled at Mombasa by African Marine. Each had two hatches with a derrick and diesel winch. A four-man crew was assigned to each barge.

The tug *Arusha* was a powerful sea-going tug supposed to be capable of towing up to three lighters in reasonable weather. When she first arrived she was not performing satisfactorily, but the trouble was discovered by a new chief engineer who found that baffle coils had been placed in the boiler tubes to reduce fuel consumption during her delivery voyage to East Africa When these had been removed the tug's efficiency increased.

However, against the strong south-easterly trade winds and with sometimes a five-knot northerly set to the current, *Arusha* sometimes had difficulty in making any headway at all when towing full lighters. It was disappointing for the crew to have Chale Point lighthouse abeam at sunset and to find it still abeam at breakfast the next morning.

The conception of the tug and lighter service on paper was a good one; the idea being that while the tug was at sea towing lighters, other lighters were being quickly loaded ready for the tug to pick them up on arrival and make an immediate turn round. Fortunately for the crew, this ideal was seldom achieved**

Whilst BI had renewed its other African routes with new tonnage by 1951,

141

the Home Line remained in the capable if crusty hands of the five "M"s whose age was exceeded on the East Africa coast only by Companhia Nacional de Navegacao's 1906-built *Nyassa* and Union-Castle's grand old *Llanstephan Castle* of 1914. Like the "M"s, their very reliability and long-standing popularity ensured their survival until they were thoroughly superannuated, but whilst these veterans ran with much younger fleetmates, the entire BI service was in the hands of old-timers. Indeed, renewal of the Home Line was a generation overdue considering BI had yet even to respond to the 1936- and 1938-built Union-Castle intermediates and that line had plans for three more such vessels, the *Kenya Castle* class of 1951-2. Post-war inflation in shipbuilding prices, full order books, labour unrest and steel shortages precluded ordering new tonnage as early as was perhaps desirable.

The crowning glories of BI's post-war programme were first hinted at by Sir William Currie, sailing from Southampton aboard *Capetown Castle* in May 1948 on a fact-finding visit to Africa. His forecast of an eventual direct 17- to 18-day U.K.-East Africa service was strengthened by the then still promising groundnut scheme.

The announcement of a £3 million order for two 14,400-grt liners (to have been named *Kenya* and *Karatina*) from Barclay, Curle & Co. was made by the yard's chairman at the 5 July 1948 launch of *Carpentaria* (1949/7,268 grt). The final contract prices for *Kenya* worked out to £1,909,168 and for her sister, £2,062,195. Laid down in January 1950, the first ship was christened *Kenya* at 2.15 p.m. on 28 November by Lady Currie. Trials in the Firth of Clyde on 11 July 1951 recorded a top speed of 19.16 knots and *Kenya* was proudly handed over at noon the next day— the 58th BI vessel completed since 1939, the 63rd ship built for the line by Barclay, Curle and the first company flagship commissioned for a non-Indian route.

After a delivery trip from Gourock with 300 guests, including Sir William and Lady Currie, *Kenya* (Captain D.R.P. Gun-Cunninghame) sailed from Tilbury on 25 August 1951 for Suez, Aden, Mombasa (September 13), Tanga, Dar-es-Salaam (21st), Zanzibar and Beira, arriving on the 27th. Between London and Port Said she averaged 17.32 knots at 119.5 rpm. Among the 273 passengers were the Earl of Inchcape, Director of Mackinnon, Mackenzie; L.S.P. Bourne, Director of Gray Dawes & Co.; and the Hon. Simon Brooke Mackay. The Calcutta head office wired congratulations to *Kenya* upon her maiden arrival at Aden on 8 September:

MANAGING AGENTS SEND GREETINGS AND WELCOME TO COMPANYS NEWEST AND LOVELIEST BABY ON HER FIRST APPEARANCE IN EASTERN WATERS STOP ALL GOOD FORTUNE TO KENYA HER COMMANDER SHIPS COMPANY AND PASSENGERS

A large crowd of early risers were on hand at Mombasa as *Kenya* made her

East African debut. On what came to be known as "BI Sunday", 16 September 1951, the new flagship and her BI sisters occupied every deep water slip in Kilindini Harbour:

Ship	Commander	Gross Tonnage
Mantola	Capt. R.R. Stone	9,065
Mombasa	Capt. R. Trimble	2,213
Kenya	Capt. D.G. Gun-Cunninghame	14,440
Karanja	Capt. C.B. Mitchell	10,294
Modasa	Capt. W.A. Busby	9,070
Tabora	Mr. A.B. Stephens	390
Kampala	Capt. C.R. Polkinghorne	10,304
Sofala	Capt.W.R.K. Clark	1,031
(on slipway)		
		56,807

It was a unique event in the history of both the company and port and doubly fitting that the Senior BI Commander that day was Captain R. Trimble in *Mombasa*.

During the maiden call at Dar-es-Salaam, a sundowner party was held aboard for the Governor, Sir Edward Twining, who expressed his hope of seeing *Kenya* joined by a *Tanganyika* before too long. Chief Engineer Hide commented on *Kenya*'s performance to the *Tanganyika Standard*: "She is a sixteen-knot ship... an ideal speed on the East African run and she behaved extremely well in a spell of bad weather for four hours in the Bay of Biscay when the seas were very high." *Kenya*'s homeward maiden trip commenced from Beira on 1 October.

With her husband, the retiring Governor of Uganda, Lady Hathorn Hall sailed on the homeward leg of *Kenya*'s maiden voyage and at 2.15 p.m. on 15 January 1952 she christened that vessel's sister ship, originally to have been named *Karatina*, as *Uganda*. The launch was successful despite strong wind gusts which jammed the hull against the slipway for 20 minutes. Trevor Philpott contributed an eloquent birth announcement of the last BI African liner built to the *Picture Post:*

> It is *Uganda*'s birthday. The latest addition to the British India family is a bonny girl of 15,000 tons, a passenger liner for the East Africa run, and she'll slide massively into the river at fifteen minutes past two this afternoon. Now, propped on the river bank, she is just so much metal, an unsanctified iron cathedral turned upside down. It's the curtsy into the dirty Clyde water that will give her a life of her own...
>
> The chaplain ends the service:..."God bless this our ship, on her all lawful occasions of the sea."... The "ready" signal is

passed up to the Chairman. Nervously, the lady-sponsor brings the hammer down on to the knife edge. The string parts. There is a crack like the thrashing of a tremendous whip as the wire rope flays loose. The champagne bottle shatters against the ship's side, spattering the guests. Astonishing fast, *Uganda* (she has a name now) slides away. A thousand tons of chain, which rein the ship to a stop within a few ft. of the water's edge, heave over and unravel in smoking pyres of dust. Not until the bow dips into the water do the watchers find the breath to cheer.

Tonight in an ornate Glasgow hotel there will be carnations and gin and French for the ladies, and native Scotch and Havana cigars for the gentlemen. There will be talk of crippling taxes, of ultimate stagnation for industry and disaster for the nation; talk of the industrial peace on Clydeside, and banter about the days when the manager's hard bowler was a sensible precaution against the rivets falling, rather too accurately, from the staging; talk of honour, which clinches the building and buying of a great ship with a word alone; talk of rearmament and steel shortages; and of Clyde craftsmanship which still out-produces America and builds 46 per cent of Britain's ships.

But the most important lady of them all won't be heeding a word. *Uganda* will lie quietly in the downstream darkness, drinking in the ecstasy of water lapping her sides.

After fitting-out, *Uganda* made 19.52 knots on the Skelmorlie mile on 15 July 1952 and at 11.15 a.m. on the 17th, BI commissioned its 450th and largest-to-date vessel. She would sadly also prove to be its last ship built for the African run and the final BI passenger vessel constructed for commercial service. No finer British liners were ever built for the East African trade than the "BI Sisters", *Kenya* and *Uganda*.

> *But you should see two sisters pass in style*
> *No farther than a fraction of a mile,*
> *The latest, swiftest of a splendid line,*
> *As like bottles of a noble wine.*
>
> A. P. Herbert

Uganda (Captain C.R. Polkinghorne) sailed from Tilbury on her maiden voyage on 2 August 1952. In what must have been a splendid sight, she passed *Kenya* in the Mediterranean on the 9th, symbolising a fabulous if final era for the BI African run. Making a noticeably quiet entrance with nary a signal flag flying, *Uganda* docked at Berth 4, Kilindini, at 10.00 a.m. on the 19th after a 16-day 12-hour passage at 17.5 knots. Mr. H. H. Robinson, Managing Director of Smith Mackenzie, was on the quayside to welcome the son and daughter-in-law of Sir William Currie who were passengers aboard.

Despite her understated arrival, the popularity that was to characterise *Uganda*'s 35-year-long BI career had already been established judging from a maiden voyage passenger quoted in the *Mombasa Times*, "In spite of the fact that we have had a very hot passage through the Red Sea and were knocked about a bit in the monsoon south of Aden, I can safely say that I have never had such a comfortable trip. They have looked after us very well." The *Mombasa Times*' Port Reporter stated "There was no doubting the feelings of her passengers about the new ship. I spoke to several and they were all unstinting in their praise of her comfort, amenities and food."

Arriving at Beira on 2 September 1952, *Uganda* sailed for home three days later.

There were no two finer ships of their size in the British Merchant Navy than *Kenya* and *Uganda* which at 14,430 grt, 539 ft. by 71 ft., were intermediates dimensionally, but built and operated as line flagships and Royal Mail ships of the proudest order. These were truly "Best of British" with perfect proportions, graceful hulls with a pleasing sheer, raked stems and cruiser sterns and enough samson posts to impart a purposeful quality. There was a marked similarity in overall appearance to Burns Philp's Barclay Curle-built *Bulolo* of 1938.

The principal distinction between the two sisters was their funnels, *Kenya's* short motor ship-like one proving inadequate when steaming into a head wind. Considerable guarantee work had to be done by Barclay, Curle to rework her flues to correct the problem of smuts falling on the after decks. Consequently no chances were taken with *Uganda's* funnel which was a full 12 feet higher. This splendid smokestack later became a cherished trademark when its riveted construction, historic livery and polished brass steam whistles stood in proud distinction against the prevailing plethora of rainbow-painted exhaust pipes, lattice-work, ski-jump and winged monstrosities of funnels.

The accommodation for 150 First and 123 Tourist (Uganda 167 First and 133 Tourist) was superior to *Kenya Castle's,* but not up to Lloyd Triestino's new *Africa* and *Europa*. The chief failing, common to British tropical liners of the period, was the lack of air-conditioning (except in the dining saloon, hairdresser's and hospital) and staterooms with private facilities. All cabins, however, were outside ones. Each ship had eight de luxe twin-bedded staterooms and six de luxe single bed cabins with private bath and toilet and four 4-berth cabins with toilet only. The remaining First Class cabins, with washbasins only, totalled 30 single-berth, 74 two-berth and 72 three-berth in *Kenya* and in *Uganda,* 30, 66 and 75 cabins respectively. Whereas both ships had eight Tourist Class two-berth cabins each, there was considerable variance in the allotment of three- and four-berth rooms; *Kenya* had 39 three-berth and 56 four-berth compared to *Uganda's* nine three-berth and 92 four-berth.

Each ship had five passenger decks: Boat, Promenade, A, B and C with

First Class occupying the uppermost two and the forward two-thirds of the others with Tourist aft. First Class deck space was on the Boat Deck as was the children's playroom, whilst the public rooms were on the Promenade Deck: the circular drawing room, card room, writing room, entrance hall, smoking room, cocktail bar and the veranda ball room. Aft were the pool and open deck space. A wide promenade was glazed forward and covered aft. The imposing 176-seat dining saloon with a two-deck-high dome was forward on C Deck.

First Class cabins, on A Deck and forward on B Deck, were generously proportioned and fitted with dressers, wardrobes and washbasins.

The Tourist Class smoking room and lounge-bar were aft on A Deck together with the children's playroom, open deck space and pool. The 126-seat dining saloon was aft of the galley on C Deck. Tourist cabins, arranged on the Bibby system, were aft on B Deck.

Both ships boasted remarkably elaborate decor and artwork and no liners of comparable size were so well fitted out. Sir William Currie, indulging in his personal affection for BI, had ensured that *Kenya* and *Uganda* were in no way inferior to the larger ships like *Himalaya* and *Chusan* he had commissioned for P&O. Whereas BI's other post-war liners had all been built for the Eastern trades and adequately decorated, *Kenya* and *Uganda* as crack Home Line mailships radiated a classic "Ocean Liner Odeon" style. Union-Castles' new *Kenya Castle* trio which emulated rather too much the migrant ship *Bloemfontein Castle* and were very plainly furnished, looked dowdy by comparison and BI had clearly stolen a march on its old rival.

Kenya's dining saloon had murals by C. Cameron Baillie of Britannia and Aphrodite while her sister had representations of London and Mombasa by R.M.D. Robertson ("Rob"), the latter panel is now in *Canberra*'s Ocean Room. Joseph Leigh Pemberton contributed a large oil painting in the romantic style, "The Grand Tour", to *Kenya*'s Drawing Room, and another of a French 19th-century hunting scene in *Uganda*'s. Both vessels featured beautiful marquetry work by Albert Dunn, a map of Kenya in that ship and one of Uganda birdlife in the other. A depiction of a BI ship on Kenya's map was composed of over 50 different pieces of hard wood whilst a single bird in the *Uganda* panel used 122 pieces.

Uganda is still remembered for her smoking room, panelled in curly figured aspen and olive ash with a carved panel showing the use of tobacco over the ages and a landscape mural by P. A. Staynes of African wildlife with Uganda's Murchison Falls as a background. The same room in *Kenya* was decorated by an oil painting "Mount Kenya" by Strom Gold, and the aforementioned marquetry map. Fine figured Queensland Maple graced the writing rooms of both ships whilst different varieties were employed in the drawing rooms, ice flame birch-cross banded with ash burr and prima vera in

146

Kenya and mottled Canadian maple cross-banded with prima vera in *Uganda*. Contrasting effects were employed in the cocktail bars; that in *Kenya* lined in figured aspen like the smoking room whilst *Uganda*'s was more modern and covered with grey-green leather.

The decoration of the Tourist Class rooms was identical in both ships. The dining saloons were panelled in weathered sycamore with elm cross-banding and Australian walnut accents; ivory sycamore and eucalyptus burr lined the lounges which were further decorated with circular mirror panels surrounded by British and African floral motifs and the smoking rooms featured panelling of Nigerian cherry contrasting with quilted maple.

Twin-screw ships powered by Parsons single reduction-geared 12,300 shp turbines supplied by three Babcock & Wilcox boilers, *Kenya* and *Uganda* maintained a 16.5-knot service speed. Each had five cargo holds (two forward, one forward of the funnel casing and two aft) having a capacity of 390,000 cubic ft. of general cargo and 25,000 cubic ft. of reefer space. Cargo handling equipment comprised six eight-ton and eight five-ton derricks and one 30-ton heavy derrick at the foremast.

"Well-bred, very well-built, well-found and well-run," (*The Patient Talks*, C.M. Squarey), *Kenya* and *Uganda* quickly endeared themselves to officers, crew and passengers and with their advent, BI's Africa run achieved its apogee.

Mantola reopened the post-war East African Home Line upon her departure from Liverpool on 21 March 1946.

A. Duncan collection, courtesy Charles Dragonette

Landaura sailed from London on her maiden voyage 5 October 1946 to Beira. A fixture on the Home Line thereafter, she carried the first shipment of agricultural equipment for the Groundnut Scheme.

A. Duncan collection

Placed on the India-Africa run during the war, *Shirala* remained a mainstay of the service until February 1947.   *P&O*

The handsome *Amra,* built in 1938 for the Rangoon-Calcutta run,was transferred to the Durban Mail in February 1947 and is shown leaving Durban with its famous Bluff in the background.   *P&O*

Also photographed against Durban's Bluff is the diminutive *Kilwa*, formerly *Kiungchow* of China Navigation, purchased by BI in October 1946 to resume the Mombasa-Mikindani coastal service.   *A. Duncan collection*

Shown in Table Bay, *Palikonda* inaugurated BI's new Australia-East Africa run in May 1947. The massive and unattractive bridge structure of the wartime-built "P"s is shown to advantage in this photo.

A. Duncan collection, courtesy Charles Dragonette

Photographed in the English Channel and looking typically immaculate, *Matiana* resumed U.K.-East Africa sailings in June 1947.

Fotoflite

The graceful *Tairea* was back on the Durban Mail in June 1947. By then she was sole survivor of the three-funnelled "T"s; *Takliwa* was destroyed by fire in October 1945 and *Talamba*, which never sailed to Africa, was bombed and sunk in 1943 as a hospital ship.

P&O

A pristine *Kampala* on trials in August 1947. She and *Karanja* were the largest British liners ever built for an India-based trade and were essentially updated versions of the pre-war "K"'s.

P&O

When *Karanja* was delivered in October 1948, BI was painting its lifeboats white instead of black (compare with photo of *Kampala*). In this view, *Karanja*, still flying her builder's houseflag, runs her trials on a murky Scottish autumn day.

P&O

153

Not until *Mulbera* and *Madura* (shown above) resumed East African sailings in March and April 1949 respectively did the Home Line revert to its pre-war monthly frequency.
A. Duncan collection, courtesy Charles Dragonette

Smallest of BI's post-war liners, the 2,213-grt *Mombasa* is shown on trials in January 1950. By March she was at work on the East Africa coastal run.
P&O

Her funnel repainted in BI livery but retaining the Bibby Line gold-banded hull, the chartered *Leicestershire* made her first sailing to Beira in August 1950.

A. Duncan collection

Of all Britain's post-war liners, few had more pleasing lines than the "BI Sisters" *Kenya* and *Uganda*. Here, proving the point, a glistening *Kenya* is captured in the English Channel.

Fotoflite, Charles Dragonette collection

155

An evocative night time view of *Kenya* at London prior to departing on her maiden voyage on 25 August 1951. *P&O*

On full speed trials, *Uganda* makes a fine sight. Surely one of the most handsome of Britain's post-war liners, her classic profile was dominated by that tremendous funnel, 12 ft. higher than *Kenya*'s.

Laurence Dunn collection

Uganda, the magnificent! Of all **BI**'s Africa ships, none was more beloved than her, in both her mailship and schoolship roles. Here, proud and pristine, she is photographed on her delivery voyage in July 1952.

P&O

Uganda, alongside at Mombasa, possibly on her maiden voyage. Her first arrival was remarkably understated, all the more so considering the dedicated following the ship would attract. *James L. Shaw collection*

At the conclusion of her maiden voyage, *Uganda* proceeded to Rotterdam where she is shown leaving dry dock. *Laurence Dunn collection*

For passengers, the voyage out to "British East" often began with the first sight of one of the "M"s in London Docks. *Mulbera* models the distinctive front superstructure and teakwood bridge of the class.   *P&O*

More than anything else, the Suez Canal thrust BI and Britain into East Africa and except from 1956-1958 and from 1967 onwards when it was closed, the canal transit was integral to the voyage out to Africa. Here, *Mantola* passes outbound.   *P&O*

At sea— *Kampala* makes a fine sight steaming off an unidentified coast in the early '50s. *P&O*

BI interiors ranged from the simple and homely; *Kampala*'s First Class lounge where the forced-draught ball vents are supplemented by ceiling fans and the fireplace is strictly ornamental to...					*P&O*

. . . the elegant and imposing; *Uganda*'s First Class dining saloon with its two-storey central section and decorations of Mombasa's Fort Jesus (this particular panel is now aboard *Canberra*) and air-conditioned comfort.					*P&O*

This *Kampala* First Class cabin was typical of BI accommodation. Note the window shutter and ceiling fans mounted directly over the berths. The upholstered chair is a comparative luxury in this 1959 view; normally wicker furnishings prevailed. *P&O*

Mombasa scenes. The island port, centered on Kilindini Harbour, was the hub of BI's Africa routes. Here the old and new of the Home Line meet in 1953 as *Modasa* (left) arrives to join *Uganda* (right) alongside. *P&O*

Mombasa scenes. On exceptionally busy days the liners would work cargo at anchor. Here *Karanja* is attended by one of BI's barges while just visible to the left, *Kenya* lies alongside.

Author's collection

Mombasa scenes. Amra underway in the harbour, 1953. Two years previously she had been converted to oil fuel and assigned to the Bombay-Mombasa service.   *P&O*

163

The little *Mombasa* was the largest vessel able to dock alongside at Zanzibar where she is shown circa. 1960.   *W.M.L. Hall collection*

Until completion of deep water quays in the mid-'50s, the liners had to anchor in the deep, protected harbour of Dar-es-Salaam as was *Madura* pictured here.   *P&O*

Durban was usually the southernmost port for BI African ships. Here *Amra* heads out to sea, past the landmark Bluff guarding the entrance to the port.   *P&O*

A brand new *Karanja* looks especially radiant amid the clutter and bustle of one of Bombay's harbour basins.   *Steamship Historical Society of America*

8. BEIRA-BOUND BY BI

You may be travelling to East Africa to take up your duties there or returning home for a well-earned spell of leave. You may wish simply to enjoy a long holiday. In every case a pleasant period of enjoyment and relaxation stretches before you from the moment the steward takes your hand luggage and shows you to your cabin.   BI brochure, circa 1958

Lying in the roadstead of an East African harbour, framed by spice-scented and palm-fringed beaches, and crowded by dhows, a BI liner with her Red Duster hanging limp in the humidity, summed up the well-ordered world she and her fleetmates helped to maintain. "Lifeline of the Commonwealth" was more credo than motto and BI ships still served as a vital link between British East and Mother Country well into the post-war era.

The commissioning of *Kenya* and *Uganda* in 1951-52, marked the completion of BI's post-war renewal programme. They came on the scene as the King's African Rifles were rounding up Mau Mau terrorists in Kenya and after the groundnut scheme had failed. Nevertheless, 55,000 white settlers called Kenya home; Uganda was, in the words of Winston Churchill, "The Pearl of Africa"; East African trade burgeoned and BI was ready to reap the benefits with a fine, largely new fleet.

Despite the groundnut set-back, high sisal prices sent Tanganyika's trade value soaring to a record £85 million in 1952 whilst Uganda enjoyed a boom market for its coffee and cotton, reaching a peak in 1955. Everywhere road, rail, harbour and communication facilities were improved. On the political front, important first steps were taken towards increasing African participation in colonial government and economics.

A Golden Age of ships and services to Africa had dawned. Union-Castle's fabled Round Africa route employed three ships sailing via the Cape and three via Suez to all the principal East African ports. For this, the one-class, 17,000-grt *Rhodesia Castle, Kenya Castle* and *Braemar Castle* were built in 1951-52. A separate emigrant run to Beira via the Cape was maintained by the new *Bloemfontein Castle*. Also serving Lourenço Marques and Beira via the Cape were Ellerman's *City of Port Elizabeth, City of Exeter* and *City of Durban,* delivered in 1952-54 and like the BI ships known for their Goanese staff.

The Messageries Maritimes' 1952-3-built *Ferdinand de Lesseps, Jean Laborde, La Bourdonnaise* and *Pierre Loti* sailed from Marseilles to Madagascar and Mauritius via Mombasa and Dar-es-Salaam. Companhia Colonial and Companhia Nacional served Portuguese West and East Africa via the Cape with the new *Imperio, Patria, Angola* and *Moçambique*. Calling at

Mombasa, Dar-es-Salaam and Beira, Lloyd Triestino's *Africa* and *Europa* were air-conditioned and at 19.5 knots, the fastest ships on the East African run. Although they sailed from Trieste, rail connections were offered to/from the U.K. and *Africa* and *Europa* were the toughest competition BI had.

Eighty years after it introduced steamship services to East Africa, the pinnacle of BI's African ships and services had been achieved. Once alone and now among many competitors, BI remained unique in offering dedicated services to East Africa which ran the gamut from express mail, coastal, towage and cargo, whereas those of other companies were though routed to other destinations. And BI's fleet was, by far, the largest trading in East African waters. Indeed, 1952 saw the number of BI East African vessels reach its greatest number, 15 in all, excluding the chartered *Leicestershire*, barges and occasional cargo ships:

Uganda	*Karanja*
Kenya	*Kampala*
Madura	*Amra*
Modasa	*Mombasa*
Mantola	*Kilwa*
Mulbera	*Kola*
Arusha	*Sofala*
Tabora	

With a combined gross tonnage of 102,055 this group alone was almost three times the tonnage of the *entire* BI fleet in 1873 (35,422 grt).

Now at its zenith, BI's Home Line had fortnightly sailings by *Kenya, Uganda, Leicestershire, Madura, Modasa, Mantola* and *Mulbera* calling outwards at Port Said, Port Sudan, Aden, Mombasa, Tanga, Zanzibar, Dar-es-Salaam, Lindi ("M"s only) and Beira. Homewards, *Kenya* and *Uganda* omitted Port Sudan and made occasional Malta calls; all ships stopped at Marseilles and Gibraltar. In those days, a First Class two-berth cabin to Mombasa cost £130 (£95 in the "M"s).

True to Sir William Currie's prediction, BI now offered a direct Britain to East Africa passage in 17 days. To Mombasa, at least, for *Kenya* and *Uganda* spent five days there working cargo, another two at Tanga and three at Dar-es-Salaam, thus only reaching Beira 13 days after arriving at Mombasa. The full voyage took 66 days with a two-week turnaround. The ageing "M"s, good in their dotage for only 11.75 knots, plodded the 6,798 nautical miles between London and Mombasa in 27 days. Averaging four months and four days, a round voyage in the "M"s was one of the longest of any liner.

Representative of a voyage in *Uganda* is this 1953 itinerary:

28 April	sail LONDON
7 May	call Port Said
9 May	call Port Sudan

167

11-12 May	call Aden
16-21 May	call Mombasa
21-22 May	call Tanga
22-23 May	call Zanzibar
23-26 May	call Dar-es-Salaam
29 May	arr. BEIRA
2 June	dep. BEIRA
5-6 June	call Dar-es-Salaam
6-7 June	call Zanzibar
7-8 June	call Tanga
9-14 June	call Mombasa
18 June	call Aden
22 June	call Port Said
24 June	call Malta
26-27 June	call Marseilles
29 June	call Gibraltar
3 July	arr. LONDON

Uganda would sail again for East Africa on 25 July after drydocking.

Typical of a voyage for the "M"s is another itinerary from 1953, for *Modasa*:

3 June	sail LONDON
15-16 June	call Port Said
19-20 June	call Port Sudan
23 June	call Aden
30 June-6 July	call Mombasa
7 July	call Tanga
8 July	call Zanzibar
9-12 July	call Dar-es-Salaam
14-16 July	call Lindi
20 July	arr. BEIRA
23 July	dep. BEIRA
28-30 July	call Dar-es-Salaam
31 July	call Zanzibar
1-2 August	call Tanga
3-8 August	call Mombasa
14 August	call Aden
17-18 August	call Port Sudan
21-22 August	call Port Said
28-30 August	call Marseilles
1 September	call Gibraltar
7 September	arr. LONDON

After making the rounds of the northern European ports for cargo and loading at Middlesbrough or Sunderland, *Modasa* would sail again from London on 10 October.

Yet East Africa could now be reached in 16 *hours,* not 17 days. Whilst *Uganda* was being groomed for her maiden voyage, BOAC's de Havilland Comet 1 *G-ALYP* thundered off from Heathrow on 2 May 1952 with 30 passengers for Rome, Cairo, Khartoum (Sudan), Entebbe (Uganda), Livingstone (Rhodesia) and Johannesburg to inaugurate the world's first jet passenger service. Although the Comet 1s would be grounded in 1954 after several tragic accidents, air competition was there to stay and would become ever more potent.

It was on the long distance steamship routes that the aeroplane began to have an effect and BI's Home Line was indeed "long haul"— 6,802 nautical miles separate Mombasa and London via Suez, 800 miles further than Cape Town from Southampton; it is 8,000 miles from London to Beira and another 800 south to Durban, 2,000 miles more distant than via the Cape. Yet the "B.E.A. Range" ports were as close together as any in the world: Mombasa to Tanga, 69 miles; Tanga to Zanzibar, 75 miles; Zanzibar to Dar-es-Salaam, 45 miles.

The India-Africa run was not exactly short-haul, either; the Seychelles are 1,772 miles from Bombay, it is another 1,015 miles to Mombasa and the total distance steamed to Durban was 4,732 miles. By 1952, *Karanja* and *Kampala* maintained four-weekly sailings on the Bombay-Durban service, and this *Kampala* voyage from that year is typical:

8 May	sail BOMBAY
9 May	call Marmagoa
14 May	call Seychelles
17-19 May	call Mombasa
20 May	call Zanzibar
21 May	call Dar-es-Salaam
24 May	call Mozambique
25 May	call Beira
27-28 May	call Lourenço Marques
29 May	arr. DURBAN
2 June	dep. DURBAN
3 June	call Lourenço Marques
5-7 June	call Beira
9 June	call Mozambique
11 June	call Dar-es-Salaam
12 June	call Zanzibar
13-17 June	call Mombasa
20 June	call Seychelles
25 June	arr. BOMBAY

And here is a 1952 *Amra* itinerary showing her service from Bombay direct to East African ports only:

22 April	sail BOMBAY
29 April	call Mombasa
1 May	call Zanzibar
2 May	arr. DAR-ES-SALAAM
4 May	dep. DAR-ES-SALAAM
5 May	call Zanzibar
6-8 May	call Mombasa
11 May	call Seychelles
16 May	arr. BOMBAY

Finally, a *Mombasa* voyage of 1959 illustrating her coastal run:

3 January	sail MOMBASA
3 January	call Tanga
4 January	call Zanzibar
4-5 January	call Dar-es-Salaam
6-7 January	call Lindi
7 January	arr. MTWARA
8 January	dep. MTWARA
8 January	call Lindi
9 January	call Kilwa
10-11 January	call Dar-es-Salaam
11-12 January	call Zanzibar
12 January	call Tanga
13 January	arr. MOMBASA

No matter how widely travelled you are there is always a thrill in the prospect of a journey by sea. It starts with the luggage labels and mounts as you climb the gangway: there's nothing quite like it.

BI brochure, circa 1958

"On Her Majesty's Service" summed up many of the passengers coming up BI's gangways and for the steady stream of Crown Agents, colonial administrators, agricultural advisors, doctors, nurses and teachers, the voyage out and back was more than just transportation of the job. It was a much-appreciated perk as coveted home leave was reckoned to commence only once one arrived back in Britain and days on passage were on H.M. Government's account. And although Union-Castle's Round-Africa ships carried their share of government trade, BI ships usually garnered the upper echelons of Whitehall's passenger custom and First Class in *Kenya* and *Uganda* often represented the smartest set in East African society.

The First Class passenger lists were filled-out by businessmen, many of whom still travelled by sea by virtue of the often invaluable contacts made during the voyage, and winter tourists. The celebrities and safari hunter types were, by the 'fifties, more likely to pose bleary-eyed for the newsreels at Nairobi Airport. Tourist Class in *Kenya* and *Uganda* was patronised by junior civil servants, missionaries, settlers and tourists on a budget.

> To stretch your legs in a turn about the deck, to laze in the sun, to swim, to play— or just to watch. Because at sea there is always something to watch. Whether it's a long dipping line of porpoises in the lazy ripples of the Red Sea, whether it's the erratic flight of flying fish in tropical waters or the bright green phosphorescence in the night ocean south of Aden, the sea is constantly providing fresh delights.

BI brochure, circa 1958

For those who stuck with the ships, life on the ocean wave was a welcome and familiar routine. Because so many passengers were frequent travellers, the shipboard atmosphere was more homely than haughty and one dressed for dinner more out of custom than to impress. Many embarking passengers were recognised immediately by officers and crew and in those gentler times when port stays were measured in days not hours it was possible for officers and crew to establish lasting friendships in East Africa Many sea staff retired to live in Africa and by the 1950s, no fewer than 14 former BI commanders lived in South Africa, including Captains H.D. Clark, W.H. Creese, K.G. Mace and C. R. Trimble; Captain J.W. Milne in Kenya and Captain Hankin in Southern Rhodesia.

In a 1959 review of BI's Eastern Fleet, K.M. Campbell wrote:

> I know that *Kampala* and *Karanja* come in for a certain amount of criticism as, on the African coast, they frequently carry South African holiday passengers, many of whom have made similar voyages in the bigger ships. There are also those passengers who, having journeyed out to East Africa in one of the large passenger liners of Lloyd Triestino, Union-Castle, etc., have transferred to a "K" class ship in Mombasa to proceed south.
>
> I agree that the difference between *Uganda* and, say, *Kampala* must, from all angles, be most noticeable to a passenger who has transferred from the former vessel to the latter. On the other hand, there is other side of the picture. On several occasions, people who had transferred from larger ships mention the enjoyment they were getting from a voyage in a smaller ship— they said it was then they really "were at sea". They commented on the peaceful atmosphere on board, and all seemed pleased at the attention paid to them by the ship's

171

officers. There is no doubt that this is a very great feature of the Eastern Fleet passenger ships, where the senior officers soon get to know all the Saloon passengers and former's courtesy and friendliness are definitely of very great value to the Company. This is by no means confined to the 1st Class. Our Indian pursers and surgeons also make a very valuable contribution to the social side of the 2nd Class.

Home at sea was ones cabin, an invariably compact, but admirably planned panelled and painted box that varied little ship to ship. When travelling BI, one booked a berth or berths, not a cabin, and thus a family of three would be assigned berths 108, 109 and 110 in a three-berth cabin. Creature comforts in First Class included a window or porthole (all BI cabins were outside ones) which was a necessity not a luxury before air-conditioning, washbasin with hot and cold fresh water, a thermos bottle with iced drinking water, comfortable berths, the lower ones arranged high above the deck to permit luggage storage beneath, a wicker chair, a chest of drawers and one wardrobe per occupant. Starched white hand towels with the BI crest hung from little hooks round the washbasin. Underfoot was well-polished linoleum and a small area rug.

The accommodation of the "C" class cargo liners was in no way inferior to that of the mailships, if the following description from *BI News*, September 1955, "m.v. *Chantala* Makes First Atlantic Crossing, Part One", by Gerald Cleveland, is any judge:

My first impression was probably the more surprising because of my automatic comparison with the accommodation I'd found on other cargo ships, none came up to this tastefully planned stateroom furnished in richly grained mahogany. A glass-topped chest of drawers with sliding shelf supported a triple mirror, its centre portion hinged to enclose three handy shelves. Below were two small drawers and oval recesses at either side for loose change, keys and what-have-you. Lights above the mirrors provided perfect illumination. In the wardrobe was a bunch of shaped coat hangers and there was deep drawer below for shoes.

In place of the customary bunk was a bed covered with a deep-quilted spread, and a light switch, and bell button conveniently located at its head. A trim mahogany shelf folded down in just the right position for an ash tray, cigarettes and a bedtime story book. The furnishings were completed by an armchair, rug and attractive draw-curtains which hung from cornices above the windows (not portholes) on two sides of the room. The windows were of double construction: to the outside

172

was a heavy glass part, and the inner frame held mahogany louvres to admit lots of fresh air and light while concealing the interior of the cabin. Both parts of the window were adjustable, as were the twin fresh- air inlets.

I investigated my shower. Any kind of private shower would be a luxury on a cargo ship, but I was in for another surprise. Shower *and* tub, a full-sized one with running hot and cold sea water and fresh water on tap A wash basin with hot and cold water stood below a frosted glass window, and there was a large mirror attached to the bulkhead. Lots of Turkish and huckaback towels were on the rails, and a bunch of disposable "razor towels" hung from an enamelled hook. Mosaic tiles covered the floor, and there were two more adjustable air vents. No effort had been spared to ensure comfort, especially in tropic waters.

The design and fittings of a BI liner reflected an ongoing battle against the wilting heat and scorching sun of the East African run. The first thing proudly demonstrated by the cabin steward upon embarkation was the working of the electric ceiling fan, often strategically placed directly over the berth, and the punkah louvre forced-draught ball vent. The window was pulled down and the wood-slated shutter raised in its place. To augment the draught once underway, the cabin doors, which had large louvred vents, could also be locked in a partially open position by means of a clever latch with a curtain drawn over at night to block the light from the passageway. Metal windscoops could be fitted in open hull portholes, but they could create a hurricane-force wind that could make a shambles of cabin and some fastidious captains refused their employment lest they marr the smart appearance of the ship. Shell plating doors were often of the half Dutch-door variety and the upper half kept opened whilst at sea. The best accommodation was sited in the superstructure which was not only more airy, but placing the cabins inboard of a narrow passageway, shaded them from the sun. All BI ships were well provided with awning stanchions and it was common to erect awnings over the fore well and poop decks to shade the deck passengers and also on the upper decks to keep the superstructure cool, especially when in port.

When working cargo alongside in Mombasa or Beira, an invariably dirty and noisy process, canvas screens were often pulled down along the covered promenade deck to keep out some of the dust whilst in transit passengers fled the ship for shopping, bathing, local sightseeing or for a quick safari to the many game parks inland. Unwelcome passengers in the form of the myriad pests and insects that infested the continent would embark via open ports or in cargo and their eradication through frequent fumigation was a never ending process.

For the BI cabin passenger, the day would begin with the arrival, at the precise time requested, of the cabin steward bearing a tray of tea or coffee, fruit and rolls; *chota hazri* or "small breakfast", and a copy of "Today's Arrangements", the printed sheet detailing the usually modest array of planned activities and entertainments.

Ron Davies, who was Deputy Purser and later Purser in *Uganda* from 1958 to 1959 and later in *Kenya* in 1961 and from 1964 to 1969, recalls the "gentle pace" of passenger life in those liner days as opposed to his later duties as Chief Purser of P&O Cruises' *Canberra*. Besides dancing to a "not very tuneful Goan orchestra", his BI passengers watched films in the veranda, lost cheerfully at bingo or the Race Meeting, or just as likely in an era when "people were content to just entertain themselves", relaxed with a drink in the smoking room or struck up what often proved lifelong friendships or business associations with fellow British East Africans.

Daytime activity aboard was at its peak in the early morning; passengers tended to rise very early on the African mailships as it was often the only comfortably cool time much of the year. The outdoor pools of *Kenya* and *Uganda* were popular gathering places for lazing and in the other ships portable canvas pools were often rigged. There was invariably a sports committee to inspire full employment of the quoits and deck tennis courts. The ships fell wonderfully silent after luncheon when that most hallowed of British tropical mailship customs, the two to four o'clock "quiet time", was observed. The traditional and copious BI afternoon tea was taken in the drawing room with violin music, or on deck round the pool. At 5.00 p.m. the BBC World Service was usually broadcast over the Tannoy.

The dressing gong was followed by a discreet knock on the cabin door to herald the arrival of the bath steward who, bearing several enormous, fluffy white towels embroidered "BISNCo", would escort the passenger, in slippers and bathrobe, to one of several bathrooms which lined the alleyways and were booked for a specific time. In each was a huge Shanks tub, filled to the top with steaming water, its surface shimmering with the gentle vibration of the ship's engines. A long, hot soak in a BI bathtub was one of the voyage's more sublime pleasures. Upon return to the stateroom, one found evening clothes laid out by the steward. Nearly everyone dressed for dinner in a BI ship; the dinner jacket was as indispensable an article of attire as the safari suit afloat and ashore for British East Africans.

British India's bill of fare, simple and straight-forward by more pretentious cruise ship standards, reflected the company's name and routes by being archly Anglo-Indian. Following its Victorian roots, a BI breakfast was always substantial and in addition to the traditional eggs, tomato and bacon, always featured a different fish course and another hot dish; often Kedgeree, spiced rice with fish. For most, a BI luncheon meant one thing, curry and there was surely no finer shipboard meal than to tuck into an enormous portion of Lord Clive Curry (among the scores of varieties offered) served with all the proper condiments, poppadums, Bombay Duck and mango chutney. Curry was so much a part of BI tradition that every Friday before the merger with P&O and perhaps afterwards as well, the principals of BI and Gray Dawes, the London agents, would sit down for a curry luncheon in the Board room, specially prepared and served by the Saloon crew of whatever Home Line ship was in London that week. Aboard ship an English dinner of mulligatawny soup, fillet of lemon sole, lamb with mint sauce or roast beef with Yorkshire pudding, apple crumble and Scotch woodcock (savouries were a fixture of every BI dinner menu) might be enjoyed in the improbable setting of Aden or Zanzibar.

A haven of refinement in often decidedly inelegant settings, BI laid a fine table with company monogrammed Mapin & Webb silverplate, Ashworth china and crisp, white linen. The practice of individual napkin rings was normally followed and each day's menus were properly printed (or stencilled) on handsomely illustrated cards, even on the smallest vessels. The service rendered by Goan stewards, always impeccably turned out in starched white tunics, was always attentive and for many serving in a BI ship was a family tradition.

The accustomed location for the First Class dining saloon in BI ships was forward in the superstructure which permitted windows to face out on three sides giving maximum light and air. This arrangement was found on the "M"s, "K"s, *Amra* and *Aronda*. Aboard the venerable "M"s, one dined shaded by chintz curtains, soothed by dark, ornately carved woodwork and served at long tables from massive mahogany sideboards. In *Mombasa* everyone ate with the ship's officers, not because it was considered especially posh, but because the saloon was shared by passengers and staff in the diminutive vessel. Grandest of all were the dining saloons of *Kenya* and *Uganda* with their two-deck-high central sections and air-conditioned comfort where meals were enjoyed whilst gazing up at murals of Britannia or Fort Jesus, Mombasa.

Again to quote from our contented *Chantala* correspondent:

The dining saloon was fully panelled in blonde eucalyptus veneers, floored in symmetrically patterned rubber, and its white ceiling reflected the light that poured in from a row of windows facing the bows. Once more I was surprised to find these neatly draped windows instead of the usual portholes, but still more to see the Oriental stewards at their tables. The Butler [as the Chief Steward was known in BI ships] told me later that he and all the saloon crew were Goanese— from the Portuguese territory of Goa, some 250 miles south of Bombay. I also learned they were all Catholics. On either side of the room were two tables for four, an octagonal table for ten running down the centre area from the windows, and an oblong one of the same size nearer the doors. The Commander, Captain Leslie W. Smith, sat at the head of the octagonal table opposite the Cadet Instruction Officer, and the Chief Officer and Surgeon also ate at this table. Passengers filled the remaining seats, and I was complimented to find I'd been placed immediately to the Captain's left. A cultivated, well-informed man, he stimulated many interesting conversations, and his prolific fund of amusing anecdotes could always be counted on for a   laugh.   Captain Smith was a most genial host. The table linen, silver and china were of excellent quality, and I could scarcely think of some need before an alert Goanese steward would silently bring it to my hand. There must have been nearly a dozen of these perfect white-coated stewards waiting on table under the Butler's watchful eye; a sharp contrast to the one or two mess boys who'd served the officers and passengers on most of the other freighters I'd sailed in. The colourful menu offered a wide selection of dishes from soup to cheese and crackers, with a choice of salads, three entrees, three cold buffet items and four desserts. I took soup, fried fillet of plaice with lemon, Cochin curry and rice, cucumber salad, gooseberry tart with cream and coffee. Everything was excellent, as it continued to be throughout the trip.

Breakfast at nine, lunch at one, tea at four, of course, and dinner at seven. Incidentally, coffee and sandwiches are brought up to the lounge every night at nine-thirty or thereabouts.

After dinner, there was coffee in the Smoking Room with its enormous leather armchairs and faux fireplace. In *Kenya* and *Uganda* there was usually dancing in the veranda or music room, or on alternate evenings, a film show in the veranda which was fitted with a special projector booth.   On warm nights, the French doors of the veranda were thrown open and the dance music mingled with the sounds of the ship as she coursed her way through tropic seas, leaving a glittering, white wake.   Then to bed, to be lulled to sleep by the gentle, reassuring throb of the engines and the hiss of the sea washing the hull.

For the last generation of British Africans, BI ships were a common thread in that vanished way of life; the first trip out in one of the "M"s, coastal cruises in the "K"s, the coffee crop going out in the "C"s, cards and letters dispatched on the Christmas Boat (the last Britain-bound mailship), the up-country boat train to Kilindini and quayside reunions and farewells. One couple met aboard *Mantola*'s maiden voyage to East Africa, fell in love, married and settled in Tanganyika. For 30 years they always took *Mantola* to and from England on home leave and when they retired to the Mother Country, it, too, was aboard their beloved "M". At the more remote ports like Tanga, the small European community might arrange dinner dances aboard the mailship, particularly over the holidays, and enjoy their Christmas pudding in the air-conditioned luxury of *Kenya* or *Uganda*'s dining saloon, or see the latest West End film.

It happened that *Kenya* and *Uganda*'s schedule resulted in their frequently arriving at Tanga on a Saturday afternoon for a midnight sailing to Zanzibar and, being a Saturday, there was usually a request to the captain from the Tanga Club for the band to play ashore for a dance. This was usually granted and the agent had no difficulty in obtaining volunteers to meet the launch at the quay to drive the members of the band to the club. However, to enable the band to be back aboard at a quarter to midnight, the agent had to break up the dance before 11.30 p.m. and to cajole members of the club to provide their cars for the return journey. Not an enviable job as, apart from the abuse from club members, there was always the threat of much worse abuse from the captain if the band were late back on board

Because of the shortage of good hairdressers at the smaller ports at which *Kenya* and *Uganda* called, the arrival of one of them was a signal for the ladies ashore to request the agents to make appointments for them with the ship's hairdresser. Great was their frustration if time did not permit for all to be accommodated!

As the local supply of fresh meat was a dubious quality, an arrangement existed in Zanzibar for the British Residency who placed an order through the agents which was forwarded to Mombasa for *Kenya* or *Uganda* when in port for suitable joints of meat and fresh vegetables. These were then landed on arrival and sent up to the Residency for the official dinner parties which were consequently always popular. **

For the P&O staff journal, *About Ourselves* autumn 1962, J.H. Gordon recalled a BI voyage to the Seychelles, "A Thousand Miles from Anywhere":
I had a most comfortable journey from Mombasa in the BI s.s. *Kampala* which took just under 3 days... I returned to Mombasa in the BI *Amra*, a somewhat smaller but also very comfortable ship with a most cheery and friendly set of Officers. The *Amra*'s passengers were, to me, most interesting. There were I think about 800-odd including Asians (in the majority) Chinese, "Genuwine Bedooine Arabs", Seychelloises, French, British and a few others I failed to distinguish. The only trouble was that the Asian Juveniles were extremely noisy and failed

177

completely to observe the "sacred silence" of shipboard life between 2 p.m. and 4 p.m. One gentleman in particular apparently had most thrifty parents by whom he was presented with new shoes in Bombay; their thrift was manifested by the fact that his shoes were about 5 sizes too big and his main pastime was running round and round the deck at high speed. I didn't like that young man though I have to admit that this was far from the case with some of the other Indian passengers. There were some really lovely women amongst them, quiet, dignified and superbly dressed.

To Indians, who comprised East Africa's merchant and trade class, the line assumed perhaps its greatest importance. Mombasa and Durban were as Indian as they were African with BI forming the principal bridge across the Indian Ocean. While the saloon galley prepared cucumber sandwiches for tea, the deck class kitchens produced thousands of chapatties. While saloon passengers in dinner dress lingered over their "sundowners" in the Smoking Room, the teeming 'tween decks presented the sights, sounds and smells of a tiny Indian village as a thousand or more passengers, with their own bedding, squatted around their tiny deck space denoted by bundles of personal effects.

The deck passenger, though disappearing, is still a feature of passenger-shipping in eastern waters: a picturesque, even enchanting, travelling companion, from the viewpoint of the saloon passenger. He brings his family with him and has the remarkable capacity of a people with a relatively low standard of living of setting up in his domestic capacity on a deck, provided with an awning above his head. The costumes are vivid in colour and design, and often eccentric. The most intimate operations of any household are conducted *en plein air.* They tie themselves up in fantastic knots of blankets, robes and such in order to sleep o' nights, these deck passengers. They are for all the world like so many patrons of Youth Hostels in Britain: quite happy, content with little, enjoying every moment of travel and sociability.

BI Centenary, 1856-1956

The company's eating arrangements for Deck and Second Class passengers were very flexible. Passengers could buy tickets 'with' or 'without' food. If they bought 'without food' tickets they purchased their meals from *vishiwallas* who were catering contractors who travelled on board. Passengers could also select Hindu, Mohammedan or European diet. The last cost a little more.**

Bandall (Mohammedan) and Dekai (Hindu), the two vishiwalla chiefs aboard the British India liner *Aronda...* have worked together in perfect harmony for 17 years. Theirs is the task of catering for the thousands of Indian passengers travelling annually between India and Africa. Each "manager" controls a staff of 17 vishiwallas.

While Dekai takes on large quantities of rice, fruit and vegetables for the Hindu passengers, Bandall is faced with the task of embarking live sheep (or goats if sheep are unprocurable), as the animals have to be slaughtered by the Mohammedans themselves. On the last trip from India he took aboard 70 sheep at Bombay and 10 more at Zanzibar. His menus also included rice, fish, poultry, fruit and eggs. Strict attention is paid to the dietary requirements of Moslem and Hindu. *Natal Mercury*, 25 August 1947

For Africans, of whom only a handful ever travelled on the ships as passengers, BI's Smith, Mackenzie & Co. agency was an invaluable training ground for a future generation of port agents, administrators and shipping executives who gradually assumed these positions from the British.

The Commonwealth commerce carried in BI ships included sisal from Tanganyika, Rhodesian copper, chrome ore, lead, asbestos, ironstone, tungsten, mica, antimony, corundum and arsenic; Kenyan coffee and soda ash, cloves from Zanzibar, copra and cinnamon bark from the Seychelles, Ugandan cotton; and Indian cement, tea and piece goods. Cashew nuts to India was a big trade, *Kampala* carrying 1,500 tons once in 1952 and *Amra* a record 3,509 tons in March 1951 from Lourenço Marques to Cochin. From home came a "Built in Britain" bill of lading and within days of arrival at Mombasa or Beira, Nairobi and Salisbury newspaper advertisements announced eagerly awaited consignments of Raleigh bicycles, Morris motorcars, Sheffield steelware, gramophone records and the *Picture Post*.

The main cargoes from Zanzibar were cloves, copra, clove oil, coconut oil, coir, chillies and coconuts. The latter were a recent addition to the exports as prior to about 1960 Ceylon had provided Britain with all the coconuts it required. However, when the price of coconuts for local consumption in Ceylon began to rise too fast the government banned their export. This resulted in U.K. importers making a quick trip to Zanzibar to make new contracts in order to avoid a disruption in the supply. Unfortunately neither the Zanzibar exporters nor the agents had any experience of shipping coconuts and the first few

179

consignments were a disaster. They were packed in sacks and stowed with other produce in the holds but when they arrived in London it was found that half had cracked and leaked and deposited sticky coconut juice over everything into which they came into contact. Due to the small tonnages of cargo from Zanzibar to the U.K. it was difficult to obtain sufficient cargo to justify a freighter call which resulted in most exports for the U.K. being carried in *Kenya* and *Uganda* and the Union-Castle passenger ships. After an initial refusal to carry any more coconuts, chief officers were persuaded to carry small consignments in their "dirty cargo" hold, usually No. 1, provided that the fresh young coconuts were no longer shipped. A government agriculture inspector was engaged to examine all shipments and eventually matters improved.

In addition to its own exports Zanzibar was an entrepot port for cargoes from the smaller mainland ports which were not served directly by ocean going vessels Ivory tusks were shipped from Tanganyika and Mozambique to importers in Zanzibar who cut them into short lengths and shipped them in boxes to various destinations. Due to their high value compared to the small space occupied, the company charged freight on an *ad valorem* basis. Another cargo from the mainland was sisal which was stored in the port transit sheds awaiting an oncarrier. After the arrival of a BI cargo ship at Sunderland the company received a report from its Sunderland agents that girls in the factory to which the sisal had been consigned were complaining that bugs were flying out of the sisal and getting stuck in their hair. As it transpired that the particular consignment had come via Zanzibar the agents were asked to investigate. When the complaint arrived it so happened that there was another consignment awaiting shipment, so I went down to the wharf to have a look at it and was surprised to see little black beetles flying round the bales of sisal. These were of course the copra bug which came from a stack of copra bags a few feet away but the problem was remedied by always stacking the sisal and copra in the separate sheds in future.

Although Zanzibar was known as the spice island, its climate was not suitable for growing onions which were in much demand for flavouring curries and rice dishes. Onions had normally been obtained from the mainland, but in the early 'fifties arrangements were made to import supplies from Pakistan. The BI brought in the first consignment and when the ship had anchored the lighters were brought alongside and the hatches opened up as usual. However, the first two stevedores who climbed down into the hold collapsed on top of the cargo and when the superintendent then went down to find out the cause of the trouble he was nearly overcome by onion gas. By the time the bodies of the labourers had been recovered they were dead. In future holds containing onions were well ventilated before anyone went down and to be on the safe side a live chicken was lowered on a piece of string. If the chicken appeared to be unaffected it was reckoned to be safe to descend.

There was an intermittent Australia-East Africa service operated by two or three ships via Mauritius and Madagascar but it did not survive later than the early 'fifties. One of the main cargoes was Ugandan cotton and as the frequency of vessels was so low, any cargo left behind was not likely to be forwarded for months to come.

There was of course always a tendency to overbook to compensate for cargo which might be cancelled at the last moment and on one particular occasion I thought that I had been over optimistic. The stevedores had crammed the last possible bale of cotton into the tween deck and by jumping heavily on the bales it was just possible to put the beams and hatch boards in position. However to my consternation there was still a small stack of bales on the quayside. When I reported this to the captain he looked at me with amusement and said that I hadn't used the cabins. 'The cabins' I said 'I did not even realise that the ship had spare cabins.' It transpired that the ship had some passenger cabins that had not been used for a long time and that I was welcome to make use of them. By placing three bales in a cabin I managed to get the last bale loaded but they had to be covered with tarpaulins because it was not certain that the deckhead was watertight. In emergencies ships sometimes carry passengers in cargo holds but this is only occasion that I know of cargo being put in passenger accommodation.**

Animals were frequent travellers in BI ships, both as cargo and as pets. Passengers could take their dogs with them, a maximum of six permitted and placed in the care of the butcher. These were accommodated in kennels on the poop deck and the owners were usually granted the privilege of walking their pets with the tacit understanding they would clean up after them. Once, recalls Ron Davies, a lady passenger in *Kenya* took her dog up to the foredeck where, in full view of the officers on the bridge, the animal did its business on the immaculate, bone-white deck. Unperturbed, the fastidious passenger

181

produced a scoop and put the offending matter over the side, a gallant gesture that earned a formal salute from the officers on the bridge wing. Animal passengers came in all sizes aboard BI:

> Captain A.G. Smythe writes that on her last inward voyage from East Africa the s.s. *Nowshera* carried a male and female rhinoceros from Mombasa to London. Although described as 'babies', they weighed a ton each and stood about 4 feet high. One of the ship's cadets attended to them, giving them their food which consisted hay and water (sometimes bran) morning and evening. They seemed quite tame and only became somewhat bad-tempered when they were cleaned out before being fed instead of after. They were landed in London for the Royal Zoological Society.
>
> *BI News*, February 1956

> I think it was Kilwa which carried a "Noah's Ark collection of animals from Mombasa to restock a German mission station inland from Lindi. The animals, two of each, had been brought out from Hamburg in a German cargo vessel and had to be transhipped at Mombasa by lowering them over the side in slings onto a pontoon. When the German missionary in charge came into the agents office to make arrangements his English turned out to be inadequate to give a list of the animals. However this problem was overcome by the missionary holding up two fingers and saying solemnly *"zwei moo-moo", zwei quack-quack"* etc.**

In 1969, *Chindwara* transported 19 giraffes, 28 eland and 7 wildebeasts from Mombasa to Plymouth for Woburn Wild Kingdom.

> Landfall becomes an adventure; a line of hills that might be a cloud mass; a lone gull, a twinkling light or a cluster of white houses outlined in the clear morning air.
>
> BI brochure, circa 1958

With Fort Jesus, built by the Portuguese in the 16th-century, dominating the Old Harbour and its dhow-careening dock, Mombasa was the hub of BI's East African network.

> Few who arrived by ship ever forgot their first impression of it for nature has ensured that the approach to Mombasa would never be less than beautiful from the sea . . . The enchantment began as the ship turned south west and approached the atoll towards what today is the Old Harbour. Here the black-ringed lighthouse on Ras Serani Point could be seen against a backdrop of brilliant but natural colour. Beyond sparkling clear waters in

182

every shade of blue, lush green foliage was lit by the sun. Gigantic and legendary baobabs, for the greater part of the year their purplish branches unclad, provided a dramatic contrast to this humid vegetation and feathery palms surrounding them. In the distance, what appeared to be a spick and span Arab town edged onto the channel. A little to the right of the lighthouse stood Kilindini House [Government House], squat, unpretentious and white.

Errol Trzebinski, *The Kenya Pioneers*

As a port and commercial centre, Mombasa was largely the inspiration of Sir William Mackinnon whose statue occupied a place of honour in the Treasury Gardens. But his greatest memorial was the ongoing commerce and progress that reached deep into the interior of Africa, borne by rails from Newcastle to the Clyde-built ships flying the BI houseflag that crowded Mombasa harbour.

It was a rare day when one or more BI ships was not alongside the Kilindini quays. These represented, until 1956, the only modern docks in all of British East Africa, although by 1952 Mombasa began to rival Beira as the most congested harbour on the coast. Having arrived at Mombasa, passengers could transfer to *Mombasa* to speed their journey down the coast. *Kampala* and *Karanja* met at Mombasa, offering a cheap and popular cruise from Durban to Kenya or the Seychelles, or linking up with BI's other Indian-based routes. The "K"s bunkered at Mombasa on both the inbound and outbound calls there.

Mombasa, too, was home port for BI's coastal services including *Sofala* and *Tabora* which were frequently employed in collecting cargo from way-ports for BI's main services.

Mombasa was flagship of this little fleet and an amazingly adaptable ship she was. With three classes of passengers and three cargo holds, she was the main link between Kenya and the Tanganyikan ports of Tanga and Dar-es-Salaam on the northern sector and between Dar-es-Salaam and the southern ports of Kilwa, Lindi and Mikindani, the latter being replaced by the new deep water port of Mtwara. Many of the Indian passengers would try to avoid paying freight on small items of cargo by taking it as their baggage, but if caught they had to leave it behind on the quay. During the rainy season the road from Dar-es-Salaam to Lindi, at the best hardly navigable, became quite impassable and, apart from East African Airways DC-3, *Mombasa* became the only means of carrying passengers. The European residents at Lindi were allowed to purchase fresh supplies of meat from the Purser to augment the local mutton.

At Zanzibar, although ocean going vessels had to anchor in

183

the harbour, *Mombasa* could go alongside the wharf because of her shallow draught. One fine day I had a telephone call from the captain to arrange for extra fenders to be placed between the ship and the quay because the ship was rolling heavily.

I was rather mystified as this was normally required only when the north-east monsoon was blowing hard, but when I went down to the dock I could see a long swell coming up the Zanzibar Channel from the south and into the harbour. We then heard that a few days earlier a devastating cyclone had hit Mauritius and the cyclone must have caused the swell which had travelled 1,500 miles.**

The Indian Ocean was normally fairly calm off East Africa, but on occasion when the monsoon winds were blowing strongly the pilot taking a ship to sea thought it prudent to stay on board and go on to the next port where the agents would arrange for him to be flown home. This happened mostly between Mombasa and Tanga as from Tanga southwards the ports were sheltered by the islands of Pemba and Zanzibar.

Zanzibar was a very popular port of call with the company's passengers and the agents always arranged excursions round the island. If the south-west monsoon wind was blowing strongly the more exposed anchorages proved a problem in disembarking passengers as jumping from the gangway to the launch could be hazardous. This was especially so for Indian ladies in their long saris. On one occasion, with the ship lifting to the swell, the captain of *Uganda* decided to shift his ship to a more sheltered anchorage which caused considerable alarm to the passengers on shore who thought that their ship was sailing without them.

A facility for passengers provided by the company's agents was the town crier. He was an elderly Arab who had been employed by the agency for more years than anyone could remember and who was summoned on the day of embarkation to go round the bazaar ringing a bell and calling out of the time of embarkation. I can not recall during my many years in Zanzibar that we ever left a passenger behind. I used to recommend to the captains of passenger vessels that, to chase up the transit passengers who were shopping in the bazaar, the ship's siren should be sounded half an hour before sailing time. This always had the desired effect as there would suddenly be a dash for the dock gates and the launches waiting by the quay.**

Until deep water quays were built in the mid-'fifties, BI ships calling at Tanganyika worked cargo and embarked passengers whilst lying at anchor. Dar-es-Salaam, despite the restrictions imposed by its narrow approach, offered a good, sheltered anchorage. There, the procedure was to moor in the lagoon stern to the beach, run lines out to the mooring buoys and drop both anchors. Whilst also affording a reasonably sheltered anchorage, Tanga, the principal sisal lifting port, had an especially fast current.

Mafia Island lies off the coast of Tanganyika and the BI service there, provided by *Arusha* and her lighters, was described in *BI News* by her master, Captain R. Baker:

> The ports we work have, so far, been the bigger ones, i.e. Mombasa, Tanga, Zanzibar, Dar-es-Salaam, Kilwa and Lindi, but we have been to Mafia a number of times. The loading point here lies in a shallow bay on the western side of the Island, and the lighter has to be beached at High Water. Then when the tide ebbs ramps are put up the side of the lighter and the cargo, usually copra or cashew nuts, is loaded by hand. Sometimes, however, we take a bit of cargo to Mafia, and then the derricks on the Watson lighters come in useful when the cargo is heavy stuff like vehicles. We have landed motor cars and a 3-ton lorry there, when the drill is to wait until the lighter has almost or quite dried out. The vehicle is then landed on to the beach and driven away. A certain rival firm though was once in too much of a hurry, and landed a tractor in about three ft. of water. This swamped the engine and they could not move it before the tide rose again and submerged it completely, which is not the treatment recommended for new tractors.

So tied up with the fortunes of the Rhodesias were the Mozambique ports of Lourenço Marques and Beira it is worth remembering that they were Portuguese. Indeed, the British persistence in calling Lourenço Marques "Delagoa Bay" resulted in the Portuguese authorities stating that any post so addressed would be returned to sender. Its name aside, this was one of East Africa's few superb natural harbours, uniquely bereft of bars and high winds. Now called Maputo and a shabby shadow of its former charm as the "Transvaal Riviera", Lourenço Marques' corniche of white-painted buildings, tidy and efficient quays and extensive rail connections into the interior made it a popular port for passengers and lines alike.

The same could never be said of Beira, chosen for its accessibility to the Rhodesias more than anything else. The harbour managed to combine the worst East African waters could offer— shoals, bars, shifting sand banks, tricky tides and a five-knot current— and its situation in a swamp promised a turn-round there with 100 degrees F. temperatures, oppressive humidity and notoriously large cockroaches. Former BI purser Ron Davies recalls Beira as "being a bit of a dump" made worse by the "woodpeckers", the African chip and paint gang who would pound off the scale with hammers with a nerve-racking rhythm and carry on through the night, and "drive everyone quite mad." After sweltering alongside for four days, crews always looked forward to sailing for home. They were the lucky ones posted to a mailship or liner which enjoyed priority berthing for Beira between 1947-1950 was one of the most hopelessly congested ports in the world. Often there would be upwards of 30 vessels riding at anchor outside the bar, one Harrison liner is said to have been so situated for 102 days. Whilst the harbour itself could only handle a dozen ships at a time and a few more could be moored to buoys and off-loaded by lighters, the problem lay as much with the inadequate rail connections as with the port itself.

The "end of the line" from Britain from 1962-1966 and from Bombay was Durban, a 307-mile run south from Lourenço Marques. Dominated by the Bluff, a 200-foot-high wooded ridge jutting out alongside the southern entrance, Durban was and remains Africa's busiest harbour and one of its best, both in terms of its natural situation and facilities. This remained an interchange port for the Union-Castle Cape Mail and BI's African and Asian routes. Durban was a bunkering station for both the Home Line and Durban Mail ships. Perhaps too efficient, the call here was "never long enough" as Ron Davies recalls for leave-hungry crew. For much of the BI fleet, "home" remained India. The head office was situated in Calcutta until 1956 although the growing importance of the Home, Gulf and African trades had reduced the number and frequency of BI services from the Bengal port in favour of Bombay, home port for the "K"s, "A"s and "D"s. This was a major transhipment port for BI cargo to and from the Orient as well as a transfer point for passengers bound for Arabia and the Gulf. There was usually a five-day turnaround here, the ships disembarking passengers at Ballard Pier and then being moved to Alexandra Dock to work cargo, bunker and store before returning to Ballard on sailing day.

The Mazagon Dock Ltd. was the great centre of ship repair and replenishment for both P&O and BI, rivalling the BI establishment at Garden Reach, Calcutta. Within its complex of dry docks, metal forging shops and vast storehouses there was little that could not be accomplished to keep ships sound, in steam and supplied. Once "out East", a BI ship seldom returned home to Britain. Annual drydocking, Lloyd's Surveys and Government Surveys were undertaken at Bombay, generator and electrical work usually handled at Durban and major refits accomplished at Singapore. The day to day minor repairs were performed by the ships engineers using on board facilities. Once in March 1965, both *Kampala* and *Sirdhana* were together, bow to stern, in Hughes Dry Dock, Bombay—986 feet of liners in a 1,000-foot basin. Well-designed to time-tested standards, properly maintained and prudently operated, a BI ship was as reliable as any afloat and major breakdowns or disruption in service were rare.

And for the relaxation and replenishment of sea staff was the BI Officers' Club in Bombay, perhaps best known for the BI Parrot, ex-*Karanja* (I), whose predilection to repeat the more colourful phases of the wardroom brought equal amusement during its retirement ashore.

...as ships [BI's "M" class] they would have been little value without their commanders, officers and other members of the crew. To their efficiency and courtesy can be attributed the success they have been throughout the years and to them goes the honour of enhancing the good name of the Line in which they serve. They have built up a tradition and many of them still carry it on. *Tanganyika Standard*

Every BI ship, whether *Kenya* or *Kilwa,* possessed an unmistakable dignity, discipline and decorum. The British officers, many of whom were lifelong "cadet to commodore" company men, were fiercely loyal to BI and jealous of its traditions. Renowned for their seamanship and experience, they knew African waters, fraught with shifting sandbars and coral reefs, intimately.

When there was a number of BI vessels in port together it was the custom for the senior master to hoist the No. 5 pennant on the signal halyard at 7.55 a.m. whereupon the other vessels had to hoist the answering pennant, and at 8.00 a.m. precisely the pennants were lowered and all proper flags hoisted e.g. ensign, courtesy ensign, houseflag, jack, etc.. If any vessel failed to observe this procedure it could cause some caustic comments about the senior master's ship. When the Commodore of the fleet was master of the coaster *Mombasa* this caused a problem as the ship, being so small, was often berthed between two ocean going vessels and was frequently unobserved.

The souls of these ships were their Indian Serangs (bosun's mates), Tindals (mates), Kalassi (seamen), Agwallahs (stokers), Bhandharys (cooks) and Goanese stewards. Hard working, devoted and obliging, they kept the paint and varnish smart, the brass polished, the Empire veneers glistening, shovelled filthy African coal into the fireboxes, manned the rail at anchor stations, and laid out your dress shirt, stiff with starch, in time for dinner.

In 1952 BI, after some urging from the Kenya authorities, decided with some reservations to commence replacing the Indian crews of the coastal vessels with African crews. Zanzibar was the place most likely to provide seafaring Africans and the agents were asked to engage a crew for *Mombasa.* There was a misunderstanding about the timing resulting in the new crew being engaged in Zanzibar a month before the Indian crew had served their Articles and were due for repatriation. This expensive mistake was not appreciated by the Managing Agents in Calcutta.

187

It was very soon found that the African, though he might be trained to be a good seaman, did not take kindly to the discipline required for the successful operation of the company's vessels. There were soon reports of all sorts of misdemeanours which had hardly been heard of with Indian crews and it became necessary for the agents to maintain a record of these offences to avoid unsuitable persons being re-engaged. In the seaman's discharge books a character reference of 'good' instead of 'very good' was a warning that there had been trouble. Insubordination was the chief problem, often caused by too much to drink. On one occasion [7 June 1960] in Zanzibar the whole crew— led by the engine room serang— walked off the ship and were astonished when the captain and officers took *Mombasa* to sea by themselves, leaving the crew stranded on the quayside.**

An inside look at the routine of a typical voyage in *Kampala* near the end of her career was published in a 1971 issue of *BI News, "*Around the Fleet— The *Kampala* and Those Who Serve in Her":

Our call in Bombay usually lasts five days and throughout this time the Purser, Alan Pilkinton, and the Chief Engineer, John Major, are frequently seen wearing rather harassed expressions wondering if, indeed, they will be able to work the expected miracle and complete their repairs and cleaning operations prior to embarkation. Somehow, despite the usual shortages of labour, emergency drill, shifting ship, and by making frequent use of the First Officer's, Graeme Wright, crystal ball, an invaluable aid to cargo work, by the morning of departure day *Kampala* is once again shipshape and Bristol fashion.

When at last the cargo loading is completed we move to Ballard Pier where almost immediately on our arrival a departure inspection is held. This is usually the sign for embarkation to begin and any number of passengers up to 1,100 may materialise so that for the few hours the scene invariably appears rather chaotic with Mr. Sid Kirtikar, the Crew Purser, attending to last minute crew changes and the ever smiling Mr. Taffy Chaves presiding at the bureau, an expert at pacifying disturbed passengers who have lost their way, baggage or children.

Eventually, and with a large sigh of relief, *Kampala* sails on another voyage and whilst Captain George Denninson is conning his ship out of harbour and preparing the vessel for sea, the Saloon Department are busy puzzling out seating

188

arrangements for the 114 seater dining saloon, arranging salt free diets and the like to satisfy the needs and requests of the Cabin Class passengers.

The voyage from Bombay to Seychelles takes five days and every morning a conference is held in the Captain's quarters to discuss the day's programme of inspections and entertainment. When the weather is fine passengers are given the opportunity to visit the Bridge and Engine Room under the guidance of Cadets Allan and McAllister who now run these tours with the polish of a Cooks' Courier.

By midday the Rounds of Inspection are complete and interest transfers to the bar or to the Dart Board where there is often a darts match in progress between the Officers and the passengers. Unhappily it is only rarely that the ship's eagle eyed sharp shooter, Terry Matthews, the 2/E/O [Second Engineer], can be with us to stave off disaster; but to keep the Engine Room machinery running as smoothly as ours must call at times for superhuman efforts and our Chief Engineer, Mr. Johnny Burnett should surely be congratulated on his achievements on board *Kampala*.

Once, on each leg of the voyage, the passengers enjoy a 'Race Meeting' and this is usually highlighted by the Captain's cocktail party before dinner. This is intended to relax the passengers somewhat and it is hoped that after a bottle of wine with their dinner, and by the time the Tote opens, their financial cramp will have been alleviated so that they will 'speculate to accumulate'. Recently Messrs. Nelson, Hughes, Chaves, Kirtikar and McAllister obliged with a novelty Officers' Race which was a great success, starting with a handicap of a spicy samoosa and a pint of ale which had to be drunk through a straw before the race could start. Another specialty is the Ladies' Race when Doctor Vakil volunteers his services to inspect the horses' fetlocks and to ensure that the jockeys have not been knobbled.

By the time we reach Seychelles our resources for evening entertainment are becoming exhausted, although the Daily Tote run by the Second Officer Tony Bennett and the Welfare Officer still maintains interest until the last mile. Our call in Seychelles is only for a few hours and it is not always worthwhile to go ashore for a visit and on these occasions Third Officer Mike Gilbert usually obliges the Intransit passengers by taking away a lifeboat for a little fishing or swimming on some secluded sandy beach.

Here however, the majority of the Cabin Class passengers disembark, many of them arriving in the Seychelles for the first time. With the huge development programme to which the Seychellois are committed, it has been necessary for the contracting firms who are building the airport, hotels and Deepwater Terminal to bring skilled people to work on the island until such time as sufficient Seychellois have been trained to complete and run these projects. By the end of 1971 it is hoped that the International Airport will be fully commissioned and that the new harbour will also be open where *Kampala* will be able to berth alongside. This will no doubt expedite the loading of the principal exports such as copra and cinnamon bark.

In the evening we again set sail, this time en route for Mombasa with a new set of faces. As many of the newly embarked passengers are proceeding on leave a holiday atmosphere prevails, and the Entertainments Team once more swing into action. Often on this leg of the voyage many of the passengers are the 'Younger Bloods' so that the evening's programme is wound up with music for dancing by the ship's band. As the senior citizens retire so the temp speeds up and the evening ends in a grand twisting session.

Two days and three nights later we arrive off Mombasa at crack of dawn and having picked up a pilot at the entrance we move alongside to discharge our cargo and say farewell or au revoir to the majority of our passengers.

Mombasa usually holds the social focus of the voyage, both the Second Officer and Second Engineer having their families living in Mombasa whilst the Third Engineer Ken Milne has just become engaged there. Nearly everyone has established contacts here but for those who have no friends to visit there is always a welcome at the Sports Club and the Golf Club whilst some of the more fortunate may sometimes go on Safari to Voi Tsavo, one of East Africa's Game Reserves situated close to Mombasa.

From Mombasa to Dar es Salaam is a short haul, usually done at night to give two clear working days in port. The *Kampala* almost invariably berths in the stream at 'C' anchorage which is nearest the Customs House and Landing Jetty. It is hoped that when the new berths are completed we will once again be able to berth alongside. As soon as the anchor is let go a pontoon is manoeuvred alongside the gangway, the few

190

remaining passengers disembark and the routine of cleaning ship for the northbound voyage recommences. At this time strange noises will often be heard emanating from the cargo spaces and further investigation will reveal that the Voice of Africa, namely Johnny Ward, is on board once again encouraging the labour to do their bit to enable us to sail on schedule.

The one night spent in Dar es Salaam entails a call at the Missions to Seamen Club which provides excellent services for *Kampala*, including a football match. The team, led by Derek Parks, Fourth Engineer and our erstwhile star goalkeeper John Grocott, Chief Electrician make up for the team's unparalleled records with magnificent team spirit which manifests itself in the bar at the end of the game.

The return call at Mombasa is notable in that it is a constant battle of wits to maintain the scheduled departure time. The main commodities exported from Mombasa to Bombay are wattle extract, sisal and cotton and we endeavour to complete as much as possible before embarkation commences. Here the problem is much different to that posed by Bombay. The currency restrictions imposed in East Africa are not quite so stringent as those imposed in India and passengers joining may bring with them large quantities of durable goods, hence, one family may join for the voyage to Bombay complete with five refrigerators and three television sets which they will claim to be accompanied baggage. The new import restrictions in Bombay have now reduced this to more manageable quantities. Facilities are also available for passengers to buy goods duty free ex bond and these are delivered to *Kampala* before sailing, to be issued after departure.

Leaving Mombasa we hope to find the ship full once again, with Third Class passengers for Bombay and a mixture in the Cabin Class for Bombay and Seychelles although occasionally we are called upon to cater to for a few Hippies and Skinheads in the Third Class but these are no longer encouraged to disembark in Seychelles, the destination of most.

By departure northbound from Seychelles contact has been lost with the outside world and news hungry passengers avidly devour the daily press sheets provided by one of our youngest colleagues, Mike Kay the Junior Radio Officer, whilst during the day the Senior Radio Officer, Paddy Bourke, broadcasts our messages with equal aplomb, giving Bombay ample warning of our arrival. In the meantime the Nursery

Stewardess, Grace McLean, looks after the children with all the skill that her years of experience have provided.

After another five days at sea, we pick up our pilot and proceed alongside at Ballard Pier to disembark our passengers and their baggage before moving once more into Alexandra Dock to begin again the routine of clean, patch and repair.

As recently as 1972 when BI's African service celebrated its centenary, ships like *Kampala* and *Karanja*, whilst larger and more sophisticated than their predecessors, were still operated much like in those pioneering days. Such was the timeless traditions of this and other ocean routes that it seemed impossible that they would rather suddenly vanish, yet now such ships and services and the life aboard seem of another age. But before the twilight of the liner era, a final 'fifties flourish of BI mailships, Beira-bound.

Hail & Farewell to the doughty "M"s. *Madura* sails from Mombasa in June 1952 on her 99th and final voyage.
P&O

An era in British Africana ended when *Mulbera*, last of the "M"s, sailed from Mombasa in February 1953 for Britain and the breakers.
P&O

The first of the "I" class and the first of a new era of BI cargo ships, *Itinda* of 1938 differed from her later sisters by not having a pair of kingposts on the forecastle and another on the poop. *A. Duncan collection*

Urlana (III) was built as replacement for her sister sunk in the war. Developments of the "I"s, the "U"s were familiar sights along the East African coast.
A. Duncan collection

Last of the four wartime-built "C"s, *Chupra* was a fairly regular caller at African ports late in her career. Note the lack of topmasts, the signal pole atop the bridge and no aft side houses which distinguished the wartime quartet.   *A. Duncan collection*

Typical of the nine post-war "C"s, *Chantala* (above) and sister *Chindwara* were the best known of the class due to their status as cadet training ships for BI and both became mainstays of the African Home Line.

Fotoflite, Charles Dragonette collection

Grand Old Lady among BI's cargo ships and the last of the original diesel-powered fleet, *Durenda* joined the African Home Line in 1954 and ended her long career on the route.

A. Duncan collection

First of the handsome "N" class cargo ships which would become regulars on the Home Line was *Nuddea* which was commissioned in August 1954. From a painting by Leonard B. Moffatt.

author's collection

The Fleet in White. In July 1955 *Kenya* introduced a new white livery for BI liners with black sheer line and boot-topping and buff masts. Here she is shown radiant in the new scheme at Mombasa that September. *James L. Shaw collection*

The Fleet in White. *Uganda* shows off her new colours which, if anything, made her funnel look even larger. *A. Duncan collection*

The Fleet in White. *Amra* in the new scheme which seemed less suited to the more matronly members of the fleet.   *A. Duncan collection, courtesy Charles Dragonette*

In a painting by John S. Smith, *Uganda* (left) passes *Nowshera*, the second of the "N"s, which entered service in 1955.   *author's collection, courtesy S.M. Payne*

Centenary Celebrations & Imperial Echoes— H.M.Y. *Britannia* and R.M.S. *Kenya* form an impressive backdrop as Princess Margaret dedicates the new deepwater quays at Dar-es-Salaam 10 October 1956. Her Royal Highness later dined aboard the BI liner.

P&O

Built for the Chittagong-Japan run, *Warla* replaced *Kilwa* on the East African coastal trade in February 1956 but had no passenger berths. Her sister ship *Warora* inaugurated the Persian Gulf-Durban run two years later. *A. Duncan collection*

Looking to the future, BI's centenary was capped by the maiden voyages of two more "N"s, *Nyanza* (above) and *Nardana* which sailed to East Africa in November 1956.

Charles Dragonette collection

The decline of BI's Africa services began with the withdrawal of *Mombasa* in August 1960. Here the trim little vessel is shown with her revised livery (post-1955) with the white strake carried one deck lower.

J.A. Smith collection

The demise of the Calcutta-Yokohama run in 1962 released the sturdy but slow "S" class trio for other duties. *Santhia*, shown here at Hong Kong, began to fill-in on the Bombay-East Africa service as early as November 1960.

A. Duncan collection, courtesy Charles Dragonette

Aronda, which operated on the Karachi-Chittagong run 1950-1960, played out her career with some Africa runs, including one from Bombay to South Africa; here she is shown at Durban in March 1961. *A. Duncan collection, courtesy Charles Dragonette*

What would become an increasingly rare sight in the Jet Age—*Uganda*, Lloyd Triestino's *Europa* and *Kenya* at the Kilinindi, Mombasa, quayside 12 October 1962.

P&O

Another bustling Mombasa '60s scene. Here a departing *Karanja* is framed by *Uganda* (left) and *Kenya* (right) 12 June 1963.

P&O

Karanja at her Kilinindi berth in 1963 with one of the "C" class cargoliners immediately aft. The great dock cranes gave a distinctly British quayside character to the port.

P&O

Kampala steams out of Mombasa, the cliffs of Kilindini in the background, 24 October 1963.

P&O

Sunset for *Uganda* as an African mailship; in December 1966 she left Durban for the last time and after 52 line voyages started a new career in 1968 as an educational cruise ship.   *P&O*

Upon the second closure of the Suez Canal in 1967, BI ships were again routed via Cape Town where *Kenya* was photographed on 23 December 1967; both ship and service had barely a year and a half left.   *P&O*

Kenya at Mombasa— her final departure from her namesake country in May 1969 marked the end of British-flag passenger service from the U.K. to East Africa. Two months later she was run on the beach at La Spezia for breaking up.

James L. Shaw collection

Kampala, first of BI's post-war liners, sails from Bombay for the Kaoshiung breakers on 29 June 1971 flying her paying off pennant and signal flags reading "Farewell".

P&O

Karanja resplendent after her refit at Singapore in 1969/70. Note that the bridge cabs have been removed and except for the first pair, the lifeboats are no longer double-banked. The black sheer line would be deleted as an economy measure circa 1973.

J.A. Smith collection

The former P&O *Salsette, Tairea* shown here leaving Cape Town, joined the BI fleet in March 1970 and was the second to last BI ship on the U.K.-East Africa run, making her last such voyage in January 1972.

P&O

Shown arriving at Bombay in 1970, *Sirdhana* played out her 25-year BI career on the East Africa run. Her last voyage ended at Bombay in May 1972 and three months later she passed to Taiwan breakers. *James L. Shaw collection*

The last BI ship to sail from the U.K. to Africa was *Chilka*, shown here at Durban, which departed London on 18 May 1972. It proved to be the ship's final voyage and she proceeded to Taiwan for breaking up in July. *Charles Dragonette collection*

EMBARKATION NOTICE FOR T.S.S. "KARANJA"

EMBARKATION for all passengers will take place on May 28, 1976 between 08.00 to 10.00 hours. Cars and heavy baggage must be handed over on May 27, 1976, at the passenger baggage hall, Kilindini.

For:

MACKENZIE (KENYA) LIMITED

Agents: **B.I.S.N. CO. LIMITED.**

This modest announcement in the *Daily Nation* (Nairobi) heralded the final sailing from Mombasa of *Karanja* on 27 May 1976 which brought down the curtain on 104 years of BI service to Africa.   *author's collection*

Karanja was sold to Shipping Corp. of India and as *Nancowry* is photographed at Singapore on 28 April 1979 after a refit there. This last vestige of BI and Africa went to the breakers in 1988.   *Chris Gee photograph*

209

9. FABULOUS 'FIFTIES

The work proceeds, and the flag flies high. The individuality imposed on this concern a hundred years ago, the high standards William Mackinnon required of his shipbuilders, his ships' companies and his staffs ashore — these have been upheld.
BI Centenary, 1856-1956

The 'fifties were a busy and prosperous time for British India— its fleet an intriguing blend of old and new, its services at their peak of efficiency and its 100-year-old traditions a reassuring constant as East Africa entered a period of transition.

For BI's African ships 1952 was an eventful year. The inbound *Kenya,* with 260 passengers, had a fire in her No. 5 hold whilst in the English Channel on 11 May and made for Plymouth where the blaze was extinguished. In October, *Arusha* went to the assistance of Andrew Weir's *Westbank* which grounded off Juan de Novo, Madagascar.

We received a request from the Bank Line for *Arusha* to go to the rescue of *Westbank* which had run her bows at high spring tides onto a dangerous coral reef in the Madagascar Channel. The Managing Agents agreed, but there were some logistic problems to be overcome first because *Arusha* did not have the endurance to proceed so far south and return without refuelling and taking on more water. It was arranged that she would have a look at *Westbank* and then call in at Mozambique to replenish fuel, water and stores before returning to attempt salvage. She sailed from Dar-es-Salaam with a couple of Coventry Climax pumps on deck which had been requested by the captain of *Westbank* to help pump out the forward holds which were taking in water. In the event the diversion to Mozambique was not necessary as the BI cargo vessel *Pemba* stopped en route for Mozambique and refuelled *Arusha* at sea, also supplying water and stores.

It was obvious that no serious attempt to refloat *Westbank* could be made until the next spring tide so *Arusha* stood by, but the time was not wasted as the forward end of the ship was lightened by dumping some of its cargo overboard. Because *Arusha* with her much lighter draught could navigate over the reef at high water, she waited for a calm day and then went alongside the bows of *Westbank* to take her anchors and lower them over the edge of the reef. This would enable the windlasses to assist the tug in her efforts to pull *Westbank* off the reef. However, although the ship's captain had made every effort to make the holes in the hull watertight, everyone was hoping that when the vessel was pulled into deep water she would not sink. Meanwhile *Pemba* had returned and again supplied the tug with more fuel, water and stores. Eventually the appropriate day and time arrived, and with the tug exerting maximum power and *Westbank*'s windlasses heaving on the anchors, she came off the reef and remained afloat. Under the Lloyds "No cure no pay" agreement the captain of the tug and all the crew received handsome salvage awards. In that 12-month period four other salvage operations were carried out by BI.**

November 1952 proved particularly trying. At Mombasa on the 17th, *Modasa* had a fire in a hold filled with 50 bales of sisal that burned for 13 hours; she finally left for London on the 24th, five days late. On the 18th *Karanja,* en route from Mombasa to the Seychelles, rescued the passengers of the disabled Seychelles Government steamer *Isle of Mahé,* 400 miles from Mahé. Southbound on her second voyage, *Uganda* damaged her port screw while entering Dar-es-Salaam on the 26th. Transferring her 70 passengers to *Mulbera,* she was drydocked at Diego Suarez, Madagascar, and after repairs resumed her voyage at Beira.

Kilwa arrived at Durban on 29 April 1952 from East African ports and thereafter replaced *Sofala* on the Durban-Mombasa coastal run. By this time *Kilwa* did not carry passengers. *Sofala* was put to a new use transporting cased petrol (shades of her wartime exploits) from Durban to Tamatave.

With the advent of *Kenya* and *Uganda,* it was inevitable that the "M"s would finally fade from the scene. Long planned perhaps, but no less poignant, for the passing of these ships which had served two generations of British East Africans truly marked the end of an era. The "Old Reliables" had rendered a combined 161 years of service to company and country, an achievement quietly and efficiently earned and thus typically if sadly overlooked, but not in their passing, if a lead editorial in the *Tanganyika Standard* can be any judge:

> The "M" boats, ever since they began their career, have somehow earned for themselves a very special place in the affection of thousands who have travelled on them as passengers and the still greater number who have watched them arrive or leave at one or other of the East African ports. Comfortable, on what one now considers "old fashioned" lines, they combined with excellent service and catering to provide travel facilities of the highest order and many old stagers even to this day, made a

point of "going home", or returning, on his or her, own particular "M" boat, looking upon her as something more than a ship —in fact, as upon a friend.

First to go was *Matiana* which left Dar-es-Salaam for the last time on 8 January 1952 and reached Briton Ferry on 16 March for breaking up. Flying signal flags reading "From *Mantola* to Dar-es-Salaam Good-bye" to which the Harbour Master replied "Farewell and bon voyage to a grand old lady", that ship, commanded by Captain Rodney Stone, made her final departure from Dar-es-Salaam on 5 March 1953 and among the vessels answering her whistle laments was *Modasa*. *Mantola* left Mombasa nine days later flying a 192-foot-long paying-off pennant and docked at London on 9 April. Sold for scrap to the British Iron & Steel Co. (BISCO) for £102,000 on 15 January 1952, *Mantola* arrived at Blyth for breaking up on the 26th.

Fetching £98,000 from BISCO on 19 March 1953 for breaking up, *Madura* commenced her 99th and final voyage from London on 4 April. Blotting her copy book on this last trip, she lost her starboard anchor on the 17th in the Great Bitter Lake whilst transiting the Suez Canal. "She's been a good old tub", said the ship's Captain B. O'Brian Martin. *Madura* turned round at Beira 21-24 May and arrived at London on 14 July and thence to Rotterdam and Hamburg before reaching the Inverkeithing yards of Thos. W. Ward, for demolition on the 27th.

"Hundreds of people, mostly Europeans, lined the sea front in Azania Drive, and blew their vehicle horns as she proudly steamed out with her paying off pennant dangling proudly behind. All the ships in port blazed away on their sirens, and flags flew from many buildings". So the *Mombasa Times* described *Modasa*'s final sailing from the port on 7 December 1953. The £61,000 contract with BISCO for scrapping was signed on the 30th and *Modasa* reached London on 7 January 1954. She poignantly passed her builders, Swan Hunter, Wallsend, and exchanged whistle salutes on the 23rd, en route to Blyth where she arrived five days later at Hughes Bolckow Shipbreakers. *Modasa*'s Second Engineer, E.D.F. Lewis, told the *Newcastle Journal,* "She was a smooth ship, never gave much trouble, and never failed to get there" whilst First Officer Wilfred Robson, aboard for only 18 months, commented "I haven't been with her long enough to feel any real pang about seeing her go, but she's been a good ship, slow, but sure".

> We bid goodbye to *Mulbera* with deep regret for her own sake and as the last of the M Class steamers which have played such a large part in the development of this territory. Godspeed.
>
> Signal from Harbour Master, Dar-es-Salaam
> 4 February 1954

Mulbera, the last of a long line of "M"s, arrived at Royal Albert Docks on 17 March. On the 26th she was sold to BISCO for scrap for £64,000.

Completing her cargo discharge at Sunderland 5-6 April, she reached Inverkeithing the next day.

Whereas, during the inter-war years, the "M"s had been sufficient to cater to BI's East African passenger and cargo trade and invaluable during the post-war period when their passenger liner priority status avoided port congestion, their demise resulted in the development of a separate African cargo service. Cargo vessels had occasionally operated from Britain and India as inducement offered, but from the mid-'fifties onwards they would play an increasing role in BI's African trade.

The Home Line cargo service ports included Newcastle, Sunderland, Middlesbrough, Hull, London, Rotterdam, Antwerp, Dunkirk, Le Havre, Boulogne, Bilbao, Gibraltar, Valencia, Barcelona, Marseilles, Malta, Port Said, Port Sudan, Aden, Mombasa, Tanga, Zanzibar, Dar-es-Salaam, Lindi, Mtwara, Nacala, Quelimane, Beira and occasionally Durban. This was essentially a four-weekly service, although sailings and calls were based on cargo inducement. Some vessels on BI's Red Sea service (U.K. to Port Sudan, Jeddah, Massawa and Aden) continued on to East African ports. There was also a seasonal (October-February) service from Indian ports to East Africa for the annual cotton and cashew nut harvests.

The East African cargo service was maintained by the first new generation of cargo ships which were the linchpin of Currie's building programme of the late 'thirties, MoWT contracted newbuildings, and post-war vessels that continued the pre-war classes. As BI assigned an often bewildering variety of its cargo liners to the East African run, a brief resumé of the principal types is worthwhile.

In keeping with the old BI design policy of "flexibility", the initial Currie newbuilding programme, begun in 1938, was characterised by large classes of vessels which could operate on most of the routes within their design capability. The first such group was the "I" class:

Itinda	(1938/6,619 grt)
Indora	(1938/6,622 grt)
Itria	(1940/6,895 grt)
Itaura	(1940/6,793 grt)
Ismailia	(1940/6,793 grt)
Ikauna	(1941/6,793 grt)

and the similar "U" class:

Urlana	(1941/6,852 grt)
Umaria	(1941/6,852 grt)

and two post-war replacements for the above war losses:

Urlana	(1946/6,834 grt)
Umaria	(1946/6,835 grt)

Numbering 11 vessels, this was one of the largest combined groups of BI

213

ships to date and was designed for general trading, especially the India/Burma based runs, although many of these ships figured in the post-war Home Line services, including those to Africa. Measuring 442.8 ft. by 57.6 ft., each had a approximate 460,000 cu. ft. (bale) cargo capacity in five holds. Built to the classic British three-island design, all, except *Itinda,* had a pair of kingposts in the forecastle and another pair right aft and all, save *Itria,* were built by Wm. Gray & Co., West Hartlepool. Originally coal burners, they were converted to oil-firing after the war and averaged 12 knots from their single- screw, triple-expansion machinery augmented by exhaust turbines. None of the "I"s had passenger accommodation.

By virtue of their number (13 vessels) and the use of two, *Chindwara* and *Chantala* as cadet training ships, of which more anon., the "C"s were BI's best-known cargo liners:

Canara	(1942/7,024 grt)
Chyebassa	(1942/7,043 grt)
Chanda	(1944/6,921 grt)
Chupra	(1944/6,957 grt)
Carpentaria	(1949/7,268 grt)
Chandpara	(1949/7,274 grt)
Chindwara	(1950/7,525 grt)
Chantala	(1950/7,551 grt)
Chilka	(1950/7,087 grt)
Chakdina	(1951/7,267 grt)
Chakdara	(1951/7,132 grt)
Chakrata	(1952/7,265 grt)
Chinkoa	(1952/7,102 grt)

Because of draught restrictions in the Hooghly River, BI was able to prevail upon the MoWT to build the initial four "C"s during the war as standard type ships were not suitable. The success of the design is reflected in 13 ships built over a nine-year span. Built by Barclay, Curle or Swan Hunter, they measured 485.7 ft. by 62.9 ft. (*Chanda* and *Chupra* were a foot shorter) and their bale capacity ranged from 420,590 cu. ft to 538,525 cu. ft.; the post-war vessels having 13,000 cu. ft. reefer space as well. Designed for the Home Line services, each was powered by two sets of six-cylinder Doxford opposed piston 6,800 ihp diesels and were good for 14.5 knots. All were fitted with comfortable passenger accommodation for 12 in four single and four twin-berth cabins with private facilities; the wartime "C"s did not offer private cabin facilities. Well-found ships and possessing a certain rugged handsomeness, the "C"s were the archetypical British cargo liner and the backbone of the Home Line services during the post-war period.

Soon a fixture along the East African coast, the "P"s comprised a group of wartime standard built ships originally ordered by the MoWT, but completed

214

for BI. The first group:

Pachumba	(1945/7,282 grt)
Palikonda	(1945/7,434 grt)
Pemba	(1945/7,449 grt)

were near sisters built by Wm. Gray, Hartlepool; John Readhead, South Shields, and by Bartram, Sunderland, respectively. The first two ships measured 447.8 ft. by 56.2 ft. whilst *Pemba* was two feet longer. All were single-screw ships powered by triple-expansion machinery and had a 12-knot service speed. Their five holds had an approximate 507,000 cu. ft. capacity. *Pachumba* had accommodation for eight passengers and the others had cabins for 12.

The next two wartime-built "P"s were not sister ships: *Pundua* (1945/7,295 grt) from Wm. Doxford, Sunderland, measuring 442.9 ft. by 56.5 ft., motor-driven, with a 480,220 cu. ft. cargo capacity, and *Padana* (1945/7,541 grt), constructed by Burntisland, measuring 436.6 ft. by 58 ft., powered by coal-fired, triple-expansion machinery and with a 518,417 cu. ft. cargo capacity and fitted with eight passenger berths.

The best looking of the wartime "P"s, *Palamcotta* (1945/6,662 grt and *Pentakota* (1946/6,672 grt), were built by Lithgows, Port Glasgow. With measurements of 446.8 ft. by 56.2 ft., they were powered by triple-expansion machinery giving 12 knots and had cargo capacities of approximately 450,000 cu. ft. None had passenger accommodation. The final "P", *Purnea* (1947/6,672 grt), was ordered by BI and not the MoWT and was essentially a smaller (431.8 ft. by 55.2 ft.), 12-knot version of the "C"s. She had a 455,624 cu. ft. cargo capacity and berths for six passengers.

Another hotchpotch of vessels, all bearing "O" names, were also regulars on the Africa run. The first two:

Orna	(1938/6,779 grt)
Ozarda	(1940/6,895 grt)

were built by Barclay, Curle and introduced what might be described as the "BI Look" for cargo liners built under Currie management, having a pleasing rake to masts and funnel, the classic three-island profile, raked stem and cruiser stern. These two had principal measurements of 441.7 ft. by 57.2 ft., five holds of approximately 490,000 cu. ft. capacity and a speed of 12 knots from single screw diesels. When not making periodic voyages to East Africa, they were usually on the Persian Gulf-Japan run.

The next two "O"s,

Obra	(1946/5,695 grt)
Okhla	(1946/5,732 grt)

were built by J. Readhead, South Shields, and were similar to *Purnea,* but powered by single-screw combination triple expansion/low pressure exhaust turbine machinery giving 12 knots and measuring 446 ft. by 57.5 ft..

Distinguished by their extra set of kingposts aft, each had a cargo capacity of approximately 500,000 cu. ft.

A famous old name in BI shipbuilding, Wm. Denny of Dumbarton, returned to the scene with the final three "O"s which were the first BI vessels built by the yard in some 30 years:

Ormara	(1947/5,444 grt)
Olinda	(1950/5,424 grt)
Ordia	(1950/5,449 grt)

These were powered by triple expansion/low pressure exhaust steam turbines and had a speed of 12 knots. Their cargo capacity was approximately 490,000 cu. ft.

With the phasing out of the "M"s in 1953, cargo ships began to fill the void with *Urlana, Padana, Pentakota, Palamcotta* and the chartered *Treglisson* (1950/5,975 grt/Hain S.S. Co.) making East Africa sailings that year.

Aronda made one Bombay-East Africa voyage, 27 March-19 April 1953, her place on the Karachi-Chittagong run being taken by *Dara* and Mogul's *Islami* for one trip each. As part of her operation on behalf of the Pakistan Government, *Aronda* had an all-West Pakistan crew and trained Pakistani cadet officers who came to regard her as their own ship. Their pride, reflected in the smart dark blue uniforms worn by her deck crew and in the particularly efficient way *Aronda* was run, was noted in a 1957 inspection report; "ship is very well kept, particularly in view of her rather arduous service. I have no comment to make on her condition save that she is a credit to the Fleet." Another report two years latter by K.M. Campbell stated, "In my opinion, the vessel which appeared to be the best maintained of the Eastern Passenger Fleet was *Aronda*. She was immaculate."

Flying the standard of the Sultan of Zanzibar, who was a guest aboard and who had travelled from Zanzibar in the vessel, *Kenya* represented BI at Queen Elizabeth II's Coronation Fleet Review at Spithead on 15 June 1953. A special Coronation cruise was offered in the ship which sailed from London on the 13th and concluded at Plymouth three days later. The previous month, *Kenya* had an amusing incident at Mombasa when she was swarmed by thousands of bees. Armed with fire hoses, her crew swept them along the decks and into the swimming pool.

The East African Railways and Harbours Administration embarked on a £60 million development programme to lessen the crippling congestion in Tanganyika ports. To serve southern Tanganyika and originally planned under the groundnut scheme, a new port was built at Mtwara which was first used by *Urlana* on 22 January 1954 which loaded cashew nuts for India. *Mombasa*, with Governor Sir Edward Twining aboard, participated in the official opening ceremonies on 15 September. Capacity at Tanga was increased by 50 per cent and construction began on three new deep-water berths at Dar-es-Salaam.

Mombasa made her maiden arrival at Bombay on 7 May 1954 for her first special survey and entered the Mogul Dry Dock on the 20th. Following repairs to keel plates and overhaul of her crankshafts, she was undocked on 1 July and sailed for Mombasa on the 15th.

One of BI's real old-timers and a pioneering ship in the fleet was *Durenda* (1922/7,241 grt), the second motor vessel built for the company and the last afloat powered by North British diesels. She finished her long career on the U.K.-East Africa cargo run. Leaving Britain in mid-May with a cargo of cement and motor vehicles she encountered heavy monsoon seas just before reaching Mombasa and arrived at Dar-es-Salaam on 5 July 1954. She sailed northbound in August and was assigned thereafter to the East Africa route.

Also on the cargo service in 1954 were *Chantala, Itinda, Palamcotta, Chindwara, Umaria, Pentakota* and *Ikauna*. Chartered tonnage included *Maidenhead* (1943/7,120 grt/Fort Eire S.S. Co.), *Sea Rover* (1944/7,063 grt/Soc. de Transportes Maritimos, Liberia), *Laurentian Lake* and *Lake Michigan* (1944/7,139 grt/Runnymede S.S. Co.), the later two ships carrying consignments of powered milk supplied by the United Nation's Children's Fund for famine relief in central Africa The two Lake ships and *Pentakota* were among a record 14 vessels handled on one day, 10 October, at Dar-es-Salaam. On the seasonal harvest cargo run from Bombay were the chartered *Ismaila* and *Urlana* whilst *Pachumba* made a special voyage in November from Dar-es-Salaam, Mozambique, Mtwara and Lindi to Malabar, Cochin and Quilon with part of the cashew nut harvest, *Itria* and *Pemba* doing likewise in December and January 1955.

Aronda again returned to the Bombay-East Africa run for one voyage in 1954 which turned round at Dar-es-Salaam 3-4 April.

Indian seamen were stalwarts of many British lines in addition to BI. In December 1954 *Karanja* arrived at Durban with 300 replacement ratings for the Bullard King liners *Umzino* and *Umgeni* and Goanese catering staff for Ellerman's *City of Paris*.

Amra was first in the BI fleet to be refitted to new Indian Government deck passenger regulations. These included a new Third Class with folding steel bunks, separate facilities for unaccompanied ladies and improved dining facilities. With berths for 222 Saloon and 737 Third Class, she sailed from Bombay on 9 January 1955.

While the "K"s were similarly refurbished at the Taikoo Dockyard, Hong Kong, Mogul Line's *Mohammedi* (1947/7,026 grt) was chartered for two Bombay-East Africa voyages beginning on 17 January and 17 February 1955. She had berths for 62 Saloon and 1,391 deck passengers. The refitted *Kampala* arrived in ballast at Bombay on 25 February from Hong Kong together with *Amra* from East Africa. This completed a unique assemblage in Bombay of all the India-Africa liners with *Karanja* drydocked there and

Shipping Corp. of India's *State of Bombay* also in port. *Kampala* resumed service to Durban on 8 March, followed by *Karanja* on 8 April; each now carried 60 First and 180 Second Class and 860 (*Kampala*) and 832 (*Karanja*) Third Class.

On her final BI voyage, *Leicestershire* left Dar-es-Salaam for Britain on 7 March 1955 and thereafter operated on Bibby Line's Liverpool-Rangoon service. The Home Line was thereafter maintained on a five-weekly basis by *Kenya* and *Uganda* in addition to the monthly cargo run, served that year by *Landaura, Palikonda, Durenda, Pachumba, Padana, Itaura* and *Itria*.

In August 1954 BI commissioned the 8,596-grt *Nuddea* which, at 514 ft. by 67 ft. and with a speed of 16.5 knots from 10,250 shp steam turbines, represented a new, considerably larger and faster type of cargoliner for the company. Second only to *Kenya* and *Uganda* in dimensions, they were second to none in appearance and whilst each differed in external details, all were particularly handsome and impressive vessels:

Nuddea	(1954/8,596 grt)
Nowshera	(1955/8,519 grt)
Nyanza	(1956/8,513 grt)
Nardana	(1956/8,511 grt)

Despite their extensive superstructures, only *Nowshera* and *Nuddea* had accommodation for two and four passengers, respectively. Built with the Australia run in mind, the "N"s soon became familiar sights in East African ports, although their size caused some anxious moments in the smaller, more difficult harbours. The second of the class, *Nowshera*, handed over on 25 February 1955, sailed to East Africa the first week of August and called at Dar-es-Salaam on 17 September.

Introduced with *Kenya*'s July 1955 sailing from London, BI adopted a new all-white livery (first tested by some of the Gulf Mail "D"s) for its passenger liners which was reckoned to reduce accommodation temperatures by seven degrees. Boot-topping and sheer line were now black and the masts, previously black to the crosstrees and mast brown above, were repainted buff. *Mombasa* retained her black hull but the white strake was carried one deck lower.

The once-thriving African coastal network began to wind down due to the collapse of the groundnut scheme, changing trade patterns and improvements in road transport between Kenya and Tanganyika. A major cargo to Tanganyika, Kenyan flour, of which *Mombasa* used to carry 200 tons a fortnight, was replaced by cheaper imports from Australia, further reducing cargo carryings. *Tabora* left Mombasa for the Persian Gulf and new owners (Gray Mackenzie & Co., Bahrein) on 12 April 1953:

Because of her small bunker capacity oil drums were
lashed to the deck with a portable hand pump and hose pipe.

Pirates had recently been active off the Omani coast attacking dhows and small craft so it was thought prudent to supply the captain with a .45 revolver and a supply of ammunition to discourage unwelcome boarders. A quantity of fishing lines and hooks were also supplied to enable the crew of *Tabora* to supplement their diet. The northeast monsoon petered out in late March and soon as the southwest monsoon wind was blowing the weather was considered suitable for *Tabora* to commence her voyage. Her first port of call was Mogadiscio to pick up a load of charcoal whence she set off for Muscat. The ship safely arrived at Bahrein, but the agents there sent the revolver back which caused all sorts of trouble with the Kenya customs as the Mau Mau emergency regulations were still in force.**

Superfluous on the East African coast, *Sofala*'s final duty was a special trip from Australia to Port Swettingham, Malaya, where she arrived on 7 April 1955. Returning to Durban on 21 May 1955 *Sofala* concluded her BI career, having been sold to African Coasters Ltd. (South Africa) six days previously, and renamed *Voorloper*, departed on the 31st for Port Elizabeth and a new career as a South African coaster.

After her final arrival at Dar-es-Salaam from Durban on 1 July 1955, *Kilwa* was put briefly back on the Northern Feeder Service and sailed from Dar-es-Salaam for Mtwara on 12 July. Under Captain V.S. Webb, she departed Mombasa for the last time on 27 February 1956, bound for southern Indian ports and thence to Hong Kong where she was sold to local breakers for £50,400 on 27 April 1956.

To replace *Kilwa* on the Durban-Mombasa run, *Warla* (1949/3,669 grt), commanded by Captain W.F. Solly, arrived at Mombasa on 27 February 1956. Together with sister ship *Warora* (1948/3,668 grt), these trim-looking 364 ft. by 50 ft. vessels were built by Burntisland Shipbuilding Co., Burntisland, for BI's Chittagong-Japan run. Four holds had a 273,650 cu. ft. capacity, but there was no passenger accommodation. Designed for economy and not for speed, the two "W"s got no more than 14 knots from their single-screw Doxford diesels.

Arusha was sold on 28 September 1956, to Falmouth Steam Towing for whom, as *St. Mawes*, she remained in service until 1983. On at least one occasion the former *Arusha* attended *Uganda* in her later role as a educational cruise ship during a call at Falmouth, an unlikely venue for a reunion of East African veterans.

It is admitted by her friends, by her rivals, and even by her enemies, that the experience of Great Britain in the maritime affairs of the world has been unique. It is simply a fact of

219

history that shipping lines based on that small island in the Eastern Atlantic are remarkable in strength and efficiency, these qualities being rooted deeply in the natural instincts of an enterprising people with a long history of stable government behind them.

It is therefore an occasion of true international importance when one of the largest and oldest shipping concerns in the world— the British India Steam Navigation Company Limited— celebrates its centenary.

Sir William Currie, G.B.E.

British India reached its 100th year in 1956 when the African routes contributed more than ever to the line's fortunes, an ongoing tradition of service that was also a living monument to the vision and courage of William Mackinnon.

That centenary year the Home Line cargo service was maintained by a truly representative collection of the principal BI vessel classes: *Chantala, Nowshera, Durenda, Palikonda, Ismailia, Landaura, Padana, Okhla, Pemba, Itinda, Olinda, Chilka* and *Nardana*. That old-stager *Durenda* limped into Mombasa on 13 March 1956 on only her starboard engine after her port motor failed shortly after sailing northbound from Tanga. The tug *Marie Felling* was in attendance as she came into Mombasa, but was not required. Although repaired and soon on her way, this proved to be *Durenda*'s last voyage under BI colours, although remarkably, the 34-year-old vessel was sold for further trading in May to Paramount Shipping Corp., Liberia, renamed *Elene* and not scrapped until 1960.

To improve their economy, both *Kenya* and *Uganda* were retrofitted with solid screws during their 1956 dry dock periods.

It was unfortunately symbolic that BI's centenary should have occurred at the same time when the Suez Canal, which had in large measure thrust the line into Africa, was itself thrown into chaos during the Suez Crisis, and coincided with Princess Margaret's Royal Visit of British East Africa whose existence owed so much to Mackinnon. Past, present and future came together that September of 1956.

The Sultan and Sultana of Zanzibar were guests at a celebratory luncheon aboard *Uganda* at Zanzibar on 13 September and the ship later hosted a centenary reception at Dar-es-Salaam. All eyes, however, were on the rapidly developing Suez Crisis. Although it was already planned that the Suez Canal be given to Egypt in 1968, that country's nationalist leader Col. Game Adbul Nasser announced on 26 July 1956 that the Canal would be nationalised at once and the income from transit fees be used to finance the Aswan High Dam project. On 30 October the Egyptians scuttled 13 vessels to obstruct the canal and prompted an invasion of Port Said during 31 October-5 November by

British and French forces aided by Israel. The once and former "Lifeline of Empire" was closed amid world indignation against the Anglo-French military action and indifference towards Egypt's seizure of private property.

Shipowners took no chances as the Suez situation deteriorated in late summer 1956 and began to divert vessels via the Cape, long before the waterway was closed. *Kenya* sailed from Britain on 11 September 1956, called at Dakar on the 17th, and reached Mombasa at 7.00 a.m. 4 October, five days off her original schedule. This caused considerable concern as the vessel was to participate in Princess Margaret's dedication on 10 October of the new deep-water quays at Dar-es-Salaam, with the Royal Yacht *Britannia* and *Kenya* alongside, and her Royal Highness was also to attend a formal dinner aboard *Kenya* that evening. The stevedores had to unload 3,780 tons of cargo in just two days instead of the usual five if *Kenya* was to make it to Dar-es-Salaam in time.

A letter to the *Daily Telegraph* by Douglas Williams gave the following account:

> On her recent tour of East Africa Princess Margaret received many gifts as tokens of loyalty and affection from the various people she met.
>
> But I think the gift offered to her by the men of Kilindini, Mombasa's waterfront,— one which she never saw and never heard of— was perhaps the most touching.
>
> It came from the African dock workers who, being informed that the ship had to be at Dar-es-Salaam by the morning of October 8, to entertain the Princess that evening, volunteered to work day and night to unload the heavy cargo the ship was carrying.
>
> The *Kenya* was due at Mombasa on a Thursday morning with 4,000 tons of cargo and 791 bags of mail. She had to sail on the Saturday morning if she was to reach Dar-es-Salaam in time.
>
> Older workers shook their heads and said it was impossible. But the dockers were not discouraged. The moment the ship had moored alongside they swarmed aboard, hoisted off the hatch covers and set to work with a will, singing and running.
>
> The whole operation went with a swing, and as the men realised they were beating all existing records, excitement rose to a fever pitch. They worked straight through to Friday afternoon and the job was completed with almost a full day in hand.
>
> The ship sailed at 10 a.m. on Saturday and when, a day or two later, the dockers saw a picture of *Kenya* lying alongside *Britannia* at the Princess Margaret Quay in Dar-es-Salaam they

were satisfied that their hard work had made it possible.

It was their gift— a simple one perhaps— but freely offered to prove their devotion to the Royal visitor.

On time, dressed overall and her white livery glistening in the African sunshine, *Kenya* was the first large vessel to dock alongside the new deep water quays at Dar-es-Salaam. Sharing the quayside was H.M.Y. *Britannia*, the two ships forming an impressive backdrop as Princess Margaret, witnessed by Governor Sir Edward Twining and other dignitaries, resplendent in plumed pith helmets and white uniforms, dedicated the Princess Margaret Quay. Brilliantly illuminated, *Kenya* was the proudest ship in the centenary fleet that warm tropical evening of 10 October 1956 when Princess Margaret, followed by Governor Twining, ascended the gangway and welcomed aboard by Captain D.R.P. Gun-Cuninghame, observed by the 150 other invited guests and 50 passengers. After a celebratory dinner in the ship's First Class dining saloon, the guests watched a fireworks display from *Kenya*'s decks. Amidst the upheaval of Suez, imperial echoes still rang true in British East Africa.

Although her outbound voyage from London on 7 August 1956 was just in time to be routed via Suez, *Uganda* took the Cape route home, calling there on 26 September.

Chinkoa, which docked at Dar-es-Salaam on 11 November 1956, was the last ship to reach East Africa from Britain via Suez before it was blocked by the Egyptians. The canal was still open when *Kenya* sailed northbound from Mombasa, but upon news of its closure, she turned back at Aden on 2 November and arrived at Cape Town on the 11th, not calling at any East African ports en route. Her original London arrival of 14 November was changed to the 27th. Henceforth the Home Line routeing was London-Las Palmas-Cape Town-Beira-Dar-es-Salaam-Zanzibar-Tanga-Mombasa.

Hundreds of spectators watched from Mombasa's sea front on 15 October 1956 as *Kampala* slowly steamed into the harbour, towed by the tug *Marie Felling*. "We came in on the starboard engine only, assisted by the tug. The fault with the port engine is not all that serious and we should be leaving Kilindini on time", *Kampala's* Chief Officer explained to reporters.

Mogul Line's *Mohammedi* made a single Bombay-East African voyage for BI in 1956, arriving at Dar-es-Salaam on 27 October and sailing for India the same day.

The centenary year was capped, suitably, by the addition of three new ships to the fleet; the 20,527-grt transport *Nevasa*, largest vessel to ever fly the houseflag, and two more of the handsome "N" class, *Nyanza* and *Nardana*, the latter started her maiden voyage to East Africa, the first such via the Cape, on 2 November 1956 and called at Dar-es-Salaam on 13 December.

Kenya's 14 December 1956 sailing from London featured the at sea premier of BI's new centenary film, "The Connecting Links". The 45-minute-long colour film, in production for 15 months, was by the Kenyan freelance cinematographer Robert Kingston Davies, and featured footage of BI ships and staff in India, Pakistan, the Persian Gulf, Ceylon, Burma, Japan, Hong Kong, Singapore, Australia, Kenya and Britain.

In February 1957, whilst on passage from Las Palmas to Cape Town, 90 miles off Cape Verde, Captain Spiers diverted *Uganda* to pass 900 ft. astern of *Britannia* carrying Prince Philip, with ensigns dipped, sirens sounding, messages exchanged and "Rule Britannia" rendered by *Uganda*'s band.

Flying along at 17 knots with a fresh breeze whipping up the waves and carrying the voices of the cheering crew away over the Atlantic, the *Uganda* swept within 900 ft. of the stern of the Royal Yacht *Britannia* which was racing away at 90 degrees. Cameras clicked and binoculars were almost snatched by the ladies who 'certain' they could see the Duke 'who was wearing a blue shirt' and standing on the after deck.

Tanganyika Standard

The Kabaka of Buganda, making one of his periodic BI voyages, sailed in *Karanja* in 1957 from Mombasa to Lourenço Marques for a hunting expedition and whilst at Dar-es-Salaam on 27 February, visited *Uganda*. In January 1960 he presented two elephant tusks to be hung in the ship's smoking room; they became familiar to future passengers and are now displayed at P&O's headquarters in Pall Mall, London.

Uganda last called at the Cape homewards on 15 June 1957 and *Kenya* arrived at Mombasa on the 25th for the first time in nine months via the now Egyptian-owned Suez Canal which was cleared of obstructions by 9 April. One of *Kenya*'s officers commented on the transit of the waterway on the 16th: "There were no incidents when we passed through the canal, and when we went ashore at Port Said we were treated with every courtesy by the Egyptians." *Kenya* had aboard 150 passengers for Mombasa and 100 for Beira.

The cargo service, held down in 1957 by *Ordia, Nardana, Nuddea, Chantala, Padana, Chilka, Chindwara, Woodarra, Nyanza, Nowshera* and *Orna*, continued to carry Commonwealth commerce from the mundane to the unusual. An unusually large consignment of cement clinker, 9,250 tons in all, was landed in a fortnight period in November at Kilindini by *Padana* and *Chilka* whilst *Nuddea* numbered among her homeward cargo on her June voyage a pair of zebra embarked at Dar-es-Salaam, a gift from Tangangyka to Princess Margaret during her Royal Tour. They were accommodated in specially-made stalls carried on deck. That year's seasonal cashew nut trade fleet to India included *Garbeta* (1941/5,323 grt) which arrived at Lindi on 20 January and left nine days later with 3,187 tons of cashews and loaded another 4,175 tons at Mtwara and 514 tons from Mafia via lighter before sailing for

Mangalore and other southern Indian ports. *Kenya* and *Uganda* began to make regular calls at Nacala, Mozambique, in 1957 after the latter vessel first stopped there on 30 March 1956.

Among the newcomers to East African ports in 1957 were *Nyanza* which arrived at Dar-es-Salaam from Britain on 13 June and on their maiden voyages, *Woodarra,* launched at Barclay, Curle on 22 November 1956 and calling at Dar-es-Salaam on 24 May 1957, and sister *Waroonga,* christened at the same yard four days later, which arrived at Dar-es-Salaam on 18 November. Measuring 8,753 grt, 520 ft. by 68.6 ft., and powered by 10,850 shp Pametrada turbines giving 17.5 knots, the "W"s were BI's last traditional cargo liners and developed from the earlier "N" class with fewer but longer hatches. Each could carry as much as 716,000 cu. ft. of cargo in five holds and accommodate 12 passengers.

Arriving at Dar-es-Salaam on 11 March 1957 on her first visit to East Africa was *Chantala*, one of BI's two well-known cadet training ships, the other being *Chindwara* and both normally on the Australian run. On this trip *Chantala* carried 39 cadets, aged 18-21 years. British India was one of the few companies to operate such vessels and *Chantala* and *Chindwara* came to occupy a very special place in the fleet, both to their young future officers and to management, particularly Sir William Currie. Giving invaluable experience, the ships were run largely by the cadets who assumed all the functions of deck and engine crew as well as officers, learning navigation, vessel handling, cargo loading, engineering as well as the routine of chip and paint. Just as important, they were imbued with teamwork and BI traditions and made lifelong friendships with fellow cadets that would endure throughout their respective BI careers.

The agents always tried to arrange sporting fixtures for the cadets at the local clubs while the ships were in port, and in Mombasa trips to Tsavo game park were also arranged. Time in port enabled the cadets to practice lifeboat handling and sailing the whaleboats which were carried on board.

Sometimes a lifeboat would be sent on ahead to the next port to give the cadets some experience of handling an open boat at sea but on one occasion things went sadly wrong. The lifeboat set off from Tanga with an experienced boatswain in charge of the cadets but the captain of the cadet ship had not reckoned on the strong northerly set to the current and the southeast trade wind which was blowing strongly up the coast. The unfortunate crew of the lifeboat tacked backwards and forwards across the Pemba Channel and gradually reached the shelter of Zanzibar Island but still had some way to go before reaching the harbour which they did five days after setting forth from Tanga. The exhausted and sunburnt crew were given breakfast by the agent and his wife before being flown on to Dar-es-Salaam to rejoin their ship which picked up its boat on its return voyage northbound. **

On 5 January 1958 BI announced a new direct cargo service from Durban to Persian Gulf ports catering to an increasing commerce of African livestock and farm products outbound and dates, dried fruits, nuts and bitumen from the Gulf.

> The main cargo northbound from Zanzibar was boriti (mangrove) poles which were brought to Zanzibar by dhow from the Rufiji River delta. These were in great demand in the Gulf area for house building due to the almost complete absence of timber and also due to their straightness and strength.**

Commencing in late February, *Warora*, sister ship of *Warla* on the Durban-Mombasa run, would maintain the Gulf service approximately every ten weeks. Before entering service, *Warora* was drydocked at Durban and a special plastic anti-fouling paint applied to her hull to counteract the corrosive qualities of the seawater along the East African coast. *Warora* first called at Dar-es-Salaam on 14 February from the Gulf, bound for Durban where she arrived on the 20th with a cargo of dates. Her maiden northbound run from the Natal port commenced on 1 March, called at Dar-es-Salaam on the 11th and continued to Kuwait, Bahrain, Basra and Khoramshahr.

In January 1958 *Amra* completed a special survey at Taikoo Dockyard, Hong Kong, at a cost of £96,000, £1,000 of which was spent on new furniture and general refurbishment of her interiors. Her shipyard berth was then taken by *Kampala* which arrived on 10 January for a 28-day, £55,490 special survey which also included redecoration of public rooms.

The Deputy Chairman of BI, E.J. Pakes, made an inspection trip of the Eastern Fleet in 1959, sailing out in *Uganda* and seeing many of the India-based ships. The "K"s came in for some criticism even after their refits:

> Visiting the "K"s after travelling in the *Uganda* and *Kenya* and going on board the Lloyd Triestino *Europa* was a depressing experience. The "K"s and the *Amra* are clean, particularly in the unberthed passenger decks, but the saloon accommodation throughout is shabby and dull. A little money spent intelligently on the cabins and the public rooms would make a world of difference especially in First Class. The cane furniture on deck all needs replacing and the opportunity could be taken of introducing something modern.

In reply, D.B. Lattin, Chief Marine Superintendent, Eastern Fleet, commented:

> I doubt if anything we can do would compete with the Lloyd

225

Triestino ships, newer, air-conditioned and superbly staffed. We may however, be competitive with Union-Castle by virtue of better service.

It is rather hard on the "K"s to compare them with ships whose principal business does not include the carriage of Indian saloon passengers. Their personal habits are quite disgusting.

We spend a good deal on the "K"s' public rooms and passenger cabins, but with the destructive carelessness of the Bombay/East Africa passenger, it is uphill work.

Kenya had a bit of a scare when on 8 June 1958 she was torn from her moorings in high winds at Beira, but her crew just managed to get her underway before she hit any other vessel. On her northbound passage, she carried home the retiring Governor General of Tanganyika, Sir Edward Twining, and Lady Twining, who embarked amidst much ceremony at Dar-es-Salaam on 17 June and were cheered off by a large crowd on the quayside.

At this time British East African ports began to be increasingly effected by labour unrest. A six-day strike by 1,200 dock workers at Dar-es-Salaam at the end of August 1958 resulted in the inbound *Amra* being able to only discharge passengers and mail on 29 August and *Kenya* having to leave behind 800 tons of cargo the next day.

The 1958 Mogul Line charter resulted in *Mozaffari* making two Dar-es-Salaam calls from Bombay, 29 November (returning via the Seychelles) and 30 December, calling at Porebunder on the return. On the cargo berth that year were *Nardana, Nyanza, Chinkoa, Itinda, Chindwara* in addition to U.K.-bound sailings from Indian and/or Australian ports via East Africa by *Pentakota, Okhla* and the chartered *Scottish Trader* (1948/5,590 grt/Trader Nav. Co.) and *La Cumbre* (1944/7,371 grt/Burie Markes Ltd.).

"Interest in our new service is exceeding expectations and has surprised all our agents, full cargoes out of Africa seem assured", was how E.J. Pakes characterised the initial success of the Africa-Persian Gulf run in its first year which warranted the addition of the chartered *Norse Captain* (1945/3,875 grt/Rederi A/S Hauk) in May 1959, the ship first calling at Dar-es-Salaam en route from Durban to the Gulf on 26 May. There was even some discussion about the possibility of positioning one of the Gulf run "D"s on the service.

Mogul Line's *Mozaffari* (1948/7,024 grt) filled-in for *Amra* and *Kampala* on the Bombay-East Africa run again in 1959 with two voyages which terminated at Dar-es-Salaam on 30 January and 4 March respectively. On the cargo service that year were *Nowshera, Landaura, Chilka, Chindwara* and *Chakdara*. With the exception of *Urlana* and *Umaria*, the "I" and "U" class ships were sold off (largely to Pakistani owners) from 1958-9.

On 8-9 December 1959 *Uganda* called at Barcelona and henceforth the Spanish port became a regular northbound call in place of Marseilles and or

Malta, the last stop there by *Uganda* occurring on 13 May.

Sir William Currie retired on 30 March 1960, and Sir Donald Anderson assumed the Chairmanship. It was more than the passing of the torch, rather the end of an era. Sir William, born in the India of the Imperial Raj and whose career in shipping began with Mackinnon Mackenzie, was the last P&O Chairman with personal and professional links with the roots of BI. Under his leadership, the P&O Group contributed to victory in the Second World War, built up a post-war fleet with the finest vessels ever to ply the East of Suez trades, and re-oriented its business towards Australia, Asia and Africa.

Sir William's nurturing of the old BI traditions was exemplified in his cherished cadet ships *Chindwara* and *Chantala* of which he said, "incalculates in these boys an esprit de corps and an atmosphere of tradition which is invaluable in later years." Now as the new decade of the 'sixties dawned, fraught with change and upheaval of every sort and on every front, such traditions and BI itself were to find themselves fighting for survival.

10. AFRICAN SUNSET

The lights, the signals die. The sisters part
But something bright long lingers in the heart:
And British breasts may be allowed to swell,
For here's a thing we still do rather well.

A. P. Herbert

Even if a far cry from "BI Sunday", company ships could dominate East African ports into the mid 'sixties, as on 6 December 1965 when *Santhia, Uganda* and *Chakla* occupied all the deep-water quays at Dar-es-Salaam. On 15 September 1966 *Uganda, Rhodesia Castle* and *Pierre Loti* shared the tranquil palm- and mangrove-shaded anchorage of the "Haven of Peace", now also a refuge for the remaining African liners amid the blowing winds of change.

Few routes in the 'sixties were dealt as many body blows as the East Africa run. The jet had siphoned off much of the Home Line traffic, but air competition did not figure much among the Third Class passengers who made up the vast majority of the India-Africa trade. The most significant factor was a rapidly changing Africa. The Mau Mau outrages and groundnut fiasco of the 'fifties were a prelude to sweeping political changes in the 'sixties. In 1960, the Union of South Africa left the Commonwealth and became the Republic of South Africa. Between 1962-64, Tanganyika (Tanzania), Kenya, Zanzibar, Nyasaland (Malawi) and Northern Rhodesia (Zambia) achieved independence. In 1965 Rhodesia declared its Unilateral Declaration of Independence.

As the Union Jack vanished from East Africa, the Red Ensign and BI houseflag which preceded it, fluttered on in a waning breeze. Trade declined as the new nations found different economic partners, nationalized their industries and often started their own shipping services. The steady flow of British civil servants, settlers and businessmen was reduced to a trickle of expatriates. Commonwealth sanctions against Rhodesia wiped out a major BI market. Majority rule African nations enacted their own sanctions against South Africa.

For its part, BI can be faulted for perhaps not re-organising the basis of its operations quickly enough and inadequately competing in the changed political and economic climate. The fleet was not sufficiently renewed with more efficient and faster tonnage and overall retrenchment saw the "I"s and "P"s merely retired without replacement. Then too P&O Group in the 'sixties with its emphasis on oil tankers and bulk carriers did not foster change and growth within its subsidiary companies. For BI's African passenger operations, however, the political changes were for the most part insurmountable and none of the traditional British or foreign flag carriers carried on as long as BI did on the African routes.

Jet trails traced the setting sun of African empires. It will be recalled that BOAC operated the jet Comet 1 from London to East and South Africa from 1952-1954. After the Comet 1 was grounded, air service reverted to slower piston-engined Argonauts, Constellations, DC-7s and from 1957 onwards, turbo-prop Britannia aircraft. Already substantial air competition was made irresistible when jet service from London direct to Nairobi was resumed on 17 September 1960 by East African Airways' Comet 4s and fares became more competitive. It would be a long time until air competition became a factor on the India-Africa run, however.

On the last charter voyage for BI, Mogul Line's *Mohammedi* sailed from Bombay to Mombasa, Dar-es-Salaam and Zanzibar and return via Karachi, 18 January-11 February 1960.

The decline of BI's African routes started with the demise of the remnants of the East African coastal run. Once so much a part of BI tradition, this was now the company's only remaining coastwise service.

Mombasa had been the object of corporate concern for some time. Not only was her trade falling off, but her crew of 85-89 officers and ratings was large for a ship of her size and costs were correspondingly high. When the need for the ship's customary six-day turn-round between voyages was queried on cost grounds, it was admitted that most of this time was needed for engine repairs, her machinery being described as being "a box of tricks." Then too, *Mombasa* had her fair share of staffing problems and her Swahili crew were never really satisfactory. Thus *Mombasa* was vulnerable when the "penny counters" in Leadenhall Street began to prune the fleet.

After carrying 200,000 passengers and 250,000 tons of cargo in ten short years, *Mombasa* left Dar-es-Salaam on her final voyage on 16 August 1960 and she, together with *Karanja* and *Kenya*, arrived at Mombasa two days later. Her first (Captain Robert Trimble) and last (Captain Frank Everett) masters were on her bridge on the 23rd to receive a farewell salute of the outbound *Kenya*, Tanga-bound, and ring up together *Mombasa*'s final BI trip to Port Reitz (the tanker berths at Kilindini) where she was laid up. She was not sold until 18 October 1961 to Pakistan's Crescent Shipping Lines and renamed *Kareem*.

The withdrawal of the BI coastal service prompted the Government of Zanzibar to position the Sultan's yacht, the 1956-built *Seyyid Khalifa*, on a similar service in December 1960 for which Smith Mackenzie was appointed agents. Accommodation was for five First Class, 21 Second Class and 406 deck passengers.

Beginning its own competing East Africa-Persian Gulf service was the

Dutch K.P.M. line with the 7 May 1960 Durban sailing of *Van Riebeeck*. In addition to those by *Warora*, BI sailings on the route were augmented that year by *Johilla* in May, *Malika* from Durban on 19 September and in December, *Pachumba* in August and *Garbeta* in October.

Although the October-March period was traditionally the busy season for the East Africa-India run, 1960 witnessed especially heavy traffic owing to, it was suggested, Asians returning to India and Pakistan due to their uncertain future as independence loomed for British East Africa This demand was evidenced on 2 September when Smith Mackenzie's Kampala office opened berthing books for the January-June 1961 period and sold-out its entire allotment by afternoon, despite a ten per cent increase in passage fares.

There was new blood on the India-Africa service, however, *Sirdhana* and *Santhia*, built for the Calcutta-Yokohama route. Like all of BI's post-war ships, these were handsome and workmanlike. Built by Swan, Hunter & Wigham Richardson, Newcastle, and preceded by *Sangola*, the 8,608-grt, 479 ft. by 62.7 ft. *Sirdhana* was delivered on 9 December 1947 followed by the 8,908-grt *Santhia* which was handed over by Barclay, Curle on 3 November 1950. It will be recalled that both called at East African ports en route to India on their delivery trips.

Powered by two four-cylinder Doxford diesels giving 14.5 knots, the "S"s were slower than the "K"s or "A"s and this would ultimately shorten their careers. In cargo capacity, however, they had no equals among BI liners: four holds of 402,000 cu. ft./11,000 cu. ft. (reefer)—*Santhia* 360,000 cu. ft./15,000 cu. ft. reefer—and it was said they could be profitable as cargo carriers alone.

Originally built to carry First, Second, Intermediate and deck passengers, *Sirdhana* accommodated 83 Saloon Class, 333 Bunked and 987 Deck and *Santhia*, 141 Saloon, 268 Bunked and 762 Deck whilst on the Bombay-East Africa run. Saloon Class staterooms, one- and three-berth or twin-bedded, were on Promenade and Bridge Decks, and amidships on Upper Deck. Public rooms comprised the former First Class lounge forward on Promenade Deck and the smoking room aft and the former Second Class lounge aft on Bridge Deck with the combined dining saloons forward on this deck.

As early as the mid-'fifties, the Calcutta-Yokohama route was over-tonnaged. Fortunately, the "S" ships proved BI's most versatile, *Sirdhana* serving on all of the India-based routes at various times. In 1955 she became a relief ship on the Gulf run, filled in for the drydocked *Rajula* on the Straits service two years later and in 1958 was chartered by the Pakistan Government for the Haj.

Santhia, too, sailed to new horizons. After relieving *Aronda* for two voyages on the Karachi-Chittagong service, 10 August-30 September 1960, she then deputised for the drydocked *Amra* and *Karanja*. *Santhia* departed Bombay on 14 November for Mombasa, Dar-es-Salaam and Zanzibar

230

followed by a 14 December departure for East and South African ports, including maiden calls at Beira on 30 December, Lourenço Marques on 2 January 1961, Durban (3-8), Mozambique (14th) and returning to Bombay via Karachi. Following her refit, *Karanja* arrived at Bombay on 11 February 1961 from Hong Kong and Singapore with cargo, but no passengers.

In addition to the superfluous "S"s, BI also had to find employment for *Aronda* which was supplanted on the Karachi-Chittagong run by the new *Shams* (Crescent Shipping Lines) in November 1960. Mackinnon Mackenzie had detailed plans in August 1960 to refit *Aronda* with 175 extra Saloon berths and perhaps an outdoor pool and other amenities for a new Calcutta, Bombay and London service to cater to budget Asian travel on the route. Unfortunately the cost of the required refit and doubts as to the viability of the run year-round precluded this intriguing revival of the long dormant Indian Home Line.

Instead, *Aronda* left Karachi for East Africa, returning to Bombay on 23 January 1961. Another East African voyage concluded at Bombay on 17 February. In what proved to be her final such trip, *Aronda* sailed from Bombay ten days later for East Africa, Beira, Lourenço Marques and Durban. She docked at the Natal port on 21 March and departed on the 25th for East African ports, Karachi, Bombay, Muscat, Dubai, Umm Said, Bahrain, Kuwait, Khoramshahr and Basra. Another Persian Gulf voyage followed from Bombay on 22 April. Following a terrorist bomb explosion on 10 April 1961 off Dubai that resulted in 212 deaths, *Dara* sank two days later. The inbound *Aronda* carried some of *Dara*'s survivors to Bombay from Dubai and *Sirdhana* was transferred to the Gulf run as a replacement. Although happily none of her fleetmates would share such a violent death, *Dara*'s loss was the first of the post-war fleet and in a way, presaged the gradual decline that would characterise the decade.

After a 1962 charter to the Indonesian Government, *Aronda* was sold for scrap and arrived at Hong Kong on 8 May 1963. Whilst being towed by the tug *Cabrilla* to Taiwan breakers, she broke adrift when the tug developed engine troubles and went aground southwest of Macao. On 13 December 1963 she returned to Hong Kong and was broken up locally.

There was growing realisation by BI management that *Kenya* and *Uganda* were falling behind circumstances and competition. Ship for ship, the BI Sisters and the Union-Castle trio never really matched the amenities of Lloyd Triestino's superb *Africa* and *Europa*. Non-air-conditioned, non-facility cabins became a hard sell when sea travel was being promoted as an ocean holiday. Union-Castle refitted *Rhodesia Castle, Braemar Castle* and *Kenya Castle* with air-conditioning and some private facilities on A Deck during August 1960-June 1961.

British India made considerable study in 1961-1962 towards updating *Kenya* and *Uganda* with full air-conditioning and conversion to one-class with the former Tourist Class public rooms converted into private facility cabins. The six suites on each ship had been retrofitted with air-conditioning by 1958 as had some areas on the Gulf run "D"s, but such piecemeal ventilation enhancement was seldom really satisfactory. A captain of *Uganda* even installed, at his own expense, an air-conditioning unit in his cabin and then sold it, upon his retirement, to the company for £50. The cost, however, to fully air-condition the ships came to £250,000 and the idea was quietly shelved. There was effort and expenditure, however, to brighten and modernise the decor of both ships, *Uganda*'s First Class bar, for example, getting new furnishings and a livelier red and grey scheme.

A year after the demise of the East African coastal run, another, shorter lived BI African route closed out with *Warora*'s final sailing from Durban for the Persian Gulf in early May 1961.

Amra docked at Mombasa and Dar-es-Salaam in July 1961 with four Indian passengers suspected to have smallpox. Two were taken to hospital in Mombasa and the other two, young children, were taken ashore at Dar-es-Salaam where over 1,000 port workers were vaccinated as a precaution.

In a bit of inter-company rivalry, P&O's *Iberia* detoured to East Africa en route from Australia to Britain and embarked 22 passengers at Zanzibar on 18 July 1961 and more at Mombasa. Although it was speculated that more such calls would be made, this proved to be the only one.

In addition to the "regulars" *Chinkoa, Landaura, Chilka, Nuddea, Chindwara, Chantala, Chakdara* on the cargo service, there were several newcomers in 1960 including *Garbeta, Chupra* and the chartered *Trewidden* (1943/7,272/Hain S.S. Co.) and *Mutlah* (1947/6,652 grt/J. Nourse Ltd.). The "cashew fleet" from India that year comprised *Pundua* and *Ardenode* (1943/7,036 grt/Mullion & Co. Ltd). The 1961 cargo sailings to East Africa were made by *Chakdara, Chupra, Nardana, Treloske* (1950/5,388 grt/Hain S.S. Co.), *Nyanza, Chinkoa, Warora and Chantala*. Additionally, *Landaura* sailed from Durban on 10 September for Beira, Mombasa and Karachi.

As announced on 24 October 1961, effective with *Kenya*'s 27 July 1962 sailing, the Home Line was extended to Durban with frequent calls at Naples. The passage took 32 days with six-weekly sailings. *Kenya* arrived at Durban for the first time on 29 August under Chief Officer T.E. Kelso who assumed command after Captain H.B.W. Cray fell ill and was taken to hospital in Beira. The ship's maiden arrival at Durban was delayed by bad weather with winds of 42-72 mph which resulted in the very unusual closure of the port, causing the liner to loiter off the coast for some hours. *Kenya* sailed northbound on the 30th.

Among the passengers aboard *Uganda* (Captain J.D. Hamilton) on her maiden arrival at Durban on 25 September 1962 were a number of immigrants to South Africa from former British East Africa including S.H. Mackay, a former oil company official, who told the *Natal Mercury* of Kenya's "deteriorating political situation" and a Mrs. K.J.T. Southbate who said "she saw the light" and was resettling in Natal.

The Durban extension gave a new opportunity for South Africans to avail themselves of the coastal run up to Mombasa and this was extensively promoted:

VISIT EXOTIC AFRICA BY BI . . .
to a world of magic. Dream away your days as a British India Line steamer transports you to lands of powder-soft shores, where the air is heavy with the sweet smell of spices and the stars seem near enough to touch!

That year also saw the end of Union-Castle's famous Round-Africa run and its replacement with a duplicate U.K.-East Africa service terminating, like BI's, at Durban.

Ending the Yokohama service and its historic Calcutta-Rangoon segment, *Santhia* sailed from Calcutta on 4 September 1962 for Chittagong, Rangoon (last passenger call for a BI ship there), Penang, Singapore, Hong Kong and Yokohama, returning to Calcutta on 1 November. On 22 October *Sirdhana* sailed on the first of two Bombay-Dar-es-Salaam trips. *Santhia*, after a major refit at Kobe, joined her on the Gulf run with occasional East African voyages. *Sangola*, however, was sold to Japanese breakers in March 1963.

Cargo sailings for 1962 were made by *Chilka, Chindwara, Chantala, Chakdara, Nardana, Olinda, Ordia, Umaria* and *Nuddea* in addition to one voyage by P&O's *Socotra*, the chartered Asiatic S.N. *Nurmahal* (which would be transferred three years later to BI), and *Inchdouglas* (1943/7,275 grt/Douglas S.S. Co.). The next year saw an increase in chartered tonnage with *Betwa* (1950/6,722 grt/James Nourse Ltd.), *Nurmahal, Cingalese Prince* (1950/8,827 grt/Prince Line), *Ganges* (1950/6,724 grt/James Nourse Ltd.) and P&O's *Cannanore* running with *Nuddea, Nardana, Chinkoa, Chilka* and *Chakdara* and most sailings terminating at Dar-es-Salaam.

To further tap the South African tourist market and satisfy demands by the Seychelles Government for increased service, *Kampala* in March 1963 joined *Karanja* in calling at Port Victoria, Mahé, the two offering a popular 28-day cruise to the island still without an airport. On 6 November *Karanja* arrived at Cape Town for the first time to embark a large party of Cape Malay Muslims bound for a pilgrimage to Mecca. *Santhia* made one Bombay-Dar-es-Salaam voyage 23 October-15 November.

The new African political climate, for a time, encouraged some passenger market segments. Asians in Africa generally held South African passports, making it difficult for them to travel by air to and from India and Pakistan and clear African airport immigration. This problem was not encountered on the ship route which became for many the best and sometimes only link between the land of their birth and their adopted homeland. In one of the first of several unhappy departures, *Karanja* was reported on 11 January 1963 to be "packing her decks" with 600 Indian refugees deported suddenly from Lourenço Marques during Portuguese-Indian disputes over Goa. As the BI liner already had another 400 embarkees at Mombasa upon arrival there on the 21st, the Indian Government arranged to have the chartered *Mozaffari* meet *Karanja* there and tranship 400 of her deportees for transport to Bombay.

Other new passenger trade brought its own peculiarities:

The early 'sixties saw the growth of the "hippie" travel routes which these people used to travel from Europe to Africa and the East. They would usually have to pay their fare to some starting point in Africa and would then travel overland through Zambia or the Congo with Mombasa as their goal. Some carried notebooks in which the most detailed information was given as to the cheapest places in each town to eat and sleep and they were not above accepting free accommodation traditionally given by the Sikhs and others to travellers.

On arrival at Mombasa they would come to the BI Agency to ask for deck passages to Bombay whence they would travel on to Nepal etc., but BI had a rule that Europeans were not allowed to travel Deck Class. This had been introduced because so many had bought deck tickets and after 24 hours at sea had asked for cabin accommodation (which was usually full) because they could not put up with the conditions of deck travel. This rule caused them much anguish because they had of course to pay a higher fare. Eventually the company gave way and said that they could travel Deck if they had previously viewed the conditions and signed a declaration that these were accepted and that they would not ask for cabin accommodation after sailing. However when female hippies started to arrive with their boyfriends BI insisted that the females pay for and travel in cabin accommodation which caused them more distress because they were separated from each other during the voyage.**

On the Home Line, however, there was a steady decline in traffic and even BI's Annual Report of 1963 noted a fall-off in outbound passenger carryings. From 1962 onwards steady losses were incurred, averaging £5,000 a trip.

The imposition by Kenya of economic sanctions against South Africa in 1963 had the immediate effect of severing BI's Durban-Mombasa shuttle, the third BI African service to succumb in as many years. *Warla* arrived at Durban for the last time from Mombasa on 21 November 1963.

If the European presence in Africa was usurped in the 'sixties, so too was the age-old Arab and Indian influence, culminating with the January 1964 revolution in Zanzibar. Amidst the upheaval, the port was closed to all shipping. *Karanja* was the first passenger vessel to call at the re-opened port and she together with *Kampala* and *Amra* were to carry the island's deported Asian population, the bulwark of Zanzibar's commerce, back to India and Pakistan. When *State of Bombay* could not make the trip due to mechanical problems, the Indian Government chartered BI's *Daressa* (1950/5,180 grt) for a special evacuation voyage from Zanzibar on 14 April via Dar-es-Salaam. This was the ship's only African voyage and she was sold on 18 August to Chandris.

Instead of the southbound Zanzibar calls, *Kenya* and *Uganda* began to serve Lourenço Marques northbound with *Kenya* making the first stop on 16 January 1964.

Chartered tonnage continued to figure in BI's East African cargo run and in 1964 included *Tremeadow* (1958/6,504 grt/Hain S.S. Co.), *Temple Lane* (1954/7,848 grt/Temple S.S. Co.) and *Leoville* (1950/5,305 grt/Skibs A/S Siljestad) in addition to *Nowshera, Chinkoa, Chilka, Chantala, Chakdara* and *Chakla,* the latter being the newest addition to the fleet (as of 16 January), the former *Swiftpool* (1954/6,565 grt) of Ropner & Co. In an effort to expedite cargo handling before the advent of containers, BI's East African Port Captain G.R. Williams and Cargo Superintendent A.W. Clarke developed the idea of "pre-slung" breakbulk cargo and this was first tested with the arrival at Mombasa of *Chilka* on 18 August.

There was new competition on the East Africa run when Pakistan's Pan Islamic Steamship Co. positioned its *Safina-e-Hujjai* on regular Karachi-Mombasa-Zanzibar-Dar-es-Salaam sailings beginning in August 1964, outside of her annual Haj service. The 1935-built former *Potsdam* which had been employed from 1947-1960 as the transport *Empire Fowey* was, at 19,116 grt, the largest ship on the East African route. At about this time, BI and the Shipping Corp. of India began to list joint sailings with SCI's *State of Bombay* and *Mozaffari.* On 24 October *Santhia* sailed from Bombay on a single voyage to Mombasa and Dar-es-Salaam, arriving on 3 December.

In a 3 November 1964 memorandum to the London office, J.W. Anson of the Bombay agency assessed the state of the India-Africa run:

[the] future of this service hinges on political development in Africa It is becoming increasingly obvious that with the drop in the movement of passengers outbound from India and Pakistan, the periodic threat of intrusion by Pan-Islamic, and the ban on trade with South Africa imposed by the East African and Pakistani governments, we shall find it very difficult to maintain our three-ship service... we can carry on with the existing pattern of service till *Amra*'s passenger certificate expires in September 1965 and decide then whether she is to be retained or not.

This was a period of considerable appraisal of BI's African ships and services as *Amra, Kampala* and *Karanja* faced special surveys within the next two years and the future of the two remaining "S" class vessels remained undecided. In a 26 February 1965 memorandum to London, the Bombay office stated that "the principal threat to our passenger service at the moment comes from Pan-Islamic" and recommended that *Amra* be retained on the East African service, *Sirdhana* kept on the Persian Gulf run and act as relief ship to East Africa and *Santhia* to be withdrawn in September. It was argued that *Amra*, despite her greater age, carried 153 more Third Class and 81 more Saloon passengers than *Santhia* and that *Sirdhana*'s greater unbunked Third Class capacity could be better used on the Persian Gulf or Straits run.

Then, in a 7 May 1965 memorandum, the Bombay office changed its mind and recommended replacing *Amra* with *Santhia*, stating "We consider the passenger traffic to and from East Africa will decline in the long run and, if this view is accepted, *Santhia* will produce better results than *Amra*." Not only was *Amra* facing a £88,000 special survey at year's end, but *Santhia* was held to be newer, more flexible and her greater cargo space could come in handy for the seasonal Mombasa-Bombay cotton trade. There remained the problem of her insufficient reserve speed which would pose problems during the monsoon. In reply, the London office stated that *Amra* remained more profitable despite having twice the fuel consumption as passenger traffic, at least one-way, remained fairly high and *Santhia*'s Third Class would require considerable upgrading if she were to enter the East African trade. It was decided on 30 May, therefore, to give both ships only minor refits to renew their passenger certificates and wait until March 1966 to make a final determination.

The after effects of the Zanzibar revolution was felt in Kenya when in 1965 Zanzibar's Vice-President and leader of the opposition party imported a shipload of Russian arms into Mombasa. The vessel was placed under arrest and Kilindini Harbour closed. This was two days before *Amra* was due with 1,000 passengers and the BI agency had to obtain special permission for their disembarkation.

After a stint on the Persian Gulf service, *Santhia* replaced the drydocked *Karanja* on one Bombay-Dar-es-Salaam-Durban-Karachi-Bombay voyage 16 June-3 August 1965, calling at Durban on July 5 via Lourenço Marques and Beira.

The Indo-Pakistani War of 1965 and its disruption of trade resulted in the immediate decision to withdraw *Amra* upon completion of Voyage 256. *Amra* departed Bombay on 25 September 1965 for Mombasa, Zanzibar, Dar-es-Salaam, Tanga and home via Mormugao, returning on 20 October, three days late owing to a delay at Zanzibar transhipping cargo from *Admiralty Crest*. *Amra*'s sudden withdrawal caused the cancellation of a planned charter voyage from Mombasa to Marmagoa for the exhumation of St. Francis Xavier. Still a splendid-looking vessel, evoking pre-war memories when she was the pride of the Rangoon Mail and a familiar, faithful friend along the East African coast, *Amra* was sold to Keelung breakers on 2 December. Of the pre-war liners, only the doughty *Rajula*, dating from 1926, now remained in the fleet.

In place of *Amra, Santhia* made one voyage to Dar-es-Salaam from Bombay beginning on 24 October 1965 and one from Karachi a month later. This proved to be her final African sailing as she departed Dar-es-Salaam on 3 December for Karachi and thence to the Persian Gulf.

As a permanent replacement for *Amra,* *Kampala* shifted to monthly Bombay-Dar-es-Salaam sailings of 12-day duration effective with Voyage 117 commencing 23 November 1965. She was programmed to depart from Bombay on the 23, 24 or 25th of every month, calling en route at Mombasa and the Seychelles, and sailing from Dar-es-Salaam on the 7, 8 or 9th of every month via Zanzibar, Mombasa and the Seychelles with a 12-day passage. The Durban service was reduced to sailings in *Karanja* from Bombay on the 14 to 17th day of even months via Karachi, Seychelles, Mombasa, Dar-es-Salaam, Beira and Lourenço Marques (a 22-day voyage) and from Durban on the 9th or 11th of odd months via Lourenço Marques, Beira, Dar-es-Salaam, Zanzibar, Mombasa, Seychelles and Karachi, a 24-day crossing. Results of a one-ship service to South Africa would be watched closely as insufficient traffic might result in *Kampala,* facing a special survey in 1967, being replaced by *Sirdhana* or *Karanja* and the Durban run consequently being dropped.

Rationalization replaced rivalry and in 1965 a new joint service was announced by BI and Union-Castle whereby *Kenya, Uganda, Kenya Castle* and *Rhodesia Castle* sailed from London to East Africa via Suez every three weeks, the same arrangement with which the Royal East African Service started before the First World War, but it proved equally short-lived.

In defiance against the Wilson Government's insistence that the country adopt majority rule, Ian Smith's Rhodesia proclaimed its Unilateral Declaration of Independence from the Crown on 11 November 1965. Britain and the Commonwealth immediately enacted an array of economic sanctions whose immediate effect was more damaging to neighbouring Zambia which previously exported all of its copper through Rhodesia and on to Beira. The Royal Navy's Beira Patrol was wholly successful, however, in cutting off oil imports landed at Beira and then conveyed by pipeline to Rhodesia. But Rhodesia simply switched to oil supplies from neighbouring South Africa and Lourenço Marques.

For BI the sanctions cut into a once profitable market, but its ships still served Beira and Rhodesians. *Karanja* and *Kampala* would now draw up alongside whichever Royal Navy frigate was on station and receive the warship's mail which was transferred by small assault boat, by helicopter or by line firing gun. In exchange the BI ships would send over the latest newspapers and magazines, all to the cheers and clicking of cameras of the passengers lining the decks, even the Rhodesian ones. For many Rhodesians the only holidays available were to South Africa, Mozambique and the Seychelles and BI won much of this business.

Only two vessels, *Temple Main* (1954/7,848 grt/Temple S.S. Co.) and *Kuartia*, were chartered in 1965 to augment cargo sailings by *Chilka*, *Chindwara*, *Nowshera*, *Chakdara*, *Chantala*, *Chinkoa*, *Chakla*, *Nuddea* and *Purnea*, by then the last of the "P"s. The next year these same vessels maintained the service in addition to the chartered *Trecarraell* (1959/6,499 grt/Hain S.S. Co.) and P&O's *Salsette*.

Chakdara, on Voyage 77 which began from London on 22 April 1966, broke down on passage between Aden and Dar-es-Salaam on 15 May. The scavange pump crank coupling bolts sheered off, possibly due to metal fatigue, sending the connecting rod through the side of the Doxford diesel, smashing the engine control and fuel piping. The scavange pump, tank tops and switchboard were also damaged. Fortunately there were no injuries. The disabled *Chakdara* was towed to Mombasa by the Aden-based tug *Svitzer* and arrived on the 28th, assisted into her berth by the harbour tugs *Marie Felling* and *Simba*. After her cargo was unloaded, *Chakdara* was towed by *Svitzer* to England for repairs, leaving Mombasa at the end of June.

There was some good news on the passenger front for a change when in April 1966 it could be reported that "recent results of the two-ship service [India-East and South Africa] have been very encouraging" and between June 1965 and June 1966, *Kampala* had carried 14,594 non-Saloon passengers and *Karanja*, 8,508. Consequently it was decided that *Kampala* would be retained and given her special survey refit.

In July 1966 BI together with Union-Castle and other shipping lines put on an "Ocean Travel Week" promotion in Nairobi. This was aimed at the rapidly growing number of people who had come out to East Africa by air and were unaware of the sea travel option. Alas, it was an increasingly undesirable alternative on practical terms, both in time and now, with the advent of non-stop jet service to and from Britain, price. Even Smith Mackenzie & Co. had a policy of sending staff home on leave by air. Worse still the Colonial Office had changed its policies whereby home leave was now reckoned to commence upon departure from Africa, not arrival in Britain. As Purser Ron Davies recalls, this resulted in "passengers leaving the sea like lemmings" as the voyage time was now on their own account.

Big changes were announced on 8 August 1966 — the withdrawal of *Uganda*, end of the joint Union-Castle operation, conversion of *Kenya* to one-class and a new routing.

Uganda (Captain J.D. Hamilton) sailed from London for the last time, Durban-bound, on 5 November 1966. Heralded by four mournful blasts on her whistle, she departed Durban on 7 December. Hoisting the signal "Good bye Mombasa and Thank You", *Uganda* left Kilindini forever on the 23rd and arrived at London on 15 January 1967. After completing 52 voyages to East Africa, carrying over 42,000 passengers and 750,000 tons of cargo, *Uganda* was laid up at Royal Albert Docks from 21 January to 3 March.

On 4 March *Uganda* departed for Howaldtswerke AG, Hamburg, for conversion from mailship to schoolship to replace *Dunera* and *Devonia* on BI's educational cruises. Substantially rebuilt to carry 920 students in dormitories and 304 Cabin Class passengers, *Uganda* made her first cruise from Southampton on 27 February 1968.

Kenya's Voyage 108, beginning on 17 December 1966, was the last to call at Beira (14-15 January 1967) and Durban on the 17th. Upon her 9 March sailing from London the ship now carried 274 one-class passengers. The Tourist lounge was converted into a large nursery and Tourist pool was also reserved for children. The First Class dining saloon was now utilised by all passengers. None of the improvements originally mooted in 1961 such as conversion of redundant public rooms to facility cabins or full air-conditioning were undertaken and it was obvious that *Kenya* would play out the waning days of the East Africa Home Line with the minimal expenditure of capital.

Now the last British liner on the East African run, (*Kenya Castle* and *Rhodesia Castle* having been withdrawn in April and May 1967 respectively), *Kenya* sailed bi-monthly from London to Gibraltar, Naples (summer only), Port Said, Aden, Mombasa and turned around at Dar-es-Salaam instead of Durban. Homewards, she called at Tanga, Mombasa, Aden, Port Said and Gibraltar. This abbreviated routing proved very short-lived when the June 1967 Six-Day War between the Arab states and Israel again closed the Suez Canal. *Kenya* was at Dar-es-Salaam when the war began and she sailed home via Cape Town (4 August), her itinerary thereafter becoming London-Las Palmas-Dakar-Cape Town-Durban-Mombasa-Dar-es-Salaam.

The Bombay office on 11 February 1966 stated that it was "most unlikely that the BI could operate three passenger vessels on this [East African] trade for any prolonged period" and that for *Santhia*, "no employment of this ship is foreseen." Consequently, after a 16-year BI career, she was handed over to the Shipping Corp. of India on 6 December 1966, and as its *State of Haryana* operated on SCI's Bombay-East Africa run for ten more years. Her erstwhile running mate, *Sirdhana*, briefly competed with two Bombay-Dar-es-Salaam voyages on 19 January 1967 and 27 February in relief of *Kampala* for her special survey refit. *Kampala* resumed service on 25 March.

On the cargo berth for 1967 were *Nuddea, Chakdara, Nowshera, Chindwara, Chantala, Canara* and, on her maiden voyage that September for BI, *Juna* (1952/7,583 grt), formerly *Cornwall* of Federal S.N. Co., whilst chartered tonnage that year comprised *Glanely* (1960/8,261 grt/Atlantic

Shipping & Trading), *Trecarne* (1959/6,499 grt/Hain S.S. Co.) and P&O's *Baradine*, the former BI *Nardana*. The next year, sailings were made by *Chantala, Chanda, Chakrata, Nardana* and *Nyanza* in addition to P&O's *Coromandel*, East African National Shipping Line's *Harambee* and *Industria* and the chartered *Tarpon Bay* (1953/7,564 grt/Tarpon Shipping Co.) and *Pearl Stone* (1956/8,000 grt/Monrovia Shipping).

Twenty-one years old in 1969, *Karanja* had steamed an estimated 1,140,000 Indian Ocean miles. On 17 January she made her first call at Nacala, Mozambique, followed by another on 1 May. *Kampala* called there on 27 September and on inducement, the port was henceforth included on a number of cargo sailings.

The unlikely prospect of any early reopening of the Suez Canal, the long Cape diversion and ever-declining trade conspired to doom the Britain-East Africa passenger run. On 8 May 1969 a new joint BI/Union-Castle cargo service was announced, but it was already the beginning of the end for the passenger run.

On her 131st and last voyage *Kenya* sailed from London on 4 April 1969. Fully booked with 240 passengers from Kenya and 60 from Tanzania and with a typical cargo of coffee, tea, sisal and copper (ironically this was also the first sailing of the joint BI/Union-Castle service), *Kenya* left Dar-es-Salaam on 7 May for the last time on a slightly revised routing via Tanga, Mombasa, Durban and Tenerife. Upon her final departure from Mombasa, the Port Authority sent *Kenya* a farewell radio message:

A sad day for Kwaheri and best wishes for future sailings. Thank you for all co-operation during years of service to this Country after which the Ship was named.

Kenya arrived at London on 7 June 1969, passing the educational cruise ship *Uganda* anchored in Gravesend Reach, amid rumours she would be converted into a trade exhibition vessel. Instead, *Kenya* was sold to Cantiere di Portovenere for scrap and left London on 24 June and arrived at La Spezia on 2 July.

The "all BI" East Africa cargo run was phased out by sailings by *Chakla*, P&O's *Coromandel* and *Chantala* and the joint BI/Union-Castle operation began in early June 1969 with a decidedly "mixed bag" of BI, P&O, Union-Castle, King, Clan, East African National Shipping Line (EANSL) and chartered tonnage: *Clan Macintyre, Ribot, Clan Grant, Chupra, Kinnard Castle, Uganda* (EANSL), *King George, Bulimba* (1959/6,796 grt) which was making the first African voyage of the handsome "B" class, normally on BI's Australia-Japan run, *Ozarda, King Charles, Tantallon Castle, Clan Alpine, King Malcolm* and *Amra* (1969/10,024 grt). The last named was the final newly built BI ship to make her maiden voyage to Africa, sailing from London on 21 November 1969 and calling at Cape Town, Nacala, Mtwara, Mombasa,

Tanga, Dar-es-Salaam and Karachi. She then took up her intended Japan-Persian Gulf service and did not return to African waters.

Proving to be the last capital investment in the BI African run, *Karanja* entered Singapore's Keppel Shipyard on 14 August 1969 for an extensive £1 million refit. This included air-conditioning and re-arrangement of accommodation to 493 Cabin (comprising three grades of First Class and a new Cabin Third with six- and eight-berth cabins) and 408 Bunked Third Class passengers. To satisfy new fire-safety requirements, Formica sheeting and metal-framed furniture replaced the old Empire woods and chintz and leather furnishings. Close-circuit television was added and in the galley modern electrical appliances supplanted coal-fired stoves. In the engine room, new a.c. generators replaced the original d.c. ones.

Thoroughly renewed and reckoned to be good for another eight to ten years, *Karanja* left Singapore on 28 February 1970. Earlier that month she, *Sirdhana* and *Rajula* were in Singapore together. After a Bombay-Dar-es-Salaam voyage, *Karanja* resumed her bi-monthly Bombay-Seychelles-Mombasa-Dar-es-Salaam-Beira-Lourenço Marques-Nacala (optional)-Durban run on 21 April.

After maintaining the Durban service in *Karanja*'s absence, *Kampala* reverted to the Bombay-Karachi-Seychelles-Mombasa-Dar-es-Salaam run. Carrying 14,875 passengers and 40,675 tons of cargo, and steaming 74,518 miles in 1970 alone, *Kampala* retained her chintz, ceiling fans and coal stoves, but had only a year's service remaining.

The remnants of the once enormous BI fleet were, like *Kampala*, either coursing towards the inevitable breaker's torch or corporate absorption into the P&O Group as the troubled 'sixties gave way to the traumatic 'seventies. Rampant inflation, Third World economic chaos, crippling East African port congestion, high labour and fuel costs, and cargo containerisation all conspired against the remaining BI ships.

Representing a final "gathering of the clan" in African ports, *Sirdhana*, *Chakdara* and *Amra* occupied adjoining Kilindini berths at Mombasa on 15 January 1971 whilst three days later *Chakdara* joined *Waipara* alongside at Mtwara.

Departing Bombay on her final voyage on 29 May 1971 *Kampala* (Captain V.P. Harvey) called at Karachi, Seychelles, Mombasa, Dar-es-Salaam (13-14 June) and returned via the last two ports, docking at Bombay on the 25th. Destination oblivion, she sailed four days later and on 24 July the first post-war BI Africa liner arrived at Kaohsiung. On the 31st she was handed over to China Steel Co. to be broken up, her fate after 24 years' flawless and faithful service during which she carried 500,000 passengers on 179 voyages.

As a result of the combined BI/Union-Castle service, the number of BI vessels on the East Africa cargo berth began to diminish substantially. In 1970

Bulimba, Chantala, Chindwara, Chupra and *Tairea* made one or more sailings in addition to the chartered *Eva, Bell Rive* and *Brighton.* The following year *Chantala, Sirsa, Tairea, Chakla, Chakdara* and *Chinkoa* were on the service. The once ubiquitous "C"s began to leave the fleet and in 1971 *Chupra, Chanda, Chindwara* and *Chantala* were sold. The demise of the latter two, Currie's cherished cadet ships, sadly symbolised the end of BI and when *Chantala* left East African waters for the last time she proudly flew a 166-foot-long paying-off pennant.

On 1 October 1971 the remaining BI passenger liners *Karanja, Rajula, Sirdhana, Dwarka* and *Dumra* came under P&O ownership and General Cargo Division management, but proudly and pleasingly they kept their BI livery and houseflag as did the schoolships *Uganda* and *Nevasa.* The last of the BI cargo vessels, too, came under the management and eventually assumed the colours of P&O's General Cargo Division in 1971-73; *Chakdina, Chakrata, Nuddea, Nowshera, Nyanza, Nardana, Nurmahal, Jelunga, Amra, Aska, Tairea, Teesta, Manora* (1970/11,177 grt), *Merkara* (1971/11,143 grt), *Morvada* (1971/11,143 grt) and *Mulbera* (1971/11,143 grt). The "mod" '70s corn-coloured hull and pale blue funnel emblazoned with the P&O logo marred their dignity, but only superficially.

Replacing *Kampala, Sirdhana* was transferred from the Bombay-Gulf run to the Dar-es-Salaam route upon her 22 February 1972 sailing. The 25-year-old liner was destined to make only three voyages to Africa, the last concluding at Bombay on 20 May. On 3 August she was sold to Taiwanese breakers.

The centenary year of BI's Africa service, 1972, ironically marked the end of the company's U.K.-East Africa run in so far as operating any BI-owned or liveried tonnage. *Tairea* sailed from London on 25 January on her final Africa-bound voyage. Fittingly, it was left to one of the gallant old "C"s to bring down the curtain on the venerable Home Line. On 5 May *Chilka* arrived at Royal Albert Docks, the last "C" to load a BI cargo for Africa, and 13 days later an era ended when she became the final BI ship to sail from England to Africa. *Chilka* arrived at Mombasa on 14 June and the next month passed to Taiwanese breakers.

Karanja was now suddenly alone, still plying the trade for which she was built, but she, too, was eventually done in by steadily declining trade, exacerbated by Idi Amin's deportation of Asians, the mainstay of Uganda's once-thriving economy in 1972.

> The Mombasa agency gave priority to all applications from its Uganda travel agents but sadly many [Ugandan Asian] were unable to find the fare as their businesses had either been confiscated by the Idi Amin regime or they were unable to sell up. When Amin prohibited the export of currency from Uganda

to Kenya, the Mombasa agency had to make emergency arrangements with the Uganda banks for the passage money to be remitted to London instead. The British Government offered British citizenship to many Uganda Asians, and although many availed themselves of this gesture, it was not necessary as the Indian Government had agreed to take as many as wished to go to India. The Indian High Commission in Nairobi and Kampala made funds available to some of these who could not afford to pay the fare to Bombay.**

The dislocation of Asians from Uganda plus the growing acceptance of air travel largely robbed *Karanja* of her principal passenger traffic. A final blow came in 1974 with the opening of the international airport at Mahé, Seychelle Islands, hitherto largely dependent on *Karanja* for its link with the outside world as well as being the principal tourist carrier. Cabin Class trade began to fall off rapidly as a result. A year later the Portuguese hastily quit Mozambique and that once peaceful and prosperous country tumbled into political and economic chaos. The East Africa that Mackinnon had laboured to create and that BI had nurtured and profited by, had vanished and with it the place and purpose of ships like *Karanja*.

Ending 104 years of BI service to Africa, *Karanja* pulled away from Ballard Pier, Bombay, on 19 April 1976 on her 173rd and final voyage. After calls at Karachi, Mombasa (4-6 May), Dar-es-Salaam and Maputo (formerly Lourenço Marques), she reached Durban on 14 May. It will be recalled that 27 years previously *Karanja* and *Edinburgh Castle,* both then on their maiden voyages, had occupied adjacent berths at Durban. Uniquely and poignantly the careers of these last two classic British African mailships would likewise simultaneously come to a close as *Edinburgh Castle*, empty and bound for the Taiwan breakers, had departed from Durban just three days before *Karanja*'s final arrival there. And the very next day (12 May) Lloyd Triestino's *Europa* sailed for Italy and ended that historic service. On 15 May *Karanja,* Bombay bound for the last time, also took her final departure from Durban. Three African mailships, outbound past the Bluff, never to return, their likes never to be seen again. After calls at Beira, Dar-es-Salaam, Mombasa (25-28 May) and Karachi, *Karanja* docked at Bombay on 9 June.

Karanja was handed over to at 2:00 p.m. on 6 August 1976 to the Shipping Corp. of India. Renamed *Nancowry* and carrying 294 Saloon Class, 200 air-conditioned bunk and 408 bunk passengers, she faithfully operated the Madras-Port Blair, Andaman Islands run. In 1979 she underwent a final refit at Singapore. Upon *Dwarka*'s demise in 1982, *Nancowry* was the last ex-BI ship still plying a liner route and fittingly one pioneered by the line. Exactly 40 years after her maiden voyage as *Karanja, Nancowry* arrived at Bombay for breaking up in November 1988.

243

The former *Karanja* has thus joined the British India Steam Navigation Company, once the sinew and symbol of the Empire east of Suez, in oblivion. Last to proudly wear the colours, the beloved *Uganda*, after valiant Falklands War service, was discarded by company and country in 1986, only to cheat the breakers and founder in a typhoon shortly after arrival at Taiwan. Lying on her side off Kaohsiung, she was a sad reminder of the vanished BI and the vanishing British Merchant Navy whose unique contributions to the development of East Africa she exemplified.

BIBLIOGRAPHY

Albion, Robert Greenhalgh. *Seaports South of the Sahara.* New York, Appleton-Century Crofts, 1959.

Bierman, John. *Dark Safari.* New York, Alfred A. Knopf, 1990.

Blake, George. *BI Centenary, 1856-1956.* London, Collins, 1956.

Cable, Boyd. *A Hundred Year History of the P&O.* London, Ivor Nicholson and Watson, 1937.

Coupland, Reginald. *The Exploitation of East Africa.* London, Faber & Faber, 1939 and 1968.

Dunn, Lawrence. *Passenger Liners.* Southampton, Adlard Coles, 1961.

Gailey, Harry A., Jr. *History of Africa Vol. II From 1800 to 1945 and Vol. III From 1945 to Present.* Malabar, Krieger, 1989.

Gibbs, C.R. Vernon. *British Passenger Liners of the Five Oceans.* London, Putnam, 1963.

Gregory, Robert G. *South Asians in East Africa* Boulder, Westview, 1993.

Haws, Duncan. *Merchant Fleet Vol.11 British India S.N.* Burwash, TCL Publications, 1987.

Hill, M.H. *Permanent Way.* Nairobi, East African Railways & Harbours, 1949.

Hook, F.A. *Merchant Adventurers.* London, A.& C. Black, 1920.

Ingham, Kenneth. *A History of East Africa* London, Longmans, 1962.

Lapping, Brian. *End of Empire.* New York, St. Martin's, 1985.

Miller, Charles. *The Lunatic Express.* New York, The Macmillan Company, 1971.

Mitchell, W.H. and Sawyer, L.A. *The Cape Run.* Lavenham, Terrence Dalton, 1984.

Morris, James. *Pax Britannica* New York, Harcourt, Brace and World, 1968.

Murray, Marischal. *Ships and South Africa* London, Faber and Faber, 1948.

—*Union-Castle Chronicle 1853-1953.* London, Longmans, Green and Co., 1953.

Pakenham, Thomas. *The Scramble for Africa* New York, Random House, 1990.

Saunders, Hilary St. George. *Valiant Voyaging.* London, Faber and Faber, 1948.

Stanley, H.M. and Dorothy (ed.). *The Autobiography of Sir Henry Morton Stanley.* New York, Greenwood, 1969.

Tzebinski, Errol. *The Kenya Pioneers.* New York, W.W. Norton, 1986.

ABC Shipping Guide

About Ourselves (P&O staff journal)

BI News

East African Railways & Harbours/Spear

Fairplay

Karachi Port News

Lloyds List

Lloyd Loading List

The Log (article Retrenchment— B.I.S.N. Co. Ltd Since the War by H.W. Dick, 31 March 1970)

Marine News

Official Steamship and Airways Guide

Sea Breezes

Ships Monthly

Shipping World

Shipbuilding & Shipping Record

The South African Shipping News

Syren & Shipping

Wavelength

Daily Nation (Nairobi)

East African Standard (Nairobi)

East Africa & Rhodesia

Journal of Commerce & Shipping Telegraph (Liverpool)

Kenya Daily Mail (Mombasa)

Lourenço Marques Guardian

Mombasa Times

Tanganyika Standard (Dar-es-Salaam)

Tanganyika Times (Dar-es-Salaam)

Cape Times (Cape Town)

Natal Mercury (Durban)

Rhodesia Herald (Salisbury)

The Sydney Morning Herald

The Times (London)

The Times of India (Bombay)

Gabriel, Robert C., Manuscript on British India S.N. Co. and notes, referenced * in text.

Hall, W.M.L., Manuscript "A Few Reminiscences of BI Agency Work in East Africa", referenced ** in text.

Records of British India S.N. Co. held at the National Maritime Museum, Greenwich:

Annual Reports, 1870-1970

Correspondence files, 1870-1962

Passage books, 1951-1969

BI Handbook, 1866-1939, 1949-1969

ACKNOWLEDGEMENTS

This book would not have been possible without the generous assistance of many individuals and institutions worldwide.

The author wishes to thank in the United Kingdom; A.M.B. Bell, Ron Davies, Iain Gillies, Alan S. Mallett, John A. Smith, and Steve Tilston, in South Africa, Brian Ingpen and Robert Pabst; in Australia, Stephen A. Kentwell; and in the United States, J. Edward Glancy, Richard Maxwell, James L. Shaw and Albert Watson III.

The more than four years of extensive primary source research that went into this book was facilitated by the collections and helpful staff of the Library of Congress (Washington, D.C.), The British Library's Newspaper Library (London), The National Maritime Museum (Greenwich), The South African Library (Cape Town) and P&O archives and Librarian Stephen Rabson (London).

I am also most grateful to those who made available rare photographs and research materials from their private collections, especially Charles Dragonette (United States), Laurence Dunn (United Kingdom) and Alex Duncan (United Kingdom).

Gordon Turner (Canada), the late F.W. Perry and Tony Smythe (United Kingdom) edited the manuscript which benefited immeasureably from their constructive advice.

A special note of appreciation to Col. Robert C. Gabriel (United Kingdom) for his generous co-operation, editing and use of his manuscript on BI ships and services prior to the First World War, and to W.M.L. Hall (United Kingdom) for his reminiscences of BI agency work in East Africa.

Last but not least, I am indebted to my brother Eric for executing the cover design and to my wife Christine for her support and encouragement during an often all-encompassing project.

INDEX OF VESSELS

Note that numbers in *italic* type represent illustrations.

A view of *Karanja* post-refit.

J.A. Smith collection

s.s. UGANDA

U.K. –
East AFRICAN
SERVICE

BRITISH INDIA STEAM NAVIGATION CO. LTD.

255

JUNE 1970

India & Pakistan/Africa

a tradition of service

BI advertising card circa 1956 (Artist John S. Smith) depicting *Uganda* (left) with *Kampala* (right background) at Durban.

Author's collection, courtesy S.M. Payne

UGANDA